江西省社会科学规划项目《新基础教育课程改革背景下江西省农村小学校长教学领导力研究》（18JYZ52）研究成果

THE STUDY OF PREPARATION AND PROFESSIONAL DEVELOPMENT OF SECONDARY SCHOOL PRINCIPALS' LEADERSHIP IN HENAN PROVINCE

中学校长领导力准备与专业化发展研究
——以河南省为例

江　娜　著

吉林大学出版社
·长春·

图书在版编目（CIP）数据

中学校长领导力准备与专业化发展研究 ：以河南省为例 ：英文 / 江娜著 .— 长春 ：吉林大学出版社，2020.4
ISBN 978-7-5692-6289-6

Ⅰ. ①中… Ⅱ. ①江… Ⅲ. ①中学－校长－学校管理－研究－英文 Ⅳ. ①G637.1

中国版本图书馆 CIP 数据核字（2020）第 057132 号

书　　名：中学校长领导力准备与专业化发展研究——以河南省为例
　　　　　ZHONGXUE XIAOZHANG LINGDAOLI ZHUNBEI YU ZHUANYEHUA FAZHAN YANJIU——YI HENAN SHENG WEI LI

作　　者：江　娜　著
策划编辑：邵宇彤
责任编辑：代景丽
责任校对：田茂生
装帧设计：优盛文化
出版发行：吉林大学出版社
社　　址：长春市人民大街 4059 号
邮政编码：130021
发行电话：0431-89580028/29/21
网　　址：http://www.jlup.com.cn
电子邮箱：jdcbs@jlu.edu.cn
印　　刷：三河市华晨印务有限公司
成品尺寸：170mm×240mm　　16 开
印　　张：13.5
字　　数：348 千字
版　　次：2020 年 4 月第 1 版
印　　次：2020 年 4 月第 1 次
书　　号：ISBN 978-7-5692-6289-6
定　　价：56.00 元

Abstract

Principal preparation and training is the key to school and system improvement. This study was intended to investigate the preparation and professional development of secondary school principals' leadership in Henan Province, China. It allows for a deeper understanding of the current status of the school principals' preparation and professional development and aims to develop constructive suggestions in improving the current status and resolving the constraints of this effort. Data was collected through open-ended questionnaires and semi-structured interviews with the secondary school principals and training providers. Observations of school principals' routine work and training programs were also conducted to support the research findings. Thirty-seven school principals participated in an open-ended survey, seventeen school principals were interviewed and six training providers were selected from different training institutes to share their experiences and perceptions in three areas: (1) The ways they prepare for their roles; (2) The challenges and constraints of their preparation and professional development; (3) The challenges and constraints of their leadership practices. All interviews were recorded digitally and fully transcribed. Inductive coding was employed, to reduce, simplify and transform the data to facilitate data analysis. A classification of themes was then undertaken and emerging patterns were verified and confirmed. This case study outlines the findings by way of triangulating the data sets. The findings of this research study highlighted various shortcomings of policy implementation and standards, accompanied with some contradictions associated with the current demands of the principal's role in meeting these demands. This research presented the following recommendations in support of policy implementation: (1) Principals' professional development policy construction, (2) Promotion of formal and informal learning, (3) Resolving challenges in preparing and developing professionalism, and (4) Solving constraints in principal leadership practices. It is with the hope that the proposed suggestions derived through this study, can be a merit in enhancing educational policies to facilitate the educational reform, as a stepping stone for further research in this area of study.

目录

CHAPTER 1: INTRODUCTION

1.1 Introduction

In recent decades, education reforms have been implemented around the world. School principals have been recognized by stakeholders and governments as the catalyst for education reform (Bush, 2012; Chen, 2011). As a result, there has been an increased interest in school principals' initial preparation and professional development towards better leadership practices inculcated in schools (Bush & Chew, 1999; Bush & Jackson, 2002; Harris & Jones, 2015). Therefore, the best ways to promote school principals' continuous progress have been the priority for national educational development strategies in different nations. With the continuous advances in Chinese educational reform, school principals' professional development is receiving unprecedented attention in China (Chen & Tian, 2006; Chen & Liu, 2012; Gao, 2016; Huang, 2014).

A primary and secondary school principal is perceived as an important conduit to promote basic educational development and implement educational reform (Bush, 2011 ; Hallinger, 2011b; Yukl, 2002), which is also a key factor in determining schools' survival, development and success (Hallinger & Heck, 2009; Huang, Liang & Lin, 2010). Thus, the preparation and professional development of primary and secondary school principals, and its significance in promoting principal leadership, is a concern of many stakeholders in China (Chen & Liu, 2012; Feng, 2003b;Guan & Song, 2000). Moreover, with the rapid social development and the global competition, school principals are facing new expectations, higher requirements and greater challenges in China (Chen, 2010; Chen & Xu, 2009; Chu & Cravens, 2012). In order to keep pace with complex and dynamic social and economic changes and to meet the ever-increasing expectations and challenges faced by schools, school principals need preparation and professional development programmes to equip them for their roles, social needs, knowledge and skills needed in the rapidly changing social-culture (Yan & Ehrich, 2009).

China is pursuing quality education and seeking ways to promote innovative education. In this context, school principals need to undergo a series of effective professional trainings to be capable of leading educational change (Chen, 2010). Schools cannot achieve their educational goals without effective leadership (Hallinger, 2011a; Hallinger & Heck, 1998; Huang, 2013). Therefore, issues concerning the nature and role of leadership must form the foundation of any discussion of leadership preparation (Hallinger, 2006). In order to assist the school principals to deal with the challenges and adopt these changes of educational reform, while pursuing professional development, it is important to study the preparation and professional development of primary and secondary school principals' leadership in China. The following sections present the background of the study, statement of the problem, purpose of the study, objectives of the study, research questions, definition of terms, significance of the study, limitations and delimitations, as well as structure of this thesis.

1.2 Background of the Study

During the past few decades throughout the world, countless research has acknowledged that educational leadership makes a difference in student learning, school development, and educational reform (Bush, 2011; Hallinger, 2011b; Harris & Chapman, 2002; Leithwood, 1996; Stuart & Philip, 1997; Yukl, 2002). A school principal plays a pivotal role in school improvement and school effectiveness, and is a crucial factor in determining school success (Hallinger & Heck, 1996; Leithwood, 2002; Peterson, 2002; Sergiovanni, 1991). Moreover, Darling-Hammond and Meyerson (2009) highlight that the school principal's selection, and their initial training and professional development has become an important focus of educational reform strategies in many nations.

In China, school principal training is perceived by the Chinese government as an important strategy to improve the educational quality, implement educational reform and achieve a successful quality-oriented education (Zheng, Chen & Lu, 2010). Since the 1990s, principal training in China has received increased attention, due to school principals being perceived as "those who are best placed to implement a range of education reform agendas driven by fundamental changes in governance, curriculum and management" (Yan & Ehrich, 2009: 54). Similarly, Hallinger (2011b: 305) affirms that "the role of school leadership in educational reform has reached the status of a truism, and has led to major changes in school leader recruitment, selection, training and appraisal." However, the changes and complexities of the socio-cultural environment pose challenges to the school principals. Therefore, in order to meet the higher expectations and requirements of school principal leadership, the initial preparation and continuous professional development of school principals are regarded as an irreplaceable methods (Feng, 2003a; Hallinger, 2003) for school principals to gain new knowledge, skills and abilities and to keep pace with the rapid changing world (Yan & Ehrich, 2009).

Today, China has entered into a new period of constructing a well-off society, but the Chinese education system is facing new challenges now and more than ever. Data from the Educational Information Management Center of the Education Administration in China, reported an escalating numbers of 299,302 primary and secondary schools in 2014 (*China Statistical Yearbook*, 2015), which makes China a country with the largest education scales in the world, which cannot be served without the support of high quality school principals. Leadership preparation and professional development is viewed as an important strategy to improve educational quality and this will be well accepted by the Chinese government. In order to achieve that goal, school principals need to be equipped with certain values, knowledge and skills gained through their initial preparation and professional development programmes. According to Bush (2011), the preparation and professional development are crucial factors in the success of schools. In line with Stuart and Philip (1997), values, knowledge and skills are needed for school principals' professional development and the achievement of desired educational goals. Moreover, Davis et al. (2005) emphasize the importance of appraising and verifying the most effective preparation and development programmes.

According to Yan and Ehrich (2009), leadership preparation and professional development in China, has caught researchers' attention mainly for two reasons: firstly, the school principal is perceived as the one who can promote school efficiency; secondly, school principals need to update their knowledge and skills to be able to adapt to the rapidly changing social-cultural environment. On the same note, Jin (2007) stated that promoting the professional development of primary and secondary school principals is the most important for establishing the fundamentals of Chinese basic education. Chen (2010: 3) reports that "with more than hundreds and thousands of principal professional development teams, they are yet to form a system for the new century, one that is mature and scientific, as a basis for discipline. Creating a characteristic Chinese 'Educational Leadership', should be a priority, as it is important for the contemporary educational researchers and historic mission."

A number of studies show that in China, "educational leadership" is in the process of exploration and development (Chen, 2010; Sun, 2009; Zheng & Li, 2007). Since educational leadership is linked to the needs of social reform, enhancing and promoting educational leadership is a necessary requirement and regarded as a modern concept of social development. In Davis et al. (2005), it is stated that effective programmes are research and context-based, however in reality, the preparation and professional development of school principal programmes still lacks a strong and coherent research base. Some studies show that leadership research is mainly dominated by Western theories, and the ideas of leadership practice are hugely influenced by Western leadership concepts (Wen, 2004; Chen, 2010).

Chen (2010) stresses that the Chinese educational leadership discipline must be based on the foundation of the Chinese context. Currently, China is in an era where the nation is undergoing educational transformation and reform. During this period, it is significant to emphasize the functions of educational leadership, where China is pursuing quality education. In order to solve the issues, challenges and achieve its educational goals, education leaders at all levels have to develop leadership awareness and inculcate effective leadership practices.

Generally, at all levels of schooling in China, education leaders over emphasize on management issues, but lack sufficient emphasis on leadership skills (Chen, 2010). Hence, it is crucial to strengthen and enhance effective educational leadership training methods. Otherwise, the educational reform strategies cannot achieve its objectives. According to Davis et al. (2005), school principals' preparation and professional development programmes seek to reform and produce qualified and sustainable principals worldwide; in this case, China is no exception.

1.3 Statement of the Problem

In 1992, the Organization Department of the Central Committee of the Communist Party of China and State Education Commission jointly published a report entitled, *"Opinions on Strengthening the Construction of the Headmasters of Primary and Secondary Schools"*

(SEC, 1992). This report proposes that the main evaluation of school principal's work should be based on morality, capacity, perseverance, and achievement. Due to the lack of evaluation criteria and theoretical proof, it cannot properly reflect the reliability and validity aspects of the principals work assessment (Chen, 2010). Moreover, it also cannot meet the requirements needed for the professional development of principals. Hence, establishing professional school principals' training system is required to train and improve principals' leadership practices and promote quality leadership (Chen, 2010; Cheng, 2004; Sun, 2009).

The study of educational leadership is developing interest in China. There appears to be a lack of research about primary and secondary school principal leadership in China, due to the lack of native research-based and contextual-based studies on the discipline of educational leadership. Instead, Chinese policy makers and scholars have transformed and replicated Western leadership theories, ideologies and practices into the Chinese context (Chen, 2010; Lee & Pang, 2011). Unlike Western countries (such as, United States, United Kingdom and Australia), Chinese colleges and universities rarely offer educational leadership as a subject (Yang, 2003). Furthermore, Chen (2011) pointed out that although China has the largest education system, the quality of leadership practices has regressed compared to other countries. The current condition cannot satisfy the needs of leadership development, as it restricts the leadership development at practice level and so the situation of Chinese leadership practices need to be improved both theoretically and practically. Therefore, improving the level of Chinese leadership practices has become a requirement of national development.

The school principal is viewed as the school leader, who is in charge of school development. Therefore, school principals must have the competency and capacity for teaching and management. As a result, it is important to select and appoint a candidate who is suitably qualified to handle the role of principal leadership. Yang (2006) states that the selection system is an important part of the principal professional development process, which endorses the scholarship of principals. Nevertheless, the selection system of principalship in China is facing a number of constraints. Some of these problems include the lack of specific criteria and provision of selection, the lack of social connections, and difficulty in administration (Hou, 2012). Therefore, perfecting the selection system of primary and secondary school principals to ensure the placement of quality principals, should be given due importance.

Currently, the overall quality of school principals cannot meet the educational development needs in China (Chen, 2010). China is facing numerous challenges to prepare and develop its school principals. The lack of adequate and excellent primary and secondary school principals has prevented the existence of an effective incentive mechanism to lead educational innovation (Jiang & Li, 2011). The educational leaders training system has not developed the standard training mechanisms and systems required to establish quality professional standards (Chen & Liu 2012). Feng (2003a) states that even with the constant development of school principal specialization, most of the training programmes are theoretical, and there is still lack of specific pertinence, applicability and guidance. From the perspective of professional orientation, the principal specialization is an independent profession, still in the process of personal growth through their own learning and development inside and outside of teaching and training, and constantly striving to improve professional standards. Past research also shows that most school principals are ill-prepared to steer a school-wide transformation of strategic planning, curriculum, instruction, teacher development, performance review and other important elements of school management (Bai, 2006; Chen & Xu, 2010).

Leadership training is perceived as an orderly and effective method used to modify the trainee's beliefs, attitudes and behaviors, expand their knowledge, update their skills, enhance their capabilities and improve their performance (Ngai et al., 2012). Leadership training is also a key factor that influences the preparation and professional development of school principals, by offering principals the opportunity to improve their management skills, update their knowledge, and enhance their competencies. However, various studies have indicated that principal training has been challenged by many problems (Bush & Jackson, 2002; Davis et al., 2005; Jackson & Kelley, 2002). One of them is that the training content and training methods are not diversified at the local level (Davis et al., 2005). In the different areas of China, principal development is disparate, thus the school principal's abilities, qualities, needs and problems are also different. Hence a single method of school principal training programme is not sufficient to meet the diverse needs (Feng, 2013; Sun, 2009).

Training content and training methods have become the key issues for school principals' professional development in China (Zheng, 2009). There is evidence to suggest that the training model is still relatively traditional, and based mainly on theoretical and thematic learning, with training content found to be relatively backward (Chen, 2010; Zhao, 2005). In line with Feng (2003a), some of the training courses and principal effective practices are disconnected. Existing school principal trainings systems need to be reformed to a more scientific and systematic training system that can continuously develop principals' leadership skills and enhance their leadership practices executed in a dynamic and multifaceted environment.

1.4 Purpose of the Study

The aim of this study is to examine the preparation and professional development of secondary school principals' leadership in the Henan Province of the People's Republic of China (PRC). This study will investigate and present the status quo of principals' leadership, and understand the phenomenon of the preparation and professional development of secondary school principals' leadership in the Chinese educational context. The goal is to develop a deep and clear understanding of the current issues, obstacles, challenges and paradoxes, gathered from current secondary school principals' perspectives and experiences in the principalship training and leadership practices. In particular, this research, through their experiences and understanding, will identify the extent to which preparation and professional development programmes impact school principals' leadership practices. Their perceptions and suggestions may provide targeted and instructional advice for improvement strategies of secondary school principals' leadership practices. This study will spur further research in the area of preparation and professional development of leadership among school principals.

1.5 Objectives of the Study

The objectives of this research study are as follows:

I.To explore how the governmental training policies impact the preparation and professional development of secondary school principals' leadership in Henan Province, China.

II.To discover how secondary school principals are prepared for their present principal leadership role in Henan Province, China.

III.To explore the constraints and challenges faced by Henan secondary school principals, in their preparation and professional development programmes.

IV.To explore the constraints and challenges of the principal leadership practices faced by Henan secondary school principals.

1.6 Research Questions

The following research questions have been formulated based on the research objectives above:

I.To what extent do the governmental training policies affect the preparation and development of secondary school principals' leadership in Henan Province, China?

II.How do the secondary school principals prepare for their present principal leadership role?

III.What are the constraints and challenges faced by secondary school principals in Henan Province, China in their preparation and professional development programmes?

IV.What are the constraints and challenges faced by secondary school principals in Henan Province, China regarding their leadership practices?

1.7 Definition of Terms

There are four key concerns that have to be front and center and the terminologies are defined as follow to allow a better understanding of this study.

I.Principal Preparation

School community can never keep in order without a leading character. Principals can only take over this substantial role when they have undergone training prior to their appointment. Principal preparation concerns on the compulsory pre-service for the new principals. This pre-requisite training aims to equip the beginners with leadership capabilities to be in position. The completion of the pre-service training is affirmed with the principal qualification certificate system which appears as a qualification and ability recognition of the principals to be on duty to rule the school community.

II.Principal Professional Development

Principal professional development concerns on the later development of principalship ability. The available training programmes available in the country are in-service training and self-directed development training. The existing training accepts participation when they are already in the role and needed a boost of energy and supports, for example Qualification Training, Improvement Training and Advanced Training. The completion of the required improvement training and advanced training will add value to their leadership experience and their qualification recognition.

III.Principal Leadership Practice

Leaders are often related to leading improvement and advancement. Whether or not the principals are able to guide the school population towards the desired and guided goals, it is important to look at how the leaders are able to utilize their own leadership skills and traits to move forward with their group of teachers and students. In this study, the leadership practice concerns on the ability and leadership style of the school principals to reach unity within his population and achieve what they are required, for instances, school education excellence, students' enrolment rate, and teacher performances.

IV.Principal Leadership Role

Leading a school population, school principals have to be always ready to cope with circumstances that come out of nowhere, either from the teachers' team or the students. School principals have been stereotyped to be the educators, managers of teacher and student affairs, and the goalkeepers to meet the reformation requirements. The leadership roles have undergone changes with the societal changes and the expectation shift onto the results from their leadership ability. The leadership roles that they are playing are to coordinating all the mentioned tasks and ensure all of them are on the right track. Extensive leadership experiences are needed when it is to deal with affairs that involve different parties: teacher team, students, the Ministry of Education, the parents and the publics. Thus, apart from being the school leaders, they are the managers of resourcing and the influential personnel in school-public relationship.

1.8 Significance of the Study

The main contribution of this study is to provide a deeper understanding regarding the preparation and professional development of secondary school principals' leadership in China.

This study will provide empirical evidence to the knowledge base and international literature, and will be a foundation for further research in China and beyond.

1.9 Limitations and Delimitations

As stated in Hallinger & Heck (1996: 7), "any attempt to integrate a body of research into a coherent framework that summarizes empirical, conceptual and methodological issues, must begin with an acknowledgement of its limitations." Due to the differences in context and the focus of schools located in the Henan Province, the findings of this study are limited to the selected schools within this province and cannot be representative of the whole province and whole of China. Nevertheless, the gross depiction will allow readers to conceptualize upon the common issues and the general phenomenon of preparation and professional development of secondary school principals' leadership in China.

This study explores the preparation and professional development of secondary school principals' leadership in China from the respondents' perspectives. Instead of using a specific model as a framework, the relevant literature about educational leadership as well as the preparation and professional development of primary and secondary school principals' leadership in China will be used to support the propositions. Therefore, the purpose of this study is not to prove any previous method and content of preparation and development of secondary school principals' leadership, but its intent is to understand the current issues, situation and challenges of the preparation and professional development of secondary school principals' leadership in China.

1.10 Structure of the Thesis

This thesis comprises of seven chapters. Each chapter represents its significance in allowing readers to have a clearer understanding and idea about the main concerns outlined in this study. The seven chapters are as follows: (1) Introduction, (2) Background of Chinese Education, (3) Literature Review, (4) Research Methodology, (5) Findings, (6) Discussion and finally (7) Conclusion and Recommendations.

Chapter 1, the introduction chapter, begins with introducing the education system in China, and pays particular focus on primary and secondary education within the Henan Province. It also traces the education reforms advocated by the Chinese Education Department, showing the renewed interest in the professionalism and leadership preparedness of school principals, in line with their succession plan.

Chapter 2 (Background of Chinese Education) focuses on the historical background of China, traces the historical development of the Chinese educational system, as well as the evolution of principal leadership in China. This chapter also looks at the effects of the changing ideologies concerning the educational system, principal leadership practices, and the influence of the political nature of this country on the school management and leadership configuration. Overall, this chapter anchors the central idea of school principal leadership, with implications on the need to enhance professionalism in line with meeting the nation's educational initiatives and missions.

Chapter 3 (Literature Review) reviews the relevant theories of leadership and provides a historical account of Chinese school leadership since the establishment of the PRC in 1949. The chapter attempts to relate leadership concepts with contemporary issues, obstacles and challenges faced by school principals. It also explores literature on principal preparation and their leadership development.

Chapter 4 (Research Methodology) outlines the research approach and design employed in this study, the population and samples of this study, as well as addressing the issue of validity and reliability of this research.

Chapter 5 (Findings) presents the detailed and systematic description of qualitative data analyzed from open-ended questionnaires, field observation report and semi-structured interviews with school principals.

Chapter 6 (Discussion) presents the results of this study and covers discussions on the professionalism of school principals and the impact of training policies on principalship preparation and professional development, in the Henan Province, China.

Chapter 7 (Conclusion and Recommendations) attempts to sum up the study with constructive recommendations, for similar research to be potentially replicated in other provinces of China.

CHAPTER 2: BACKGROUND OF CHINESE EDUCATION

2.1 Introduction

In order to have a better understanding of the preparation and professional development of secondary school principals' leadership in China, it is important to look at the Chinese educational system from a historical's perspective. The political nature of a country is usually associated with national educational ideologies and its educational system. As stated in Crossley and Watson (2003), it is not fair to isolate educational factors from its political, social, economic, and other environmental elements in the growth process of education.

Different contexts have different influences on principal leadership practices. Kwan (2011) states that contextual elements should not be ignored in the study about school leadership development. Hence, this chapter provides an insight to the Chinese educational system as well as a review of the preparation and professional development of school leadership in China since the establishment of the People's Republic of China until today.

2.2 Basic Facts of China

China is a sovereign nation located in the east of Asia. As one of the four most ancient civilizations in the world, China is a nation rich with more than 5,000 years of history. Spanning across about 9,600,000 square kilometers, China is one of the biggest countries of the world. China has all kinds of landscape, ranging from the mountains of Tibet to Hainan's blue sea; and from the Inner Mongolian steppe to the stretch of Yunnan rice paddy plantations. Despite diverse local dialects, Mandarin is the main language used by the 1.35 billion inhabitants of China, making it the world's most widely used language.

China comprises of 23 provinces, 5 autonomous regions (Sinkiang, Tibet, Inner Mongolia, Guangxi, Ningxia), 4 direct-controlled municipalities (Beijing, Shanghai, Tianjing, and Chongqing) and two special administrative regions (Hong Kong and Macau).

The People's Republic of China (PRC) was established in 1949 under the lead of Mao Zedong. Marxists' and Mao Zedong's ideologies have led to the construction of socialist China. Since the establishment of PRC, several crucial events changed the course of Chinese history. Events such as "The Cultural Revolution", the "Great Leap Forward", and the "Reform and Opening-up", not only have had a great influence on Chinese social policies, economics, and politics, but also a great impact on the Chinese educational development (Hu, 1991; Tsang, 2000). The economic reform began in 1978. Since then China's economy has been growing rapidly. In 2016, it was the second-largest economy in the world by both nominal total Gross Domestic Product (GDP) of 11,392 billion US dollars and a "Purchasing Power Parity" (PPP) of 21,269 billion US dollars (World Bank, 2016).

China is viewed as a potential superpower by many nations. Its present political system is labeled as "people's democratic dictatorship" (Zhang, 2013); its ideological system is known as "socialism with Chinese characteristics" and its economic system is perceived as a "socialist market economy" by Chinese leaders (Chen, Gao & Zhou, 2009). The Chinese education that is under the Chinese government's control, is influenced by these ideologies. It is in this context that the Chinese educational system has evolved through its widespread territory, coping with very different cultures, climates, and different levels of development. The context of this study is based on the Henan Province, where China's civilization began. Located in the central part of China, with an area of 167,000 km^2 (64,479 sq. mi), Henan is the third most populous province in China with a population of more than 94.36 million (*China Statistical Year Book*, 2015). Moreover, according to the Henan Province Bureau of Statistics (2016), Henan ranked fifth in the economic aggregate of China. Nevertheless, Henan is still considered as one of the less developed regions in China. In 2015, China was reported to have 9,370,500 primary school students, 4,048,100 junior high school students and 1,943,100 senior high school students (*China Statistical Year Book*, 2015).

2.3 The Chinese Educational System

China's educational system is divided into several stages depending on the age of the pupils. It begins with early childhood education, followed by primary education, secondary education, then tertiary education. As of 2014, this system was composed of 209,881 nursery schools with 40,507,000 pupils; 201,377 primary schools with 94,511,000 pupils; then 67,851,000 students went to the 65,876 secondary schools; and lastly 3,856 colleges and universities gathered 35,543,000 students (*China Statistics Year Book*, 2015).

Since the establishment of the PRC, China's educational system has evolved according to the political environment and historical changes. The Chinese government has been promoting educational reform and development, and has transformed the populous country into a strong resourceful country, equipped with the largest educational Chinese system in the world. The following section reviews the progress of the Chinese educational system since the establishment of the PRC.

2.3.1 People's Republic of China (1949—1976)

The establishment of the PRC in 1949 arose with the closure of semi-colonial and semi-feudal social conditions in China. At this time, the country was isolated and overwhelmed by the West, hence, education became an important tool to rapidly achieve industrialization, enrich the nation's ascendancy to achieve national goals. School principals at different phases, were given different functions by the Chinese government.

In the early days of the PRC (1949—1956), the main mission of the new government was to restore the national economy. During this period, the Chinese educational system followed the Soviet Union's educational pattern (Feng, 2006; Zheng, 2003) by introducing a simplex school-running system, with schools being the "institutions of socialization" (Feng, 2003a). The educational goals were to recover and develop the new educational system by fostering cadres and teachers to take the lead on deploying industrial construction, establishing specialized colleges and schools and reconstructing the national school structure (Chen & Hong, 2007). Under this mission, the "Institute of Education Administration" was the first training center established in Beijing (Feng, 2003a). The training content used at this institute, reflected the social and political development needs of the national educational system and covered topics of philosophy, psychology and pedagogy. During the following decade, several other training institutes were established, and the local government used the same training methods and content to develop their school leaders and promote school education. During the early establishment of the PRC, the school principal training lacked in expertise and resources.

In 1956, China established the socialist basic relief system, and created conditions for the emancipation and the development of productive forces. During the process of socialist construction, the Chinese chairman Mao proposed Four Modernizations: agriculture, industry, national defense, and science and technology (Di, 2014; Tsang, 2000). These new orientations were introduced to meet the needs of social development, and improve the quality of education. The school leader played the key role in promoting the development of education under the governance and control of national leaders. When the Socialist Transformation Movement ended in 1956, the Communist Party of China stepped into a period that involved the total reconstruction of socialism. Following this, the education system underwent a "great leap forward" with the implementation of the Fourth Session of the National Education Administration. During this period, the professional development of teachers' and school principals was downplayed and neglected (Tsang, 2000; Wang, 2002). During the Chinese "Cultural Revolution" (1966—1976), China sustained serious losses economically, culturally and educationally (Cai & Du, 2003). Social development was extremely restricted. "The Cultural Revolution" focused on the economy and on politics, and advocated to abrogate education (Thogerson, 1990).At that time, students spent most of their time in political activities and school activities were based on the dictatorship of the proletariat. School systems were termed as "a proletarian school system" (Sui, 2012; Thogersen, 1990). The negative influence of "the Cultural Revolution" on education, science, and culture was extremely profound. Countless intellectuals were persecuted, schools were closed, and many research institutions were revoked (Cai & Du, 2003; Sui, 2012).

"The Cultural Revolution" led educational careers into a period of stagnation and backward development. The functions of education were completely denied (Sui, 2012; Tsang, 2000). School principal trainings came to a standstill (Feng, 2003a). As a result, the headmaster's role became insignificant and lower qualified individuals were appointed to take responsibility of schools. This resulted in very low quality education (Kwong, 1988; Lin, 1993), as the level of professionalism among school leaders could not meet the demands of the four modernizations.

After the Third Plenary Session (1978), The CPC (the Communist Party of China) Central Committee attempted to recover the Chinese education. According to Wang (2002), the school management and educational structure during this era, did not have a strong foundation. Moreover, there were inadequate numbers of schools, a lack of qualified teachers and a severe lack of teaching and learning equipment. According to the 1982 census statistics, 235,820,002 people, (around a quarter of the Chinese population), were illiterate or semi-literate (*National Bureau of Statistics of China*, 1982). This was a serious constraint to the development of education and modernization. Since the establishment of China in 1949, the political leaders have emphasized that education should serve and support politics. This is evident from Deng's speech presented during the National Conference on Education in 1978 (Deng, 1978: 1): *"schools should follow political direction as priority; schools should strengthen on revolutionary order and revolutionary discipline."*

2.3.2 Educational Reform and China's Open Policy (1978—2014)

During the reformation, the modernization of China's education started to establish itself with educational reform at the core (Fai & Wang, 2008). The development of education during this period evolved through three stages. The first stage (1978 to 1984) began with the "National Conference on Education" hosted in Beijing by Deng, the Chinese vice-chairman and reformist, on 22 April 1978 (Cheng, 2012). Deng proposed the following suggestions for educational reform and development to improve the quality of education:

I.To enhance the level of teaching for the Sciences, Social Sciences and Humanities in order to better serve the socialist construction. Deng particularly emphasized that developing Science and Technology was a priority;

II.To send a large number of students overseas to learn advanced technologies beneficial for the country's development;

III.Teachers to be given due respect and authority (Deng, 1978).

Learning experiences from developed countries became an important resource for educational reforms in China (Fei & Wang, 2008). In the mid and late 1980's, Chinese education began to progress through theoretical research and practice, and gradually formed the characteristics of China's educational philosophy (Fai & Wang, 2008). The strategic development of China's education, its educational reforms, as well as the level of curricula and teaching was fully emphasized (Chu, 2008). From 1978 to 1984, restoring order was the main goal of education, which emphasized on the importance of knowledge for economic construction (Tsang, 2000). In 1979, the school principal training institution was re-established. This institution provided trainings and developed talents in a shorter frame of time, and this appeared as the new feature of school principal training (Feng, 2003a). With the recovery of educational order, education at different levels developed rapidly, and the basics of an educational system was thus formed.

With the improved educational structure, the government allocated educational resources to improve the quality of education during this time. However, the government allocations were provisioned for the minorities, and this brought about serious inequalities in educational allocation (Cheng, 2012; Tsang, 2000). From 1985 to 2002, the second phase of educational reform flourished. In May 1985, the Chinese central government issued *"The CPC's Decisions on the Education System Reform"* (CPC, 1985). This was the most important document guiding educational reforms in the 1980s (Feng, 2003a). This document clearly stated that, *"Education must serve the socialist construction, and that the socialist construction must rely on education"* (CPC, 1985). It also raised the curtain on the comprehensive educational reforms applicable (Cheng, 2012). At this stage, reforming the educational structure was the main mission of the educational reforms strategy. However, the educational system had to adapt to the economic system for appropriate and simultaneous reform (Wang, 1994).

The central Chinese government then implemented the nine-year compulsory education, restructured secondary education, and developed vocational and technical colleges (CPC,1985). Under the school management system, the principal assumed a full responsibility of the school. At this stage, the focus was on the internal distribution policy reform of primary schools and secondary schools to start implementing a staff appointment system and a school reward system. Educational reform initiatives placed emphasis on process efficiencies, and after the new educational order was established, schools administrative and managerial efficiencies were greatly improved. The *"Outline of Chinese Education Reformation and Development* (OCERD)*"*, also pointed out that the expanse of education, has improved the education quality and school efficiencies. Primary and secondary schools began to focus on "exam-oriented education".

In 2001, with the promulgation of the *"Compendium of Curriculum Reform of Fundamental Education"*, a new curricula reform was implemented in primary and secondary schools to emphasize on quality-oriented education. The OCERD also reported on the resultant outcomes to be attained at the end of the 20th century: A nine-year compulsory education to eliminate illiteracy among young and middle-aged people in China. The OCERD explicitly indicated that education should be directed towards quality-oriented education and this reformation strategy has been emphasized since then.

When China joined the World Trade Organization (WTO) in 2001, the Central Committee of the CPC and the Chinese State Council, proposed a new educational strategy, "invigorating the country through Science and Education." Since 2003, the nation has been focusing on educational reform. With the social development and the continued economic growth, educational investments have grown substantially and school operations have improved remarkably. The Chinese government has prioritized an action plan for invigorating education in the 21st century. Then in 2006, the Chinese government promulgated the 11th "*Five-Year Plan*" with the aim of prioritizing the development of education and human resources. A jargon of "scientific development" , introduced by the Chinese Communist Party's Sixteenth National Congress and the Third Plenary Session of its Sixteenth Central Committee, became the basic guiding principle of educational policy-making, educational reform and development since 2003.

In 2010, the *"National Medium and Long-term Plan for Education Reform and Development (2010—2020)"* proposed that education should prioritize the development of an educational system featured with Chinese socialism characteristics (CPCC, 2010). The plan pointed out that quality improvement is the core task of education reformation and development. This plan also sought to advocate educators into running a school, and encourage teachers and principals to take on bold practices. It also looked at perfecting the training system and developing the training plan, which helped cultivate, strengthen and improve the professional competencies of the primary and secondary school principals.

2.4 The Phylogeny of Primary and Secondary School Principal Training

The primary and secondary school principal trainings had experienced critical changes in social reform during the past decades in China. The Chinese government proposed different policies and strategies for developing school principal leadership. The following sub-sections highlight the main policies and documents issued by the Chinese government at different historical phases.

2.4.1 People's Republic of China (1949-1988)

With the establishment of the PRC, teachers and principals played significant roles in restructuring China. Hence, the Chinese government started to pay attention to teachers and principals training. In March 1952, the government promulgated a set of school regulations that clearly outlined the roles of the "headmaster" in charge of the system. After 1954, the Chinese government started to pay attention to teachers and principal training. At this time, the school principal' s role was mainly managerial. In 1954, the Chinese central government issued a set of "*Instructions*" known as *"Improvement and Development of Secondary School Education"* . These instructions stipulated a systematic plan to train principals in batches and by rotation. Along with this set of Instructions, the first training programme was conducted by the Ministry of Education. According to Feng (2003a), the objectives were to improve the political and ideological outlook of school principals in order to execute school administration under a new educational system. A number of promising school principals who were eligible for school administration and national educational development underwent this training programme.

In the following year, the first education administrative training center was established in September 1955 in Beijing, after being approved by Chairman, Mao Zedong. According to Feng (2003a), the guiding principle for running a school was to balance out between politics and professionalism, while combining theory with practice. The training content of this one-year programme consisted of philosophy, pedagogy and psychology (He et al., 1997). Since the training content was mainly dominated by political ideology, school principals were asked to be government cadres rather than professional personnel (Feng, 1996).

From 1958 to 1979, it was a period of inactivity, due to the social unrest between the "Right-leaning Ideas" and the Chinese government, which led to the 10-year "Cultural Revolution" . Because of the political unrest, school principals' leadership positions were seriously affected. In 1959, the Central Institute of Educational Administration was shut down because of political pressure. During "the Cultural Revolution" , all the school principals training institutions were closed and all the school principals training programmes were completely stopped by the government (Feng, 2003a; Jia, 2012). After "the Cultural Revolution" , all the social systems and social orders needed to be re-established. The quality of school principals could not keep pace with the Four Modernizations, and so the Chinese government began to focus on school principals trainings. Since 1980, the school principal training in China went through three main stages, which are an adjustment and recovery period, the transformational period and the rapid development period (Wu, 2009).

In August 1982, the State Education Commission of the People's Republic of China issued an official document known as *"The Opinion on Strengthening the Training Work for Ordinary Education Administrative Cadres"*. This document contained the philosophy, goals, requests, content, and methods of school principal trainings in China (Feng, 2003a). However, according to Wu (2009), the training targets were found to be too general:

"To improve the ideological and political qualities, educational theoretical level and management skills."

"To make the cadres training work institutionalized and regularized."

(Source: People's Education, 1982: 45).

Furthermore, because of the lack of targeted training programmes for primary and secondary school principals, principals were not well prepared for their roles. In 1980, the Education Administrative Institute was re-established in Beijing as the "Central Academy of Educational Administration" (Jia, 2012). Since then, training work resumed and rapidly developed in China. In October 1982, China's State Education Commission introduced a revised version of the previous document named, *"The Opinion on Strengthening the Training Work for Administrative Personnel of Primary and Secondary Schools"*. The objectives of this revised version, were to improve the ideological and political qualities, educational theoretical level and management skills, and to ensure that the cadres training work is institutionalized and regularized. In August 1987, China's State Education Commission officially re-issued *"Opinions on Strengthening the Construction of the Headmasters of Primary and Secondary Schools"* and stipulated that training centres are important bases for educational leaders' professionalism and development (SEC, 1992).

From 1980 to 1988, the Chinese government paid particular attention to the professionalism of educational management work. While numerous training programmes for educational leaders were organized, the role of school principals was not given due importance. Whatever trainings were conducted, it was based on political theories, educational theories and management skills. These training methods were also simple "chalk and talk" methods, as described by Chen (2011). Furthermore, Feng (1996) pointed out that many training institutions lack modern technology and advanced training methods.

2.4.2 Educational Reform (1989-2016)

Due to the lack of targeted training programmes, primary and secondary school principals were not well prepared for their roles under China's educational reform. To improve the level of school principals and enhance their training, a series of documents and policies were issued throughout the last 26 years. The researcher conducted a document analysis to review and assess these official documents and government policies, 11 documents based on the policy contents and priorities highlighted in Table 2.1.

Based on Gong (2012) and Zheng, Chen and Lu (2010), there are four categories of training policies concerning primary and secondary school principals according to the changes of policy contents. The first category, Type I, refers to the national macro educational policy documents. The second category, Type II, refers to the training implementation documents issued by the National Education Administration. The third category, Type III, is about the educational cadres training plan documents, and the fourth category, Type IV, is about personnel policy documents. School principal trainings were not merely about the training contents and training methods, but it was based on a policy package related to the national education development plan, basic educational reform policy and personnel system. The national training policy embodies the basic understanding, requirements and purpose of the primary and secondary principal trainings (Zheng , Lu , Chen, 2010).

Table 2.1 Policies on School Principal Trainings in China

Document Names	Policy Focus	Policy Category
Opinion on Strengthening the Training for the Principals of Primary and Secondary Schools (1989)	· Framework of school principals training · Appointed qualifications for training · Principals' appointment and evaluation	Type II
Opinions of the State Education Commission on Post Training for Headmasters of Primary and Secondary Schools (1990)	·Job training and implementation	Type II

Continued

Document Names	Policy Focus	Policy Category
Requirements and Position Requirements of Headmasters of Primary and Secondary Schools in China (1991)	· Job training certification for principals	Type IV
Opinion on Strengthening the Team Construction of Primary and Secondary School Principals (1992)	· 5-year job training rotation for school principals	Type IV
Opinions of the State Council on the Implementation of the Outline of China's Educational Reform and Development (1994)	· Implementation of primary and secondary school principal training plan · Implementation of post-holding certificate for primary and secondary school principals	Type I
Training Regulations for Primary and Secondary School Principals (1999)	· Establishing an integrated framework for school principal training · Establishing the relationship between school principal training and educational reforms	Type II
Opinion of Ministry of Education on Further Strengthening and Improving the Training of Primary and Secondary School Principals (2002)	· To promote the basic education reform and development · Recommend training materials for school principals	Type II
Action Plan for Education Revitalization 2003—2007 (2004)	· To combine educational cadre training and life-long education	Type I
National Eleventh Five - Year Plan for Cadre Training of the Educational System (2007)	· Emphasis on quality-oriented education for school principal trainings · To promote trainings	Type III
Professional Standards of Headmasters for compulsory schools (2013)	· To define the basic trends of school reform and development	Type II
Opinions of the Ministry of Education on Further Strengthening the Training of Primary and Secondary School Principals(2013)	· To improve the training system (content, methods, evaluation) and quality of principal training	Type II

In December 1989, the State Education Commission promulgated the policy, *"Opinion on Strengthening the Training for the Principals of Primary and Secondary Schools"* (MOE, 1989). This was the first systematic and complete guiding document for primary and secondary school principals training. In this document, school principal training was perceived as the strategic intent to comprehensively implement Communist Party and national educational policies. It also established a basic institutional framework for school principals' training and development (Gong, 2012; Lu, Chen & Zheng, 2010). Meanwhile, the government introduced the *"Multimillion Primary and Secondary School Principal Training"* project. China's school principal training entered the phase of standardization and systematization (Chen, 2010). At this time, the characteristics of the school principal training were fundamental, universal and compulsory (Guo, 2007).

In 1991, the State Education Commission issued another official document—*"Requirements and Position Requirements of Headmasters of Primary and Secondary Schools in China"* (SEC, 1991). This formed the basis for school principals' selection, appointment, assessment and training. The document defined the four main responsibilities of school principals. Firstly, the main duty of the school principal is to implement the national educational guidelines, policies, laws and regulations. Secondly, the school principal is viewed as a democratic manager, who is tasked with developing teachers' initiatives, motivation and creativity. Thirdly, school principals are required to manage their schools by leading and organizing educational activities, and building collaborative relationships with parents and the broader communities. Lastly, the school principal is expected to play a guiding role in facilitating school educational development and create a good environment for educating students. In order to enhance the quality of school principals' trainings, universities were expected to collaborate with local authorities to design training programmes and provide trainings, according to the directives of the Ministry of Education (Chen, 2010; Feng, 2003a). From 1991 to 1995, qualification training was the main training method. Both aspiring school principals and in-service school principals needed to participate in trainings, in order to be certified.

Since 1995, professional development programmes have been carried out on the structure of national, provincial, city and county levels under the coordination and organization of the Ministry of Education in China. In 1998, the Ministry of Education promulgated, to have training and continuing education for all the primary and secondary school principals and full-time teachers, in order to consolidate and improve the system of primary and secondary school principal trainings and the post-holding certificate system, within three years (MOE, 1998). In December 1999, the Ministry of Education officially issued policy entitled the *"Training Regulations for Primary and Secondary School Principals"* (MOE, 1999). This was the first administrative regulation that legally endorsed school principal training in China. It also defines the content, form as well as the training responsibilities for school principals. This document has stipulated that new school principals are required to be certified with official training qualifications, before they serve as a school principal. For those who wish to retain their position as school principal, will have to be re-trained every five years (MOE, 1999). In order to match this training policy, the local government established training policies and training systems to support school principals training development (Guan & Song, 2000).

In May 2001, the State Council issued the policy *"Decision of State Council on the Reform and Development of Basic Education"* (State Council, 2001). This official document is intended to improve and regulate the management system of primary and secondary school principals in accordance with the law. This document also contains the criteria regarding the appointment system and the necessary qualifications required of primary and secondary school principals. In February 2002, the *"Opinion of Ministry of Education on Further Strengthening and Improving the Training of Primary and Secondary School Principals"* (MOE, 2002) was implemented to further perfect the training system and improve its quality by strengthening the programme pertinence and effectiveness. Efforts to build principal's professionalization are driven by reform and innovation.

In September 2009, the revised document entitled *"The National Eleventh Five-Year Plan for Cadre Training of the Educational System"* was promulgated by the Ministry of Education. The objectives of this document defined four general aspects of the training:

I.To fully implement large scale and high quality training programmes for educational cadres;

II.To monitor the educational system and build a collaborative, diversified, and effective training method;

III.To enhance the training system by promoting a scientific, systematic and normative training method;

IV.To fully utilize high quality training resources.

This revised document also pointed out that the key issues are how to improve the training quality, innovate the training mode and expand training types.

At present, school principal training in China is largely governed by the macro guidance of the Ministry of Education (Chen, 2010). There are four national training institutions, thirty-one provincial training institutions, over two hundred municipal training institutions and more than two thousand training institutions in China (He, 2011; Yan & Ehrich, 2009; Zheng et al., 2013). Training centres were set up to organize, plan, coordinate and guide school principal trainings and help improve their quality and efficiency. Trainings assist school principals to develop the correct ideology for running a school. According to Chen (2010), this was done previously by a principal training network system.

Before the 1990s, Chinese school principal trainings used apprenticeship methods, as qualified teachers were then selected as school principals (Feng, 2003a). Since 1990, school principals formal training has improved greatly. The Chinese government has organized a large number of training programmes for school principals' professional development. More than one million school principals participated in these training programmes (Feng, 2003a). During this period, the government authorities also issued a series of documents that clearly defined the roles, responsibilities and competencies required of school principals. The school principal training system has become more scientific and systematic with collaborative and diversified training methods introduced. Through the years, principals' professionalization was gradually established. As their training evolved towards institutionalization and standardization, school principals were valued for their independent roles. Through an open and diversified training system, the training content met the basic demands of social change, and this greatly enhanced the quality of education. At present, there are three types of certificate training programmes provided for school principals:

I.The 300-hour "Qualification Training" professional certification for newly appointed principals;

II.The 240-hour "Improvement Training" for principals equipped with certified qualifications;

III.The "Advanced Training Seminar" is for a select group of outstanding principals (*gu gan xiao zhang*) who wish to enhance their leadership skills and knowledge.

(Source: MOE, 1999; Yan & Ehrich, 2009; Zheng et al., 2013: 490).

The trainers for these courses are usually university lecturers like research fellows and professors, who train principals in the philosophy of education, curriculum management, computer and information technology and educational administration. Besides, they also instill in principals the values of effective school management and the ability to lead schools with passion, vitality and compassion. Other activities of these programmes include face-to-face lectures, group discussions, school visits, internship programme and submission of a project paper (Chen, 2010). These trainings are organized by the Chinese government. However, it is known that school principals are not allowed to select their preferred training institution during the period of induction and improvement training (Lv, 2011).

2.5 School Principals' Preparation and Professional Development

This section elaborates on the major issues concerning school principal's preparation and professional development in Henan Province, China. The following sub-sections further describe the preparation roles of secondary school principals, their qualifying credentials and the principal training system, which includes training curriculum, training method, training evaluation, training funding and training timeframe.

2.5.1 Principal Preparation

The principal as the prime leader of a school needs to be well equipped to manage their changing and challenging leadership roles. Presently, there are three forms of strategies that prepare secondary school principals for their leadership roles: pre-service and in-service trainings and self-directed development strategies. Among the principal trainings available include Qualification Training, Improvement Training, Advanced Training and other forms of training. Specifically, Qualification Training is the prerequisite leadership preparation programme that equips school principals with the necessary leadership roles. Improvement Training and Advanced Training are the training programmes held to continuously promote school principals' professional development (Chen, 2010; Chen & Liu, 2012; Chu & Yang, 2009; Huang, Liang & Lin, 2010).

The self-directed development strategy refers to school principals who are seeking additional ways to improve and develop their leadership capabilities and extend their leadership expertise (Tang et al., 2014; Wilson & Xue, 2013). With Liang's (2005) research in Beijing, the results illustrated that school principals' leadership practices were based on their previous experiences. Walker & Qian (2015) also stress the importance of building human relationships and forging strong bonds with other principals. This is regarded as an effective way to promote leadership practices. Furthermore, Sun, Cheng and Deng (2015) also pointed out that training and reading are very important for the professional development of school principals.

2.5.2 Principals Qualifying Credentials

The principal qualification certificate system is the qualifying criteria and professional standards prescribed by the Chinese government. This certification prepares and trains principals for their leadership roles while equipping them with professional values, knowledge and skills (Jia, 2005). In China, most of the school principals are selected from qualified teachers (Liu & Li, 2012). According to the *"Training Regulations for Primary and Secondary School Principals"* , new school principal candidates must obtain a training qualification before they serve as school principals. As for those who want to keep their position as school principal, they have to be re-trained every five years (MOE, 1999). However, Jia (2005) argues that the school principal's appointment system and certification is merely a formality, because this qualification certificate has not been legalized. At present, the principal qualification certificate system still remains under the policy category, and is not conducive for the implementation of school principal training. Moreover, according to Tian, Meng and Fu (2012), there seems to be a disconnection between the school principals' credentials system and the school principal trainings. Nevertheless, the certification exam is not very strict because it is well known that once the school principal candidates are selected, they will definitely receive their certifications, regardless of their performance. Besides, it has been reported that some of the school principals receive training certifications, without participating in any training (Xia, 2011b).

Although, Chinese government has promulgated a series of regulations on primary and secondary school principal qualification training, school principals' qualification standard continues to use the standard implemented in 1991. The following are the conditions stipulated by the *"Requirements and Position Requirements of Headmasters of Primary and Secondary Schools in China"* (1991):

I.The academic credentials of primary school principals cannot be lower than secondary normal school principals;

II.The academic credentials of secondary school principals cannot be lower than college degree principals;

III.The academic credentials of senior secondary school principals cannot be less than principals whom are bachelor degree holders.

Comparing the credentials system with developed countries, Chinese school principals' qualification standards do not consider the school principals' administrative experiences (Liu, 2010). The *"Instructive Teaching Programme for National Qualification Training of Primary and Secondary School Principals"* was promulgated in 2001. This establishes the primary and secondary school principals' credentials system. According to Yang (2005), the document aims to promote the overall understanding of the school principal's occupation, their roles, rights and duties, as well as their leadership and management ability.

2.5.3 Training Curriculum

The training curriculum is the crucial part of school principal training. Chu (2009) defined training curriculum as the scope of teaching content. Various studies confer that training curriculum has a direct impact on school principals' job performance (Rao, 2015; Wang, 2011; Xu, 2011; Zhou, 2015). Principal training has been a tool to prepare the school leaders for their on-the-job needs. Thus, knowing the curriculum of the training will enable the readers to have a basic concept of what are the skills and knowledge embedded in the training and targeted to inculcate into their soft and hard skills.

2.5.3.1 Principal Training Curriculum Development in China

In 1989, China began to develop a clear training curriculum for principals (Zhang, 2011). Every five years, the Ministry of Education implements a new curriculum and teaching material according to their national economy and political development plans. During the exploration phase of *"The Eighth Five-Year Plan"* (1991—1995), the main training content of principal trainings comprised of political theories, education policies and regulations, basic educational theories, teaching and school management. At that time, the curriculum was standardized and unified (Zhang, 2011), and the training content was centred on the post requirements of primary and secondary school principals'. The teaching plan and the training content were simple and basic, and were linked to the political literacy and theoretical knowledge (Rao, 2015).

The consolidation phase in *"The Ninth Five-Year Plan"* (1996—2000) addressed the requirements of market economy, technology reform and quality-oriented education. These concerns were embodied in the training content. The curriculum setting became more flexible and innovative. During this period, the training content began to shift from knowledge to practice. *"The Tenth Five-Year Plan"* (2001—2005) training curriculum addressed the new curriculum reform, which included students' moral development and mental health. In addition, the training curriculum emphasized the education reform, and individual needs of school principals' professional development. The *"Eleventh Five-Year Plan"* (2006—2010) addressed the issues of how to push forward the educational reform and implement quality-orientated education (Wang, 2013, Zheng, Chen & Lu, 2010).

The role of the principal was clearly defined during this period (Chen, 2010). The *"National Eleventh Five-Year Plan for Cadre Training of the Educational System"* (MOE, 2007)addresses the school principals' training curriculum, more comprehensively. It covers laws and regulations, school management, curriculum reform, educational assessments, campus safety, hygiene management, information technology applications, funds management, system reform and developing a harmonious campus (Rao, 2015).

For the *"Twelfth Five-Year Plan"* (2011—2015), the curriculum incorporated more advanced ideas and concepts and was found to be more systematic and hierarchical (Xu, 2011). The training content shifted the school management problems from the macro to microcosmic. During this period, the professional standards of school principals at different levels were promulgated:

I.Compulsory Education School Principal Professional Standards.

II.Regular Senior Secondary School Principal Professional Standards.

III.Secondary Vocational School Principal Professional Standards.

Over the various periods, the training curriculum had different characteristics. Before the *"Eighth Five-Year Plan"*, the training curriculum was designed pragmatically. Its purpose was to train the school principals to become school management specialists. During the implementation of the *"Eighth Five-Year Plan"*, the Ministry of Education clearly defined the training curriculum. As for the *"Tenth Five-Year Plan"*, the training curriculum comprised of a combination of an elective course and compulsory course, guidance course and local course, and required course and school-based course (Xu, 2011).

2.5.3.2 Training Curriculum Overview

At present, there are three major types of training programmes: Qualification Training, Improvement Training and Advanced Training. These training programmes are established based on the central model and requirements stated in the *"Training Regulations for Primary and Secondary School Principals"* (MOE, 1999). Taking the training curriculum of the pioneering training providers in Beijing Normal University as reference, the curriculum will be elaborated according to the three training types.

I.Qualification Training

Being a head teacher of a Chinese secondary school, he or she should be socialist ideology literate and politically proficient. This major requirement has a remarkable presence ever since the establishment of PRC (Chen, Gao & Zhou, 2009; SEC, 1991), apart from being physically fit and with a qualifying educational background. Thus, the subject of constructing Chinese socialism and educational practice takes the lead of the training curriculum for the beginner in principalship. The participants will then be educated with modern approach of educational theory and leadership practices, inclusive of educational psychology, counseling skills and application of leadership theory in education. Owing to the obligation of achieving educational reform, national law and governmental policies that are enforced on the education system will be studied and reviewed in one of the course item. Apart from classroom activities, model school visits and a six-month management practice internship are included to add value to the participants to practice what has been preached. Reports to conclude the training and passing the examination will end the beginner training with a professional certificate.

II.Improvement Training

After completing the 300-hour training, the school leaders who are already in position to serve the school community will nevertheless are exhausted with problem solving cases and affairs that often demand on skill advancement and knowledge boosting. The improvement training has a flexible course structure and the participants can choose among the elective courses offered. The basic courses at the stage offer two different natures of course contents: theoretical awareness and applied skills. Theoretical knowledge has never run away from the Marxist philosophy of education where the social functions of education are highlighted to meet the current societal demands (SEC, 1991). Applied skills, including effective leadership application, are educated through the study in depth of scientific approach of school management and educational research to perform school evaluation for school excellence. Elective courses were outlined to provide freedom to the school principals to opt for the knowledge supplement according to their needs, for example educational counselling, foreign educational ideology study and modern educational technology for local education research. The participants are required to produce an introspective report to reflect on their knowledge harvest and the planning for their school management by the end of this 240-hour training.

III.Improvement Training

Improvement training offers a themed seminar based training for school principals with good appraisal with their excellent school management and research abilities, most importantly being keen to sharpen their leadership and management ability and keep up-to-date their research experience. The advanced training allows the school principals to be more specifically equipped with the desired knowledge and be practical by the end of the training. The seminar titles being offered this far are categorized into managerial seminar, strategic research skills towards education reform, stress management, and school excellence diagnosis workshop. Since this training is under a conditional participation, the participants need to be well rounded in their performance to be eligible for the training. The participants' evaluations are subjected to the training requirement and are varied according to the course outline.

2.5.3.3 The Current Issues of Training Curriculum

Over the past decades, the training curriculum has been continuously revised. However, there are still many problems that need to be solved. Chu (2009) highlights some of the challenges of the school principals training curriculum:

I.Subject-centered curriculum setting;

II.The core curriculum is not prominent;

III.The existing training curriculum does not pay enough attention to macro strategic management and microscopic classroom management;

IV.Teaching materials, qualification-training materials and improvement training materials are not divided according to hierarchy. This results in the preparation and professional development programmes being not clearly defined;

V.Training content is subject-centered but lacks the practical curriculum;

VI.The training materials are too traditional and unitary, and not appealing to school principals.

The current curriculum setting does not meet the school principals' professional development needs, as the school principal training has been subject-centered rather than based on actual needs (Feng, 2003a; Han & Dong, 2014; Wang, 2011; Wang, 2013).

Also, one of the biggest concerns is that the training curriculum is not connected to school principals' leadership practice (Chu, 2010). The content of the training curriculum is stipulated by the Chinese government. As a result, the training content is found to be less congruent with school principals' actual demands (Militello & Berger, 2010; Tian et al., 2012; Wang, 2013). At the macro level, Rao (2015) pointed out that training content is important for theory and policy. Moreover, training content lacked a robust research foundation, training institutes and trainers that can subjectively design its content. Furthermore, there was no consideration given to school principals who require different knowledge and skills at different stages of their professional development. Gu (2011) also argued that the training content seems to strongly focus on theoretical aspects and not enough on practical delivery. Wei & Jiang (2011) further add that the training content is not aligned to the educational reform needs and the school principals' development needs. Since the training curriculum is regularly updated every five years, the trainers are required to undergo training first, before they begin to train school principals (Wang, 2011). The question that arises in school principals' professional development is how to utilize the theories learnt from these trainings to solve practical problems, and how to improve school principals' analytical abilities.

School principals appear to have poor initiative as they rely too much on the education administration departments (Zhou, 2015). Moreover, Wang (2014) claims that there is no post-training follow-up with principals and vice-principals, while Gu (2011) indicated that the national training plan conflicts with the provincial training plans. Militello & Berger(2010) also found that training topics were sporadic and repeated, which the training theories did not tally with school principals' leadership practices. Instead, the traditional theoretical part of the training mainly relied on educational experts' report and the systematic analysis of the school context (Xia, 2011a). Since school principals did not have adequate experiences in leadership practice, it is difficult for them to understand the theories systematically. According to Song (2014), the conflicts that arose had an effect on the school principals' training.

2.5.4 Training Methods

The training methods of the principalship development are guided under certain training theories and training ideologies. Based on specific training objectives, a suitable training strategy was used to design the training process and structure operating procedures (Lu, 2014; Zhang, 2011). Besides that, the training method is a tool to achieve the objectives of school principal training, as well as for implementation purposes (Huang, 2013; Yang, 2011). Effective training methods can also continuously improve school principals' professional quality for example and are emphasized in both the *"Notice of the Education Department of Henan Province on Further Strengthening Education Cadre Training in the Province"*

(Department of Henan, 2010) and the *"Opinions of the State Council on Strengthening the Construction of Teachers' Ranks"* (State Council, 2012).

2.5.4.1 Principal Training Methods

During the past decades, school principal trainings in China have undergone various developmental stages. Since the implementation of the *"Eighth Five-Year Plan"*, principal trainings were divided into three stages: compensation training, needs-based training and innovation training (Xia, 2011a). During the *"Eighth Five-Year Plan"* and *"Ninth Five-Year Plan"*, the education background of the majority of primary and secondary school principals, was relatively low and these school principals lacked theoretical knowledge of education. Refresher courses became the main training methods for school principal trainings. As for the *"Ninth Five-Year Plan"*, theme training was the major component of school principal trainings, with some additional compulsory and elective subjects added on (Zhao, 2005).

With the application of information technology in teaching, training methods started to place emphasis on school principals' varied needs. Desire-based training became the mainstream in school principal trainings during the *"Tenth Five-Year Plan"*. The thematic lectures, educational diagnosis and research-based case studies were widely used in school principal trainings throughout year 2001. During the *"Eleventh Five-Year Plan"*, tutorial training methods were used for school principal training (Xia, 2011a; MOE, 2007). During the *"Twelfth Five-Year Plan"*, training aimed to cultivate a large number of outstanding principals in the territory, to encourage a balanced development of education. Currently, school principal training method mainly includes the following: subject-oriented training method, problem-based training method, participative training method, action research method, and network based training method, educational consultation training method and school improvement based training method. A combination of theory, practice, problems and reflections go into developing a diversified training method (Xia, 2011a; Zhou, 2015).

Although, training methods look diverse, Dong (2014) and Zhou (2015) claimed that the trainings are ineffective. The Education Administrative Department incorporates unified training objectives, training materials and training syllabus into the school principal trainings (Dong, 2014). Training methods emphasize more on formalism, whereby most of the training programmes are based on listening activities (experience sharing), observations through campus visiting and "aural activities" (Wang, 2014). In the actual teaching process, training institutes pay more attention to theory. Although training methods are a one-way delivery of the educational theory, it lacks communication and interaction between trainers and trainees.

Training methods rarely pay attention to school principals' initiatives. Ignorance of the principals' subjectivity during the training process, results in the school principal being passive and obedient, especially at county and city levels, where the atmosphere is more oppressive (Fan, 2009; Han & Dong, 2014). Traditional training methods emphasize on knowledge delivery to solve school principals' common problems. Militello & Berger (2010) revealed that the training method design is not based on school principals' actual experiences, and that it neglects the school context and principals' background, which are subject and material-centered (Han & Dong, 2014; Lu, 2014; Wei & Jiang; 2011).

Nowadays, school principal trainings in China are more scientific and systematic by using more diversified training methods (Han & Dong, 2014; Wu, 2009). Nevertheless, Zhou(2015) argues that each training method has its restrictions and functional limitations, and is not compatible with each other. Tian et al. (2012) revealed that training institutes have been looking for ways of improving their training methods, but there has been no fundamental breakthrough as yet. Furthermore, network-teaching resources have not been fully developed and utilized (Han & Dong, 2014).

2.5.5 Training Evaluation

Training evaluation is a crucial part of school principal professionalization and it is an effective mechanism to promote school principals' professional development (Chu & Cravens, 2012). The purpose of training evaluation is to improve training resource allocation and monitor the training plans. Training evaluation helps training institutes to develop the training content and training methods, define school principals' training needs and improve the pertinence and effectiveness of training (Wei, 2015). Training evaluation also enhances and improves the quality of school principal training. Although school principal training in China has rapidly developed during the past decades, studies on school principals' training evaluation are still at the start-up phase and have not established a feasible evaluation system (Chu & Cravens, 2012; Zhang, 2012).

China has not established systematic training evaluation standards for school principal trainings (Xia, 2011b). Training evaluation is not based on the training objectives but according to school principals' subjective feelings, their personal impressions, evaluation report forms, the completion of training plans and training summaries, in order to draw conclusions (Tian et al., 2012; Xiao, 2011b). According to Wei & Jiang (2011), training evaluations mostly are superficial, localized and simplistic. The uncertainty of objectives in trainings is still prevailing collectively. Since the training evaluation process is not of scientific quality, the outcome of the training results may not be as credible (Chen & Lv, 2012).

Training evaluations were carried out randomly, without observing any strict requirements (Chu, 2009). It was also discovered that training institutes did not strictly implement a post-holding certificate system. Instead, there were cases where by selected school principal candidates received training certificates, without participating in training. Training evaluation was a mere formality. According to Wang (2014), training institutes do not have a long-term tracking system in place to monitor training evaluations, of the school principals who participate in trainings. This is commonly understood about the school principals' evaluation system.

Furthermore, the *"Training Regulations for Primary and Secondary School Principals"* clearly point out that the education administrative department of the State Council is responsible for the macro control of primary and secondary school principals' training (MOE, 1999). The education administrative department of provinces, autonomous regions and municipalities is officially responsible for the training plan, the supporting policies, the training implementation, inspection and evaluation (SEC, 1999). However, in reality, training evaluations are conducted by training institutes rather than these education administrative departments. At these training institutes, training teachers are responsible for assessing the training methodology and training content (Liu, 2011). The education administration department carries out some routine checks but this is not considered as a professional training evaluation. Most of the training programmes conducted by training institutes emphasize on summative assessment rather than formative assessment (Wu et al., 2015; Yuan, 2008; Zhao & Wang, 2007).

In 2015, the "*Cadres Education Training Regulation*" was issued by the Central Committee of the Communist Party of China. This regulation stipulates standards for the management system, training content, training method and training evaluation. Article 56 states that *"establishing and perfecting the cadre training evaluation system, strengthens the evaluation of cadre education training institutions, its programmes and curriculum"* (CPC, 2015). Moreover, school principal training evaluation is merely based on the evidence of participants' attendance and their written examinations. This is due to the lack of unified and specific evaluation criteria. The general evaluation criteria to assess school principals' job performance are based on the following dimensions, "morality (德), ability (能), diligence

(勤), and achievement (绩)" (Jia, 2004; Zhao & Wang, 2007). Evaluation methods have not yet established quality standards to execute formative evaluation (Hu & Wang, 2009; Zhang, 2012) As a result, the training evaluation is formalized and superficial and has become challenging to promote school principals' professional development.

2.5.6 Training Institutes

In a training system, training institutions form the organizational foundation of system operations (Chu & Yang, 2009; Chu et al., 2009; Hu, 2013). Therefore, training institutes 'and trainers' specializations have direct impact on the quality of school principal training. At present, all training institutes (national-level, provincial-level, municipal-level and county-level) run primary and secondary school principals' trainings at different levels, supported by universities, colleges of education and normal universities (Zheng et al., 2012).

In China, education administrative departments assign training institutes, because primary and secondary school principal trainings are monopolized by the Chinese national administrative power. This results many social institutes and private sectors not being able to provide in school principals' training. However, Chen et al., (2011) reported that 35% of school principals had participated in non-government training institutes. With the continuous changes in training policies, non-government training institutes embarked upon the school principal training market. In 2011, *"The Tenth Five-Year Plan of National Educational Cadres Training"* proposed to apply the qualification certification system to cadre training bases and establish an open and efficient cadre training system. This showed that Chinese school principal training institutes had begun to shift from a "closed" training institute to that of a more diversified and professional establishment.

Full-time faculties and part-time teachers are the main resource for most of the training institutes (Chu, 2009; Zheng et al., 2012). The *"Training Regulations for Primary and Secondary School Principals"* (1999) clearly pointed out *"principal training institutes shall implement the combination of full-time and part-time teachers."* Currently, there are two prominent issues regarding training instructors. According to Chu (2009) and Song (2014), China has been facing a shortage of excellent experts and trainers for school principal trainings. It is also reported that trainers have a direct influence on the quality and effectiveness of principal trainings. Highly competent training teachers are an assurance for the delivery of improved quality in school principal trainings. However, Chen, Chai, Fang and Lv (2011) pointed out that trainers' teaching and their academic qualification levels are rather low. Many of them are not qualified and are not capable of training work. This results in low quality training. Some of the training managers lack the knowledge and skills for training purposes, and are not familiar with the educational rules and policies (Cheng & Ji, 2009; Fan, 2009; He, 2008).

In China, school principal training mainly relies on the national higher education institutions. Thus, most of the training teachers come from universities or colleges, while the rest consists of educational administration department officers and senior school principals. The quality of training institutions also has an impact on the quality of training managers and training resources (Liu, 2014; Zheng et al., 2012). The shortage and low quality of training teachers has become one of the important reasons that affects the quality and effectiveness of trainings. Besides, the quality and quantity of training instructors are a mismatch with training tasks. Chu (2009) pointed out that 56.7% of the training institutes were without full-time trainers, while Qian (2007) stated that the overall quality of training lectures is not high.

Militello & Berger (2010) also pointed out that trainers were not professionally equipped on the subjects they taught. Principal leadership requires practical guidance. However, in reality, most of the trainers lack practical experience in training school principals. Most of them, who come from universities and education scientific research departments, are mainly engaged in theoretical research. They do not know much about the specific conditions regarding school principals' leadership practices. The majority of the trainers have superficial knowledge about the nature and features of school principals' practices, which cannot satisfy the actual needs of school principals' professional development. Moreover, the number of trainers at county and city levels is relatively low, especially high quality professional trainers who are proficient in school principal management (Fan, 2009).

Another setback is that Chinese scholars pay less attention on trainers (Chen & Lv, 2010). Although, there is rarely any research done in the area of professionalization of training institutes, the cognition of school principals' professional development remains at the level of training content and training methods used. School principal trainings have not been separated from teachers' trainings and other educational trainings (Chen & Lv, 2010). Chen (2009) pointed out that principal training institutes need to establish their core competency, in line with training needs.

2.5.7 Training Funding

There is a training fund that safeguards school principal trainings. *"Compulsory Education Law of the People's Republic of China"* stipulates that the compulsory education fund is the responsibility of the government departments at all levels (MOE, 2006). Nevertheless, the limited training budget is another obstacle that poses a challenge in most of the areas of the Henan Province. Especially, training institutes at county level are with limited funds and poor conditions. Han et al. (2014) reported that only 21.1% of the respondents perceived that the training funds were sufficient, 32.2% respondents felt it was "barely enough", 36.3% respondents deemed training funds as "not enough", and 10.4% respondents reflected "not enough at all". Chang (2005) also indicated that the lack of funding is the leading cause of school principals, not willing to participate in principal trainings.

Moreover, the *"Training Regulations for Primary and Secondary School Principals"* stipulates that the training funds of trainers and school principal trainings cannot be less than 3% of the total salary of faculty members and staff of schools (MOE, 1999). However, due to training funds, whether abundant or not, they are closely related to the local economic development (Dong, 2010). This is especially true in underdeveloped areas, usually without an abundant disposable educational expenditure for school principals. On the contrary, school principals in underdeveloped areas have greater demand for training than school principals who come from developed areas. Furthermore, school principals are not very enthusiastic about participating in trainings because they have to pay part of the training cost, despite having a training fund. This has dampened their enthusiasm for involving in school principals' training. Dong (2010) also indicated that government agencies freely take administrative controls and that soft budget constraints are impeding the management of training funds. Several research studies have indicated that trainings have high costs but low effectiveness and are the key determinant of school principals' professional development (Chang, 2005; Wang, 2010).

2.5.8 Training Time

There is a general believe that the effective use of time can improve the efficiency of school principals leadership performance (Claessens et al., 2007; Grissom et al., 2015; Hall & Hursch, 1982; Hallinger & Heck, 1998; Jamal, 1984; Orpen, 1994). However, the fact remains that Chinese school principals are preoccupied with administrative and management affairs, having to attend meetings and maintaining social networking. It makes them have less time to think about school development or their personal development (Chu, 2009; Liang, 2005; Zhang, 2012). According to the survey reported in Sun et al., (2015), school principals spent 45.98% of the time on daily administrative management affairs and 13.87 % of the time in activities concerning continuing education, which include training and reading.

In Chang (2005), the research findings showed that 19.78% of the 182 school principals did not want to participate in trainings due to their busy schedule. Zhang (2012) pointed out that although school principals appeared very busy, their working efficiency was not as high. Liang (2005) showed that school principals spent most of their time with administrative management affairs. The investigation of 60 school principals by Zhu (2009) concluded that most of the school principals could not finish what they planned to do. They were also mentally and physically exhausted after work, and they did not have time for rest. At times, these school principals cannot carry out their original plans because of unforeseen circumstances that arose. The failure of effective time management has left negative impact on the principal's leadership practices.

2.6 Impact Factors of School Principals' Leadership Practice

2.6.1 School Principals' Incentive Mechanism

According to the Organizational Behavior Theory, "incentive" is defined as a psychological activity that involves an individual's intrinsic motivation towards desired goals (Baker et al., 1988; Bloom & Milkovich, 1998; Eisenhardt, 1989). According to Chu and Yang (2002), an incentive system includes a promotion system, compensation system and assurance system, which serve as an intrinsic motivation for school principals' professional development. It implies that a good incentive mechanism is able to attract more personnel to pursue the school principalship as an occupation (Chu, 2005; Yang, 2003).

Chu and Yang (2002) stated that a promotion serves as an effective way of reflecting upon the professional values of principalship. It also enables the accreditation of professional expertise in the field. Obtaining professional status and reputation is the pursuit of professional practitioners, who aim at improving their professional development. A reasonable compensation system can also motivate school principals' enthusiasm about their leadership. Wu (2009) confirmed that the implementation of performance-based salaries has a positive impact on school principals' performance. Nevertheless, studies on the school principal's incentive mechanism showed that principals tended to have very low levels of job satisfaction

(Hu, 2006). This was evident among secondary school principals who were not satisfied with their salary levels. For some new school principals, their salaries were lower than teachers' average salaries.

Studies by Chen & Lv (2010), Qian (2004) and Shi (2003) further pointed out that the assurance system of primary and secondary school principal training is referred to in order to achieve the quality standards of principal trainings. According to Gong (2000), stimulating school principals' enthusiasm to attend training is the precondition and guarantee of school principals' training quality. Without providing incentives for school principal trainings, school principals generally displayed a negative attitude towards training. According to Chang (2005), 51.7% of 182 school principals left early or did not take part in training. Only 22.2% of school principals participated with full attendance.

The incentive mechanism was established firstly in Shanghai in 1993. In order to evaluate principals' leadership practices, Shanghai was selected for executing the first pilot project, and implementing the *"Principal Rank System"* . This was an incentive system that divided school principals' rank into five levels and twelve grades. In 1996, based on the experimental results of Shanghai, Beijing conducted another pilot project, which divided school principals' rank into five levels and ten grades according to school principals' leadership performance. Ultimately, in 2001, the *"Decision of State Council on the Reform and Development of Basic Education"* (State Council, 2001), was tasked at implementing the school principal rank system. With the rank system being constantly promoted in China, different regions had made their own different rules on the rank system.

The rank wage consists of graded salary, basic wage and performance pay. The Rank system advocates de-administration, intended to transform school principals from "post" to "profession" , and highlight school principals' predominance in their professions. Linking remuneration to school principals' leadership performance, largely enhanced school principals' enthusiasm. Essentially, the Rank System is a catalyst for school principals' growth, and it has a profound influence on principals professional development. According to the Rank System, school principals may be either promoted or demoted. Their overall performance is the benchmark standard for their appointment, salary, evaluation, rewards and sanctions received.

China has not established an effective incentive mechanism for school principals' professional development. Yu (2012) describes the status quo of school principals' incentive mechanism as *"not valued by superior administrative departments, not recognized by school principals, not guaranteed by system and funds; does not have internal conditions and external resources"* (p. 61). In reality, school principals' leadership performance does not really link to their compensations received.

2.6.2 Principals' Responsibilities, Rights and Interests

Since 1985, the *"Principal In-charge System"* has been implemented in China's education system. It stipulates that the school principal is the highest person in the hierarchy, who is the school's legal representative, and who is responsible for internal school work with management autonomy. Bao (2004) and Feng (2003b) explained that the "*Principal In-charge System*" is led by a higher authority, fully responsible to the principal, and democratically managed by faculties. However, many studies indicated that the *"Principal In-charge System"* has not been properly put in place (Feng, 2003b; Li, 2011; Li et al., 2006; Lu, 2003; Wang, 2014).

Chinese scholars generally believe that school principals' responsibilities mainly include political responsibility, economic responsibility, legal liability, management responsibility and ethical responsibility. Precisely, political responsibility refers to the thought and behavior of principals that should reflect the will of the state, conscientiously implement the nation's education policies, responsible for the ideological and political work of teachers and students. Economic responsibility means that school principals have the financial responsibility towards the school's assets, and the balance of income and expenditure. Legal liability refers to school principals whom are responsible for the issues that arise during the process of school management and operation. Management responsibility means that school principals bear the prime responsibility for the orderly operation of school work, including strategy-making, decision-making, and staff recruitment. Ethical responsibility refers to the managerial responsibilities of the school principal in handling public organizations. Principals have the subjective and objective ethical responsibility to achieve public interest (Ge, 2003; Xiong, 2010). However, in reality, policies provide a conceptual description of the "*Principal In-charge System*", without providing a detailed division of their responsibilities. The Principals' responsibilities are described as too broad and not clearly defined.

Yu (1999) summed up that principals should have five functional authorities, which are the right to set up agencies, personnel management, use funds, teaching management and school property management. Institutional setting gives the school principals the power to set administrative and operational matters according to the school needs, for example, the setup of an academic staff office, or student's affairs office. Personnel management refers to the full management of school staff, including the setup of a school team cabinet, staff recruitment and staff dismissal. The right to use funds refers to principals having the power to govern the educational funding and donations as well as the use of funds for facilities and school property maintenance and repair, in accordance with the policies, laws and regulations. The right of teaching management empowers the school principals to conduct teaching and learning activities, develop teaching plans and programmes, integrate school curriculum programmes and develop school-based curriculum. Property right refers to the rights that principals have to use school properties and monitor any illegal disposal of school properties.

Under Article 28 of the *"Compulsory Education Law of the People's Republic of China"*, school principals are subjected to being appointed as teachers or other staff roles, as well as the rewards and punishment schemes (MOE, 2006). Xiong (2010) further argues that the principal's rights are limited to the internal management of schools, especially in underdeveloped regions. In addition, the schools tuition fees and social donations received for the schools' self-financing, is not for the disposal of the principals. Most of the schools are facing constraints of shortage in funding. The school principal also does not wholly own the rights to management and financial matters. Xiong (2010) also pointed out that under the influence of various factors, principals' power is weakened and limited, and cannot be truly exercised.

Principals' interests are associated with the economic rewards they receive due to their positions, responsibilities and performance. The *"Compulsory Education Law of the People's Republic of China"* stipulates that the government at all levels should protect the interests of teachers and implement social security benefits to improve their working and living conditions (MOE, 2006). The policy also stipulates that the average wage of teachers should not be lower than the local average wage of civil servants. However, there are still no policies or regulations that guarantee school principals' interests. Over the years, principals' salaries are generally executed according to teachers' professional and technical positions wage. There is no wage protection system established for school principals (Lv, 2004). As it appears, principals are still not treated as an independent profession by the Chinese government. A school principal is considered as a part-time teacher and principals' occupational status is not reflected in the government's interests.

To sum up, policies do not clearly define principals' responsibilities, rights and interests. With their limited rights, principals' interests are not embodied in their profession. As a result, there is an apparent imbalance in the current school principals' responsibilities, rights and interests.

2.6.3 The Development of Teacher Teams

The Institute of Rural Education, (Northeast Normal University) issued a report entitle *"China Rural Education Development Report* (2013—2014)". This was a huge research involving 3,433 teachers. The research findings showed that there were 51.2% of teachers who went to the village schools according to the initial configuration, 56.9% of them transferred to county schools in the secondary configuration, and 36.7% of rural teachers expressed that they wished to leave their current positions. Among the teachers in the county, there were 67.3% categorized as "upward mobility", 28.2% were under "parallel flow", and only 4.5% thought of as "downward mobility". 77% of the urban teachers did not want to teach in remote rural schools. 80.2% of the students wanted to become a teacher and only 38% of them were "willing to teach in rural areas". Teachers were found in low performing schools, rural schools, high-performing schools, and urban schools. Numerous studies demonstrated that the shortage of teachers had seriously hampered the development of education.

There are several reasons for teacher shortage. It is a common problem currently faced by many rural schools. In recent years, various parts of Henan are expecting the number of approaching teacher retirements, to bring about a sharp increase in teacher attrition. Besides, teachers leave their teaching post for various reasons, which also contribute to the shortage of teachers. Despite downsizing the number of teachers, supplementary teachers are relatively difficult to obtain. Teachers are usually not willing to teach in rural areas due to the geographical isolation, difficult working conditions and backward economy. To be more precise, teachers are aware that their wages differ significantly between economically developed areas and that of economically less developed areas, as well as between different types of schools.

Teachers prefer to work in urban areas and in high-performing schools. Teachers' teaching tasks are very heavy in rural areas, where each teacher is required to take on multiple disciplines and multiple grades. Furthermore, the contradiction of staff allocation for government-affiliated institutions, remains very prominent. In November 2014, the State Commission Office of Public Sectors Reform, the Ministry of Education and the Ministry of Finance jointly issued the *"Notice on the Unified Standard of Authorized Strength of Urban and Rural Schools"* (MOE & MOF, 2014). The purpose of this move was to unify the authorized standards for primary and secondary schools in rural areas with that of urban area standards. However, many schools in rural areas are facing the problem of the huge drain of students. According to the China Rural Education Development Report 2015, primary pupils in rural areas have reduced by 26,050,000, while junior high school students in rural and township areas have decreased by 11,902,000 and 27,540,000 respectively. As a result, numbers of students in rural schools often face the trouble of teacher vacancies, which has a serious impact on the improvement of quality teaching.

The quality of teachers is an essential factor in determining the success of curriculum reform and educational reform (Li, 2005). Although, new curriculum reform advocates that teachers cannot only be executors of curriculum implementation, but also builders and developers. However, there is a huge gap between teacher quality and curriculum reform, due to the lack of knowledge among the majority of teachers regarding curriculum development. As a result, teachers are not capable of accomplishing the requirements of educational reform and developing the school-based curriculum (Li, 2005). Furthermore, various studies have found that teachers lack professionalism; they appear to have low levels of research capabilities and are poorly equipped with modern educational philosophies (Tang & Xu, 2000; Wang, 2007; Zhang, 2005). This is particularly found in undeveloped areas, where the teaching quality is rather weak, because teachers do not have enough knowledge in modern educational technology, and lack research awareness (An, 2013; Guo, 2013; Ma, 2015).

There is an imbalance in the teaching quality between developed areas and under-developed areas and this has become a significant concern. Numerous research studies have demonstrated that teachers differ according to seven dimensions: professional attitude, professional knowledge, professional competence, the philosophy of education, curriculum quality, psychological quality and information literacy. There is also evidence to suggest that the quality of teachers living in the city and county, is much better than teachers living in rural areas (An, 2013; Ma, 2015; Wang, 2007; Zhang, 2005). Due to the intense competition of teaching jobs in cities and towns, the education level and quality of teachers in urban areas is much higher than rural teachers. According to Li (2005), the education level of key (demonstration) school teachers was significantly higher than normal (general) teachers. The data also showed that key demonstration teachers with bachelor degrees and master degrees accounted for 40.9%, while the average (general) school teachers only accounted for 31.4%.

2.6.4 Education Innovation

At the macro level, educational innovation can promote the economic, social and cultural development of a nation and enhance the core competitiveness of a country (Li, Wen & Liu,

2008; Liao, 1999; Zeng & Li, 1999). At the micro level, educational innovation is critically required for the improvement of school effectiveness and school quality (Wen, 2006; Yang, 2000). It is undeniable that the principal plays an important role in educational innovation under the background of education and curriculum reform. Changes in educational ideology comprehensively promote quality-oriented education and the conversion of internal operational mechanisms of schools, depending on school principals' innovative consciousness, innovative thinking and innovative ideas. However, education innovation is confronted with great resistance and challenges.

From the perspectives of stockholders, people are reluctant to try new things, and are more willing to stick to conventional habits and traditional models. Some are hostile and offensive towards innovative changes. Innovative changes refer to schools that undergo a series of changes and reform. Generally, teachers, students and parents lack confidence in the implementation of innovative changes, because it touches on the core of the school system and their interests (Jiang & Li, 2011; Xu, 2008; Yang, 2000).

People's hesitation, uncertainty and anxiety felt about the innovative capacities of organizations and individuals, can affect and stifle its execution. From the perspective of school principals, they receive less support, in terms of human, material and financial resources. This results in innovation executors falling into the dilemma of "make bricks without straw" (Yang, 2000). However, the efficient execution of school innovation must be resourceful. One of the important factors that suppresses educational innovation is that principals are not daring to think, say or do things, because they are afraid of making mistakes. Jiang and Li (2011) further pointed out that innovative principal training is an urgent requirement for basic education reform.

2.7 System Implementation for Principals' Preparation and Professional Development

Institutional factor has become a core factor that has an influence on the effectiveness and efficiency of education management in China (Sun & Qi, 2014; Yang, 2005). Since the implementation of *"Opinion on Strengthening the Training for the Principals of Primary and Secondary Schools"* (MOE, 1989) in 1989, China has gradually established the school principal qualification and training systems. The establishment and implementation of these systems have an influence on school principals' professional development. However, there are many deficiencies and imperfections found in the system implementation of school principals' professional development.

Firstly, the school principals' management system is not complete. There is no clear standard regarding school principals' selection, appointment and promotion. Moreover, the existing standards cannot meet the requirements of the principal professional development. Secondly, the existing systems are a mere formality. Thirdly, the supporting policies of principals' preparation and professional development are inadequate and difficult to facilitate. In addition, the existing policies lack the inner link between each other, which restricts the implementation of training polices. More importantly, principal training lacks legal protection. As Ma (2005) pointed out, the imperfection of training policies has a negative impact on school principals' selection, recruitment, evaluation as well as reward and punishment.

2.8 Quality-oriented Education and Curriculum Reform

China's basic education is not able to satisfy the demand of social changes (Chen, 2010). Hence, the Ministry of Education of China had decided to implement an educational reform initiative by carrying out quality-oriented education and curriculum reform programmes. The *"Decision on the Deepening Educational Reform"* and the *"Promoting of Quality Education"* was jointly enacted by the Central Committee of the Communist Party of China and the State Council (CPCC, 1999). Traditional Chinese education system reveres authority. It also places emphasis on high-stake examinations and teacher-centered pedagogy (Dello-Iacovo, 2009). In 1999 the State Council of the Chinese Central Government further added that China should establish "a vital socialistic education with Chinese characteristics".

Quality-oriented education is known as *"Su Zhi Jiao Yu(素质教育)"* in Chinese. It is the principal guiding concept of education reform in China, translated into English as "quality education". *"Su Zhi Jiao Yu"* is concerned about students' well-rounded development, which includes "morality (德), intelligence (智), physical health (体), artistic attainment (美), and labor (劳)". In China, *"Su Zhi Jiao Yu"* is perceived as the solution to change the situation of examination-oriented education. According to the Ministry of Education website, *"Su Zhi Jiao Yu"* refers to the *"philosophy of putting people first and pursuing an overall harmonious, sustainable development and the strategy of revitalizing China through human resource development".*

The purpose of *"Su Zhi Jiao Yu"* is to meet the national needs, enhance the competitiveness of schools by promoting a school-based management, encourage school curriculum autonomy and increase pupils' participation (Walker, Hu & Qian, 2012). After the policy got fully promulgated in 2001, quality-oriented education has been widely implemented at all levels of the Chinese educational system. According to Fan (2013), educational leadership is the central focus of educational reform. Schools need diversified investment models and running patterns to meet the needs of national human resource development. Additionally, to some extent, people desired a diversified education (Fai & Wang, 2008).

The examination-oriented education has been rooted in Chinese society for more than 1, 000 years and has dominated its educational system. It was perceived as the ladder towards power, wealth and social status. Its emphasis was on learning by rote, which stifles the creativity of students. Using this unified standard to cultivate talents, it led to the primary and secondary schools of disorderly competition and the break away from the needs of social development (Ye, 2011). Due to the extensive drawbacks of examination-oriented education, a curriculum reform was proposed under the banner of "quality-oriented education."

The Chinese government has considered the new curriculum reform as an important strategy to satisfy the needs of social development and achieve quality-oriented objectives. Meanwhile, the Chinese government enacted two documents, *"Central Committee Opinions on Further Strengthening and Reforming Moral Education in Schools"* (in 1994) and *"Action Plan for Education Revitalization"* (in 1999), to vigorously promote curriculum reform in terms of system, structure and content. The kernel of the curriculum reform is to transfer traditional knowledge delivery in order to satisfy the different learning needs of students based on their interests and talents. This new curriculum is more connected to students' real life. The shift is described in Dello-Iacovo (2009) as:

"A shift from attaching importance to knowledge delivery to the emphasis on forming active learning attitude, making the process not only to acquire basic knowledge and skills, but also the process of learning to learn and form the correct values at the same time."

The shifts in curriculum have raised many issues and challenges for school principals, such as how to prepare their roles under the new curriculum. Li and Zhao (2006) argue that if a school principal, as the leader of an educational unit, only focuses on administrative roles, there will be a lack in instructional leadership abilities, which makes the promoting of new curriculum reforms very difficult. Curriculum leadership was proposed under this condition. The capacity to implement curriculum reform is one of the criteria to evaluate school principals' performance.

The curriculum reform changed the centralized management pattern to a decentralized one, implementing curriculum management at all national, local, and school levels (Li, 2013; Xie, Ma & Zhang, 2013). The Ministry of Education is responsible for the overall planning, management strategies and national standards of the basic education curriculum. The educational administration at provincial level can separately formulate provincial curriculum plans and standards according to the national policy and local context. Schools can select and exploit the curriculum based on their context and students' needs and interests (Li, 2013; Qin, 2003). Chu and Cravens (2012) stated that there are countless Chinese elementary and secondary schools facing transformational challenges in terms of school management. Therefore, the school principals training patterns need to progress from an emphasis on the exam-oriented education to a quality-oriented education.

2.9 Summary of the Chapter

The Chinese education system as well as the preparation and professional development of school principals has experienced a radical change since the establishment of the PRC. These changes had an impact on the educational objectives, educational policies, and educational reforms. Under this remarkable change, school principals needed to shift their roles from traditional managers to excellent leaders. The evolution of the educational and training systems has had an immense impact on leadership practice. Therefore, this notable change requires an enhancement and development of the professional skill set, such as how school principals should be prepared and developed in terms of professionalism, under new educational policies and new educational missions.

CHAPTER 3: LITERATURE REVIEW

3.1 Introduction

This chapter attempts to provide a theoretical overview of educational leadership and how it relates to and supports school principal preparation and professional development. The chapter begins by exploring the definitions of leader and leadership. It then looks at literature on educational leadership to draw associations with principal leadership in the field of education. Finally, the chapter closes with a review of supporting leadership theories that underpin the study of school principal preparation and their professional development in the realm of educational leadership.

3.2 Definitions of Leader and Leadership

What is leadership? Stogdill (1974: 259) pointed out that *"there are many different definitions of leadership as there are persons who have attempted to define the concept."* Basically, leadership is perceived as one who can lead a group of people towards accomplishing their common goals (Chemers, 2014). Bass and Stogdill (1990) presented 12 kinds of representative definitions about leadership, in the "Handbook of Leadership" which summarizes leadership as follows: leadership is the core of any organizational structure; it has an impact on subordinates' work efficiency. Leadership is also viewed as an influence-exerted process; a form of persuasion; a relationship, based on power.

Burns (1978) considers that the follower is an important factor of leadership, where leaders try to persuade followers to strive for certain goals. These goals reflect common values, motivation, aspiration, demand, and ambition between leaders and followers. Skowronek (1993) asserted that leadership is the capacity and process of affecting others to complete tasks. Aligned with the definition provided in Bolman and Deal (1991), it was agreed that leadership makes an impact on personal behaviors in order to profit the entire organization. Northouse (2012) believes that leadership is the emphasis on the manager's adaptability and flexibility for changes.

Maxwell (1993) defined leadership as the activity that influences people to strive willingly and enthusiastically for their organization's goals. Leaders are influential in guiding the targeted group to reach the same objective. Chinese educators, Winston and Patterson (2006) synthesize the definition of leadership as a comprehensive concept, which is goal-oriented. By means of the management, leadership is the language and action that commands and influences others or group process. According to Robbins, Judge, Odendaal & Rood (2009), leaders establish direction by *"developing a vision of the future; they align people by communicating this vision and inspiring them to overcome hurdles"* (p.290).

Although, there is no united definition of leadership, the following elements are perceived as the fundamentals of leadership: (1) leadership is a process (Bass & Stogdill, 1990); (2) leadership leaves impacts (Bolman & Deal, 1991; Maxwell, 1993; Skowronek, 1993); (3) leadership involves a group of people (Chemers, 2014); (4) leadership is associated with desired outcomes. Based on the literature reviewed, the researcher of this study views the nature of leadership as a process of interaction between leaders and followers, which involves the blending of leaders personality characteristics, behavior and authority, with the perceptions and motivation of followers, within a dynamic environment.

Leadership Theories

In the past 100 years, studies on leadership theories and theoretical foundations have been explored in various contexts and from different perspectives (Horner, 1997; Stuart & Philip, 1997). The controversy about how one becomes a leader has been frequently debated, and different theories of leadership have emerged over the past decades. The factors influencing leadership practice and how to improve leadership efficiency have been the research kernel. Since the 1940s, behavioral scientists and psychologists have been doing research on leadership from different perspectives. After decades of evolution, the study of leadership has been through morphology, ecology and the dynamics of leadership. Northouse

(2012), in the book entitled *"Leadership: Theory and Practice"*, describes 11 leadership theories that were collectively viewed as different pieces of the leadership puzzle. After the second half of the 20th century, a multitude of leadership theories had developed over time (Goksoy, 2015). The following subsections account for some of the leadership theories commonly found in various leadership studies and are relative to the educational leadership of the school principals.

3.3 Educational Leadership

Educational leadership research has accelerated since the last century. Rapid social and cultural changes require a deep understanding of educational leadership theories. Educational leadership theories are focused on how different leadership practices influence student achievement, teacher work satisfaction, and other components associated with school development (Bush, 2011; Leithwood, 1994). Nevertheless, there has been increasing importance given to training and developing school principals, as various studies claim that "principals contribute to school effectiveness and improvement" (Hallinger & Heck, 1998).

Leadership is a social influencing process and can be defined differently based on the intention and the target group to be influenced. In this context, educational leadership, as suggested, is to relate to the school organization and how the leadership can unite the single unit in the school to achieve the same goals. The existing researches often highlight about the central power unit – the school principal— to be the only application of educational leadership. However, there are informal sources of leadership who are indirectly influencing the individual in the school population, for instances deputy principals, heads of department or even a unit leaders in the organization. They tend to influence their peers and the students through their social influence or their knowledge and distinctive views. Not to forget the teacher colleagues also are viewed as a potential leadership influence (Macbeath & Dempster, 2009).

The multiplicity nature of leadership and the varied functions that the leadership possesses result in different perspectives to study about it. In this study context, the educational leadership is attempted to be associated with six leadership views: (1) Trait Theory of Leadership, (2) Behavior Theory of Leadership, (3) Contingency Theory, (4) Path Goal Theory, (5) Transformational Leadership Theory, and (6) Distributed Leadership.

3.3.1 Trait Theory of Leadership

Trait theory is perceived as the earliest form of leadership theory, and is also well known as the *"Great Man"* leadership theory (Higgs, 2003; Northouse, 2012). The argument about "leaders are born" and "leaders are made" led to further exploration on the attributes of leaders. Trait theory associates great leadership with people who possess particular physical characteristics, personality and aptitudes that distinguish them from non-leaders (Robbins & Judge, 2012; Stogdill, 1974). Bass (1990) synthesized the literature on leaders' traits and identified six important key traits of leaders that can influence leadership efficiency: cognitive capacities, personality, motivation and needs, social capacities, problem-solving skills and tacit knowledge.

Trait theory declares that innate characteristics or traits make leaders different from followers. Judge, Bono, Ilies and Gerhardt (2002) suggest that trait theory can recognize underlying leaders among the non-leaders. Much focuses were placed on the personal characteristics of leaders (Goksoy, 2015). It was found that Stogdill (1948; 1974) listed 32 traits of leaders, of which none of them could be modeled as effective leadership. However, Yukl (2002: 236) supported the basic premise of the trait theory with the notion that *"a person must possess a particular set of traits to become a successful leader"*.

Since the past century, trait theory has continuously been an evolving branch of leadership theories. Nevertheless, the modern trait theory promotes that leaders' characteristics and traits can be learnt or trained. Kirkpatrick and Locke (1991) demonstrated the six important traits of leaders as drive, motivation, honesty, self-confidence, cognitive competency, and assignment knowledge. In the 1970s, there was no consensus about the personality and physical properties of a leader that would have an impact on all situations. However, as education reforms, the image of an ideal leader has shifted to be based on one's individual beliefs, experiences, and needs.

Costellow (2011) suggested that leadership traits are one of the influential variables to the picture of an ideal school leader. School parents may always opt for head teacher with outstanding traits, such as courage, personality and intelligence as they perceived the possession of mentioned traits are likely to ensure high quality school and relationship management . Quoted from Costellow (2011) 's findings: *"Students need a principal who is able to take care of their social and emotional developmental needs to help them develop life-skills and become better learners* (Kress, Norris, Schoenholz, Elias, & Seigle, 2004)".

Thus, the leadership traits of a school principal leave an important presumption of the school community in assessing the leader's ability and whether or not he is a good leader and manager. We might admire particular traits of someone but are not able to predict the ability and effectiveness of his leadership functions.

3.3.2 Behavior Theory of Leadership

Behavior theory focused on leader's behaviors and it was developed in the 1950s. Behavior theory resulted through the pursuit for effective leadership (Goksoy, 2015). According to behavior theory leadership can be learned and so more attention is paid to the behavioral style of leaders. Behavior theory is about identifying the key factors that influence a leader's behavior, aimed at becoming an effective leader (Goksoy, 2015; Horner, 1997; Yukl, 2002). Studies on attitudes and behaviors of leaders grew popular at that time. In the behavioral leadership theory, the leadership style focused on interpersonal relationships and their responsibility towards the personal needs of staff (Goksoy, 2015). The main outcome of the behavior theory developed various interests concerning leadership styles, new patterns of management, and the Managerial Grid Theory (Moorhead & Griffin, 1998; Yukl, 2002).

Initially, the pioneering study of behavior theory actually began in 1945 at Ohio State University. The purpose of the research team, who grounded this theory, was to identify the observable leadership behaviors and the perception of the followers towards the leaders's behavior (Bass, 1990; Northhouse, 2012). Twelve years later after extensive research, the "Leader Behavior Description Questionnaire" (LBDQ) was developed (Hemphill & Coons, 1957). The LBDQ was a questionnaire that was designed to measure two essential leadership behaviors, namely "*consideration behavior*" and *"initiating structure"* .*"Consideration behavior"* is about the respect, trust and understanding that leaders project onto their subordinates. This is also called people-oriented behavior. Whereas, the *"initiating structure"* concerns task accomplishments, whereby leaders set regulations and outline the roles and group activities for their subordinates to know what is expected of them in line with task-oriented goals. Hemphill and Coons, (1957) found that high initiating structure and low consideration were the least effective leadership behaviors of an organization. The results showed that a leader, who demonstrates a balanced performance of both structures, can increase working efficiency and job satisfaction among their subordinates.

In 1964, the Leadership Grid was developed as a leadership style model that assessed the effectiveness of a leader (Blake & Mouton, 1964, as cited in Horner, 1997). The Leadership

Grid aimed at identifying universal leadership behaviors that can be adapted to different situations. There are five types of leadership styles in the Leadership Grid, which was used to assess leaders. These include: (1) the "indifferent leadership style", described as leaders who do not care for both people and the production; (2) the "dictatorial style", described as leaders showing high concern for people, but low concern for the production; (3) the "accommodating style", described as having high concern for people and low concern for production; (4) the "status quo style", described as having moderate concern for both people and production and (5) the "sound style",described as having high concern for both people and production.

Behavior theory aims to study the influence of leadership styles and behaviors on leadership efficiency. Behavior theory emphasizes on building good working relationship between leaders and subordinates. This theory tends to relate more to the leader effectiveness, unlike the trait theories that focused on the development of one to be leader through the possession of specific traits. Yukl (2002) argues that the behavior theory oversees the behavioral influence of the leaders on the subordinate' job performance. However, it is notable that leadership is dynamic and cannot be separated from a particular context. For example, a head teacher with a high initiating structure and consideration behavior, nevertheless his teacher colleague would follow his guidance at pleasure. It is not deniable that high leadership effectiveness is attributable to a leader with good and widely accepted behavior, as predicted by the behavior theory of leadership. On the other hand, Horner (1997) pointed out that leaders should be receptive of environmental changes, so that they would constantly adhere to the objectives aimed for organizational development. Leaders with the similar behavior will not result in the same effectiveness, thus appropriate style should depend on situation they are being put in.

3.3.3 Contingency Theory

Contingency or situational leadership theory purports that different situations require different leadership styles (Goksoy, 2015). The contingency theory was a new type of leadership theory that emerged due to social and cultural changes that evolved over time. At this time, leadership efficiency within an organizational culture setting was a developing interest (Schein, 2010). The contingency theory arose through the claims that leadership may be differently applied in different situations, and that there is no best approach to leadership, as it depends on the particular context and situational factors. The theoretical core of the contingency theory is about identifying the most appropriate leadership style and management strategy for a particular situation. The key element of effective leadership takes into consideration contingency strategies (Horner, 1997; Yukl, 2002). This is supported by Blanchard (1985) that there is no best leadership form, but only the most appropriate leadership form.

Fiedler (1964) proposed the *"Contingency Model of Leadership Effectiveness"* . This model assesses the leadership effectiveness of leaders' , through their combined traits and behaviors exhibited in particular situations. The *"Least Preferred Co-worker Questionnaire"* (LPC) was designed later by Fiedler in order to measure individuals' leadership style according to situational factors (Yukl, 2002). The LPC model considers all factors that collectively determine the effective leadership, such as the leader-member's relationships, the task structure, position and nature of the organization. Fieldler (1967) highlighted the eight possible combinations of the contingency model, ranked by order of effectiveness towards different situations. When the leaders and members have good relationships, task structure is clear, and position power is strong, then the leadership is most effective. However, it is not effective when the leader-member relations are bad but task structure is low, and position is weak.

Contingency leadership theory is relative to the school principals who are capable of knowing the interest of their teacher team and students and providing assistance sufficient to ensure desired achievement (Blase & Blase, 1999). The original situational leadership theory states that leaders should change their leadership styles according to the changes of their subordinates and the environment. Effective leadership occurs when leadership styles are compatible with subordinates' maturity levels (Hersay & Blanchard, 1969; Hersey, 1985). Maturity level in this context refers to the different combinations of ability and willingness that people show in their workplace. Therefore, leaders must be able to distinguish and understand the subordinates' maturity levels in order to achieve organizational effectiveness. "*Situational Leadership II*" is the second generation Situational Leadership Model revised by Blanchard and his colleagues in 1985 due to some key concepts of situational leadership that could not be applied in real leadership practices (Blanchard, Zigarmi & Zigarmi, 1985). Situational Leadership II advocates that leaders should develop subordinates' self-motivations to achieve organizational goals by combining personal goals and organizational objectives. Situational Leadership II asserts that effective leadership can motivate subordinates' initiative, enthusiasm and creativity and that good leaders can help subordinates develop their competency and commitment (Blanchard, Zigarmi & Zigarmi, 1985; Graeff, 1997; Robbins & Judge, 2012).

Enthusiastic school principals will have a lower chance to have any demotivating teacher colleagues as their leadership will always be a motivating factor in their working interaction and mutual achievement.

3.3.4 Path-Goal Leadership Theory

The path-goal leadership theory, with reference to House (1971), is not a leadership perspective but a theory about how followers are motivated by the leader to achieve the designated goals and the central idea is to focus on the impact of follower motivation to the follower's satisfaction and performance (Northouse, 2016). The theory advocates that effective leaders should assist the followers with clear goals and select the best path to achieve both personal goals and organizational goals, through the path of targeted goals (Evans, 2002; House, 1996; Schriesheim & Neider, 1996). Research shows that the satisfaction and performance of subordinates cannot be isolated. Subordinates' satisfaction determines their job performance. Therefore, subordinates' satisfaction can be a motivating factor for effective leadership.

Four leadership styles were identified in the original path-goal theory, which are directive, participative, supportive and achievement-oriented leader behaviors (House, 1996; House & Mitchell, 1974: 83). The directive leadership style is effective when tasks or projects are unstructured or complex and subordinates are inexperienced. Participative leadership focuses on mutual participation, where group members share their expertise and ideas in decision-making. Participative leadership works best when tasks are complex and team members are experienced. Supportive leadership focuses on relationship building and showing sensitivity to team members needs and best interests. Achievement-orientation leaders set challenging goals for their team members by motivating them to attain the goals and reach the highest level of competency.

The path-goal theory claims that leadership can be flexible to cope with what the situation demands. Hence, leaders need to be flexible to change their leadership styles, contingent to the environment and subordinates' characteristics (House, 1996). Being the head of school community, it is challenging to demonstrate all the mentioned leadership styles concurrently. However, blending the bright side of each style into daily interaction and communication with the teachers will enable the teammates to be inspired to reach the collective goals – students' performance.

3.3.5 Transformational Leadership Theory

Transformational leadership was first coined by Downton (1973), however it emerged widely after James Burns (1978). Burns demonstrated that the transformational leadership theory can inspire the enthusiasm of followers, create a connection and raise the level of motivation and morality in both the followers and the leaders themselves. In 1985, Bass expanded on the transformational and transactional leadership models and included the concept of Laissez-Faire (Clark, 2011). According to Bass (1985), transformational leaders inspired their followers by raising their awareness towards their organisational goals, encouraged them to go beyond their self-interest for the sake of their organisation and were able to address higher level needs.

3.3.6 Distributed Leadership

The concept of distributed leadership emerged in the 1950s, but was introduced in the educational field since 1990s due to the reformation of educational management systems. The early theorists of distributed leadership believed that leadership is distributed in some way or the other (Camburn et al., 2003; Gronn, 2002; Harris, 2008). Chen and Xu (2009) viewed leadership as a collective behavior happening within an educational context, where the school principal distributes leadership functions among organizational members who oversee the completion of internal management issues and external coordination. On the other hand, Hatcher (2005) argues that within schools, the notion of distributed leadership may overlook the dynamics of power and influence, whereby leadership may be distributed but power and influence may not. Distributed leadership advocates that leadership should break away from organizational hierarchy, and build upon shared leadership practices instead (Malloy, 2012). In fact, Gronn (2009) suggests broadening the distributed approach of this hybrid leadership to "leadership configuration". Due to the increasing challenges of school work load, the school principal as an individual cannot take all the responsibilities. However, Goksoy (2015) adds that distributed leadership is not about sharing administrative roles, but rather the sharing of decisions by school authorities regarding their subordinates.

According to Dinham, Aubusson & Brady (2009), leadership functions effectively through team work. Furthermore, Gronn (2009) and Harris (2008) assert that distributed leadership helps people develop their potentiality to be leaders' emphasis on the common performance of personnel. Harris (2008) also indicates that distributed leaders can make individuals realize their potentials and values by participating in the decision-making process. Similarly, Ogawa and Bossert (1995) also pointed out, leadership is a distributed practice embodied in leaders' working context rather than an individual activity.

Even if distributed leadership has been perceived as a perfect blue print for educational leadership, the empirical evidence about how it impacts school improvement is still insufficient, according to Hallinger & Heck (2009). On the same lines, Harris (2005) pointed out, distributed leadership need to be empirically studied rather than just treated as an abstract theory.

3.4 Roles of School Principals

"The head teacher plays a highly significant role in school management, and is the central decision-maker. Preparing, inducing and developing head teachers are a major responsibility of the education service." (DES, 1990, cited in Coleman, 1996: 3)

Originally, the role of the principal was to manage school related affairs. With social changes, traditional leadership is no longer helpful in the current social context. School principals are not only educators and managers, but are required to oversee school development and meet the requirements of educational reform. They are also needed to be problem solvers, resources finders and culture builders (Leithwood & Poplin, 1992; Wahlstrom & Louis, 2008). For these reasons, a growing number of researches pay attention to how school principals are prepared for their roles. However, according to Lattuca (2012), numerous school principals administer their schools, without being well-prepared for their roles. Therefore, understanding the roles of school principal is essential for designing preparation programmes and for the future development of school principals.

Leadership is not just about the authority held by individuals. According to Chirichello (2010), there has been a deficiency in the number of qualified principal applicants. Moreover, the roles and responsibilities of school principals are shifting with the continued social changes. Principals are expected to administer staff, monitor students, interact with parents, manage the school budget, build relationships with other agencies and communities, as well as be knowledgeable with the laws related to these activities (SEC, 1991). In a school institution, the highest standard requirements are set upon the school principal, who is required to meet the demands of all internal and external factors (Jiang, 2006). Moreover, the *"Compulsory*

Education Law of the People's Republic of China" stipulates that *"the principal shall assume overall responsibility for the school and shall conform to the qualifications stipulated by the state"*.

In the *"Professional Classification of the People's Republic of China"* , the principal is described as an independent profession. The principal is the one who has the power of managing and taking decision. In China, the main roles of school principals are denoted in the list below:

· An organizational manager.

· The decision maker who is in charge of school affairs and managing educational resources.

· An educational leader.

· A facilitator who builds interpersonal relationships with staff.

· The headmaster is expected to attend to staff' s personal needs, to develop cooperation among staff, to create a democratic and harmonious atmosphere in schools, and to promote creativity in teaching.

· The moderator of conflicts.

The school principal is responsible for solving potential conflicts and be an agent of reform (Liang, 2005; Jiang, 2006; Liu & Li, 2012; Chen, 2010). In society, schools are expected to strive for excellence and stay efficient. The document *"Requirements and Position Requirements of Headmasters of Primary and Secondary Schools in China"* also stipulates that the school principal is the legal representative, school leader, educator, and manager (SEC, 1991). The basic duty of a school principal is under the lead of the government administrative department or school board (private schools). The school principals are to be entirely responsible for teaching affairs, school administration and for improving the level of school management. The core objectives of school principals are to lead, educate and manage their schools according to the standards set by the state and pledge to instate quality education.

The major responsibilities of school principals are to establish their school philosophy and set the vision and goals of the school (Chen, 2010). The principal should plan and establish the strategic development of the school together with the school management team and school board members. Zhao and Wei (2000) further add that school principals should adopt innovative and creative methods of technology required for school management purposes.

Apart from that, school principals are accountable for ensuring that their schools always abide to the regulatory framework and national plans for the education reform and development (CPCC, 2010). School principals are regarded as the public relationship officer of the school, and the one responsible for building and maintaining good relations with parents, other schools, community organizations, and be able to create a conducive social environment for school development (MOE, 2013). All these standards show that the roles of a school principal have changed. Hence, as school leaders, principals are required to keep up-to-date with matters regarding educational reforms, and be equipped with innovative educational ideas that can promote improved efficiency. All of these depend on the foresight and macro decision-making abilities of the school principal.

3.5 Theoretical Framework of School Principals' Preparation and Professional Development

The theories of leadership have been well discussed in the subsections above, and now it is time to look at the theoretical framework of this study. The nature of the principal preparation and professional development was evolved based on two theories: the Principal Growth Pattern Theory and the Human Resource Development and Management Theory. The school principal leadership preparation and development is likely to be anticipated under the principal growth pattern: preparation period, adaptation period, competent period, mature period and innovation period (Wu, 2009). Thus, this study reviews the school principal's preparation in line with the prediction of this theory, which is generally adopted in China (Ying & He, 2005).

The Human Resource Development and Management Theory has to deal with the provision and assessment of training and development programmes in organisations (Mcguire, 2014). In this study, this theory lays a framework for exploring and examining the principal training program and to assess the management of the program in order to identify the challenges arise from its implementation. This is especially important that frequent review on the training program brings improvement to the training providers, school principals and indirectly to the school organisation as a whole (Swanson, 2001). The following subsections will discuss briefly about the theory for a better understanding.

3.5.1 The Principal Growth Pattern Theory

According to the Principal Growth Pattern Theory, it is important to take pre-service training to gain basic theoretical foundation and management abilities for school principal candidates to qualify for their jobs. They will learn to understand how to scientifically manage a school and have the right competencies to lead their school. Presently, principal candidates lack the knowledge of leadership theories. According to Wu (2009) and Chen (2010), school principals have their own school running ideology; they have a strong theoretical foundation and abundant school management experiences as well as having a good understanding of the regular patterns of school management.

During the *"Seventh Five-Year Plan"*, China's National Education Committee conducted a research on "*Chinese school principals' growth pattern in primary and secondary schools*" (The Training and Management of Primary and Secondary School Principals, 1992). The research findings show that the growth of Chinese primary and secondary school principals goes through four stages, which comprise of a pre-service session (about 5—7 years), an adaptive phase after being employed (about 2—4 years), a competent period (about 3—5 years) and a proficient period (starting about 10—15 year after pre-service beginning). In China, researchers appealed for the school principal training content to be based on the growth pattern theory (Chen, 2010). With different phases of school principal growth, the training needs are also different. School principal training should be based on the needs and characteristics of the different development stages, so that the trainings are more targeted.

The development of school leadership is also based on the Growth Pattern Theory. This theory has been implemented as a guide for school principal training, which is considered important by many scholars in China (Chen, 2010; Wu, 2009; Ying & He, 2005). Normally, the development of a school principal is based on theoretical studies, as practice gradually develops over time. The development period can be divided into five stages: pre-service preparation period, post-adaptation period, competent period, mature period and the innovation period (Ying & He, 2005; Wu, 2009; Chen, 2010). Peterson (2002) pointed out that school principals' preparation and development programmes can meet individual needs, at different stages of a principal's career. It can also equip the school principals with the acquired knowledge gained from training programmes conducted in authentic settings.

3.5.2 Human Resource Development and Management Theory

Human Resource Development Theory (HRD) is a modern concept of management recognized internationally. HRD involves large-scale complex tasks and tactical activities carried out to promote a successful organizational culture and attain organizational goals

(Lepak & Snell, 1999; Werner & DeSimone, 2011). The human resource management process includes human resource planning (selection, recruitment, placement, training, and evaluation), compensation management, performance management, as well as employee relations (Bratton & Gold, 2012). Training is the main method for human resource development (Mcguire, 2014). According to this theory, the school principal is an important human resource for running a school. Swanson (1995: 208) defined human resource development as "a process of developing human expertise through organizational development and personnel training and development for the purpose of improving performance."

HRD theory advocates that organizations can help employees improve their individual performance and meet challenges through trainings (Werner& DeSimone, 2011). HRD also considers training as indispensable. Similarly, school principal training is perceived as a strategic priority in developing school principals' capacities towards school improvement and development (Bush & Chew, 1999). As Wang (1999: 63) stated, *"School principal training is a human resource development activity, and it is a part of modern life-long education."* The aim is to improve the knowledge, skills and to change the work attitudes and behaviors of school managers, thus developing their potential to improve management quality and efficiency. Providing relevant or skill targeting enrichment and training has been a merit to the school principals (Chen & Xu, 2010). Thus, it is under the understanding of this theory that, the human resource department is encouraged to prepare and establish self-enrichment programmes or necessary trainings as to improve their working efficiency, increase their competency and reduce waste.

Human Resource Development Theory was seen as necessary for one's profession (Swanson, 2001). Therefore, in order to promote school principals' professional development, school principal training system should refer to Human Resource Development and Management Theory to improve school principals' working efficiency and promote their professional development.

3.6 Summary of the Chapter

In summary, this chapter reviewed related literature on educational leadership practices, and theories that are relative to the principal leadership development. The studies reviewed have generally expressed about the primacy of school principals and recognised the importance of promoting the continuous development of school principals for improving their professional growth in leading the learning and academic success of their schools. Some other studies have also provided useful insights on school leadership research, highlighting the benefits that principals and schools can gain through the professional development opportunities provided for school leaders.

CHAPTER 4: RESEARCH METHODOLOGY

4.1 Introduction

This chapter explains the research methodology employed in this study. In order to meet the research objectives, answer the research questions, identify and analyse the preparation and professional development of secondary school principals' leadership in China, the qualitative research methodology is used. For its research design, a multiple-site case study is used in this study to enable cross-site comparison. This chapter will present the rationale for this research design, the population and sample, the research instrumentation, data collection methods, and analysis procedures. This chapter will also discuss the research setting, ethical issues, the pilot study, and the validity and reliability of this research.

4.2 Research Orientation

This study uses an interpretive research paradigm, where according to Denzin and Lincoln (2011; 1998: 3) the researchers' job is *"attempting to make sense of, or interpret, phenomena in terms of meanings people bring to them"*. An interpretive methodology of a qualitative inquiry is naturalistic, where researchers study the subject matter in real world settings without any effort to manipulate the phenomena in order to make sense of the phenomena under study (Creswell, 2012; Merriam, 1998) The phenomena in this study is secondary school principals' initial training and professional development in China, together with a specific case study located in Huojia, Shangqiu and Zhengzhou of the Henan Province.

A case study design is used as it fits with the characteristics of interpretive inquiry in this study (Yin, 2013).

Based on Merriam (1998)'s study, there are four essential characteristics of qualitative case studies: particularistic, descriptive, heuristic and inductive. The particularistic aspect of a case study concerns a specific situation, event or phenomenon. In this present research study, the focus is on secondary school principals' leadership preparation and their professional development in the Chinese educational context. The Heuristic approach enables a deeper insight and new understanding of the phenomenon of a case from different perspectives. This study presents the perceptions of respondents from various backgrounds and experiences, regarding secondary school principals' leadership preparation and professional development in Henan Province, China. One of the types of qualitative research methods that uses an inductive approach is thematic analysis, used to analyse recurrent themes, ideas and notions from the qualitative data. The process of thematic analysis involves the identifying of themes that emerge from the data. This process of searching through the data is repeated to identify further themes and categories that are repeatedly verified, confirmed and qualified (Creswell, 2013).

Document analysis, open-ended questions, semi-structured interviews and field observation were the methods of analysis employed to assist the researcher in the data collection from secondary school principals in Henan Province, China. Document analysis in a Chinese educational setting was used to provide the basic knowledge required about China. Open-ended questionnaires were distributed purposively to thirty-seven school principals in order to identify the issues that might be useful for this study and for further investigation. Semi-structured interviews with seventeen principals and six training organizers were conducted, where the researcher explored emerging themes as described in Merriam (1998). In order to get first-hand data, the researcher also went to three training institutes to conduct field observations, to find out how school principals are trained, and what exactly happens in real situations.

4.3 Case Study

A case study is defined as a phenomenon that exists within a bounded context where researchers study complex phenomena within their context (Huberman, 1994; Merriam, 1998; Miles & Yin, 2013). The case study design in the current study involves a total of seventeen Chinese public secondary schools chosen from Huojia, Shangqiu, and Zhengzhou, where six schools were selected from Huojia and Shangqiu respectively and five schools from Zhengzhou. This study is based on a single case study with multiple sites. The secondary school principals from the chosen schools were selected as case studies in this research.

The case study approach enables the researcher to gain deeper understanding about the preparation and professional development of secondary school principals' leadership and its contextual situation in China. The case study approach is perceived by Yin (2013: 1) as *"an empirical inquiry that investigates a contemporary phenomenon within its real-life context"*. On the contrary, a quantitative method is too precise and numerical for capturing the school principals' experiences, views, and feelings about their preparation and professional development. It cannot fully grasp the phenomena and processes involved (Punch, 2009). Hence, case study is chosen rather than a mixed-methods approach is, because case study enables a detailed exploration of the phenomenon within its genuine state, that "especially when the boundaries between phenomenon and context are not clearly evident" , as supported by Yin (2013: 13). However, Davis et al. (2005: 3) further clarify that "the preparation programmes need in-depth research into the implementation and coherence of programme features" . Therefore, a qualitative method as it features comprehensiveness, holistic, and abundant descriptiveness will be employed in this study, as suggested in Berg and Lune (2004).

This case study aims to understand from a distinctive lens the respondents' views, experiences and feelings about the preparation and professional development of secondary school principals' leadership. This allows the researcher to explore the multiple realities of the same kind of environment principals evolve in (Denzin & Lincoln, 2011). This is consistent with the researcher's point of view "in understanding how people interpret their experiences, how they construct their words, and what meaning they attribute to their experiences" (Merriam, 2009: 5).

4.4 Research Sites

The research setting in this study is a representation of the study environment, in which the researcher explores the school principal landscape in Henan Province, China. With the diverse economic and demographic contexts in the Henan Province, it was not feasible to cover all schools in this province. The selection was narrowed down to seventeen schools from the Henan Province, with six schools each from Huojia and Shangqiu, and another five schools based in Zhengzhou.

These cities were specifically chosen for various reasons concerning the suitability of this research study. Zhengzhou was selected for its location and its wealth of educational resources that attract elite students from all over the province. Zhengzhou is the capital city of Henan, with the most populous province in China with 77,872,000 inhabitants (*China Statistical Year Book*, 2015). It also implies that Zhengzhou has the largest student population in China. According to the *Henan Statistical Year Book* (2013), there are 980 primary schools with 705,194 students and 371 secondary schools with 460,887 students in Zhengzhou. Shangqiu is a moderately developed city, located in the east of Henan Province. There are 2,412 primary schools with 774,692 students and 446 regular secondary schools with 516,155 students (*Henan Statistical Year Book*, 2013). Shangqiu is a typical region like many other regions in terms of economy and education development level in Henan Province, thereby being selected as the case of this study. Huojia is a county with a geographical area of 473 square kilometres and 430,000 inhabitants, located in the Henan Province. It has 26 secondary schools, and is a less developed area compared to Shangqiu and Zhengzhou, with less educational resources and lower school principals' quality. Huojia, Zhengzhou and Shangqiu have different levels of development and its respective ways of how different matters are handled, specifically principal training.

4.5 Sampling Procedures

The researcher had selected seventeen secondary school principals from 2 cities and county (Zhengzhou, Shangqiu and Huojia), across the Henan Province. A purposive sampling technique was employed in this study and thirty-seven school principals were chosen to respond to an open-ended questionnaire. Purposive sampling was the sampling strategy chosen to ensure representation of noteworthy participants necessary to address the research questions that guide this study. This sampling strategy has the similar design as the qualitative research in Sumintono et al. (2015) as it shared the same research objective as this study. The samples chosen in the research are from a broad range of characteristics and are responsive to the research objectives. Sampling purposively in this study allows the engagement of the participants who are able to meet the specific criteria. According to Punch (2009) many factors should be considered in purposive sampling and it is especially important to look at the settings and boundaries of each case study. It is for these reasons that the selection of cities, school locations and principals' leadership performances were considered at the beginning of this study.

Despite of the large population of school principals in the three selected cities, 37 school principals were given their response through the open-ended questionnaires and 17 were chosen for in-depth interviews. This sample size design for a qualitative study is appropriate for most study, as validated by a clinical research (ANON, 2011). For a qualitative research, unlike the quantitative research that focused more on the sampling of probability, it demands on the in-depth examination of the purposeful samples which is exemplary a "information-rich cases" (Morse, 1989; Patton, 1990; Sandelowski, 1995). Sandelowski (1995) has highlighted on the design of sample size of a qualitative research to be statistically "non representative stratified (Trost, 1986)" to enable the inclusive of respondents with varied demographic characteristics to achieve "representative coverage and inclusion" . This particular requirement is achieved in the research as participants are from varying demographic data and are able to provide response which is rich in information and from different perspectives.

4.6 Pilot Interview

Initially, an unstructured interview protocol was designed and piloted with school principals in order to obtain their general views, concepts, and understandings about their leadership preparation and professional development as secondary school principals and to organize the research design for the main study. The pilot interview was conducted from October to December 2015. Five participants were selected: three secondary school principals and two officers from a training institute. According to Yin (2013), a pilot study helps the researcher to enhance the quality of data collection and further discover the relevant issues that may arise during the data collection phase. The feedback received from the pilot interview helped the researcher to improve the interview protocol and enhance her interviewing skills.

The actual interviews were conducted during the months of January to March, 2016. Prior to this, the researcher ensured that the semi-structured interview questions were amended based on the pilot interviews conducted. To further ensure data reliability, the interviews were self-administered by the researcher. Before the interviews were held, the researcher had contacted the participants to obtain their consent to participate in this research study and to fix a date for the interview schedule. All the interviews were conducted in Chinese, to suit the language preference of the research participants under study. The interviews were also recorded and transcribed in Chinese. Subsequently, the researcher went to three different training institutes to conduct field observations at the county, city and municipal levels.

4.7 Data Collection Methods

The purpose of this section is to explain and elaborate on the data collection methods used in this study. According to Creswell (2012), multiple sources like open-ended questionnaires, semi-structured interviews and observations can present a holistic understanding of the phenomenon under study. There are four subsections that present on the method employed to collect research data: (1) documentation, (2) open-ended questionnaire, (3) semi-structured interviews, and (4) observations.

4.7.1 Documentation

As Bowen (2009) pointed out, documents provide background information and historical insights, which can help researchers understand what is underpinning the phenomenon. Merriam (1988: 118) states: *"documents of all types can help the researcher uncover meaning, develop understanding, and discover insights relevant to the research problem"*. In this study, the two types of documents selected are categorized as exterior and interior documents. Exterior documents include publications issued by the Chinese government and the Ministry of Education in the past decades, for instance, government pronouncements, training policies, laws and regulations. The interior documents come from selected schools and local education bureaus. They comprise of rules, regulations, reports, portfolios and plans regarding school principals' preparation and professional development. The documents from each selected school and local education bureau provided historical and contemporary information regarding school principals' preparation and professional development. In order to access these exterior and interior documents, the researcher is required to get official permission from the respective government department and school principals.

4.7.2 Open-ended Questionnaire

An open-ended questionnaire was utilized in this study. According to Gillham (2008), open-ended questions can supplement a semi-structured interview. According to Punch (2009), open-ended questionnaires enable large amounts of information to be collected in a short period of time. Open-ended questions also allow respondents to boldly express themselves in writing, due to the confidentiality clause. Moreover, open-ended questions allow the respondents more time to think and reflect before penning down their responses. The open-ended questionnaires (see Appendix D) were administered to 37 secondary school principals to capture their perceptions and views about their experiences and their perspectives towards the school principals' initial preparation and professional development. The open-ended questionnaire was developed based on the research questions to ensure the objectives are achieved. The questionnaire was being reviewed prior to its utilization.

4.7.3 Semi-structured Interviews

Semi-structured interviews with school principals and training providers were conducted immediately after they have completed the open-ended questionnaire survey, in which only seventeen out of thirty-seven secondary school principals were chose due to their suitability to the study. These were the research samples selected purposively to participate in a one-to-one semi-structured interview. In addition, six training providers were also interviewed. As the implementers of school principals' trainings, the training providers are involved in the whole process of training. Identifying the issues and challenges regarding school principals' preparation and professional development from their individual perspectives further validates the research.

All interviews were conducted in Mandarin and each interview lasted between 60 to 90 minutes. These interviews queried about the topics and issues related to the preparation and professional development of secondary school principals' leadership practices. The interview questions had been furnished after the completion of the pilot study to ensure the appropriateness of the question to the study objectives. According to Creswell (2013), interviews are the most popular data collection tool used in qualitative research. Moreover, Punch (2009) added that interviews are an excellent approach to understand people's insights, values, and definitions of circumstances and constructions of reality.

4.7.4 Observations

Observations are also a prominent method for data collection in qualitative research. Field observations were conducted in this study as it provides a holistic perspective of the contextual settings (Punch, 2009). The researcher conducted observations at selected school principals' training classes and seminars. However, prior permission was obtained from the Chinese Educational Department before carrying out site visits. The researcher also had asked permission from each of the school principals to remain in their campus, to carry out further observations on how the principals execute their jobs. This enabled the researcher to observe how the school principals were prepared for their daily routine work and discover how they equipped themselves for their professional leadership roles. The researcher also witnessed regular meetings and informal talks chaired by these school principals. The researcher also obtained permission to observe the principals training classes.

4.8 Data Analysis

During the field study, the researcher took note of the behaviors and activities of the participants as well as general observations of the surroundings. Data collection and analysis phases were carried out consecutively. The data analysis phase began after the completion of the observations and interview sessions were held with the chosen respondents. During the data analysis phase, the qualitative data obtained through the observations and interviews were transcribed, coded into different categories and analysed according to the research questions and research objectives of this study.

4.8.1 Transcribing

All interviews were recorded using a digital voice recorder during the transcription phase; interviews were transcribed by listening to the audio recordings and transcribed into written transcripts. According to Davidson (2009), the audio recordings need to be transcribed into written form, as it is the written representation of speech that facilitates a more thorough analysis. Bailey (2008) also pointed out that data transcribing involves judgments, data interpretation and data representation, and that transcribing is not a straightforward technical task as it seems. In this study, all interviews were transcribed verbatim, in Mandarin. After the transcriptions were done, they were sent to the participants for further checking and clarification. When the "member checking" process was completed, the data was then translated to English to facilitate the thesis writing process.

4.8.2 Coding and Categorizing

Coding is a process done during the qualitative data analysis phase whereby the raw data is reduced, simplified and transformed into a more manageable form to facilitate the analysis and interpretation of qualitative data (Bazeley, 2013). According to Punch (2009), there are three types of coding methods: open, axial (or theoretical coding), and selective. Coding is also used to generate abstract conceptual categories for theory building purposes (Strauss and Corbin, 1990). A thematic analysis was employed after the codes were categorised into broad themes, to analyse the roles of school principals, examine the principals' views about their leadership preparation and development. The results from the analysis also enable the identification of the challenges that these principals encountered with their leadership practices. Data from questionnaires were coded "R" , "I" comes from interview with principals, while "T" represents training organizers.

4.9 Validity and Reliability

Validity and reliability is given importance in any research (Yin, 2013). According to Noble and Smith (2015), qualitative research is frequently criticized for lacking scientific rigour and transparency in the analytical procedures. It is also criticized as merely a collection of personal opinions subject to researcher bias. Therefore, besides the attempts taken to minimize researcher bias, the fundamental concepts of validity and reliability in qualitative research are necessary to ensure credibility of the research findings. In assessing the reliability of qualitative research findings, the credibility of results is based on the soundness of the research process in relation to the appropriation of the data collection methods used and the integrity of the final conclusions. In this study attempts were made to also ensure that the research subjects selected to participate in this research, did not have any connection with the researcher. To further deal with issues of reliability and validity, triangulation is used to control bias and improve the validity and reliability of the research findings.

In this study, multiple sources like document analysis, open-ended questionnaires, semi-structured interviews and field observations were triangulated, as indicated in Merriam, (1998). Member checking was the other strategy to ensure the credibility of this research. Once the study was completed, the interpretation of the findings was sent to the respondents to verify that the interpretation of their viewpoints is authentic and reliable. Participant feedback or member checking, as described in Denzin and Lincoln (2011), can also be used to also check the researcher's inferences of the findings. According to Mays and Pope (2000), member checking can minimize the biases and the incidences of misinterpretation of the researcher. It can also determine the accuracy and completeness of the research.

Before running this study, the research instrument was pilot tested in order to detect any flaws, and to make the necessary revisions to the interview protocol, before conducting the study (Punch, 2009). Two educational leadership experts from the Institute of Educational Leadership of University of Malaya (UM) had reviewed and validated the interview protocols prior to utilizing it. This is to ensure that the questions are in line with the research objectives and research questions. In addition, two bilingual (English and Chinese) language experts checked and verified the translation of interview questions and open-ended questionnaires to ensure the consistency of the questions and objectives. As a further measure of validity, three principals with more than ten years of principalship experiences provided their opinions on the guiding questions of the interview protocol and open-ended questionnaires.

4.10 Ethical Issues in Qualitative Research

Empirical research in education inevitably carries ethical issues, because it involves collecting data from people, and about people (Punch, 2009). "Harm, consent, deception, privacy and confidentially of data" were also summarized by Punch (2009) as the main concerns of ethical issues. In this study, the researcher attempted to reduce the Hawthorne Effect, as described in Berg and Lune (2004) by trying to ensure that the participants felt at ease about participating in the interviews by arranging to conduct the interviews at their place of work, based on their availability of time and convenience. Participants were also assured that the interviews were only used for purposes of this research study and that all the information they shared were highly confidential and anonymized in this study.

4.11 Summary of the Chapter

This chapter aimed to outline the qualitative methodology for use in this study to explore and understand the preparation and professional development of secondary school principals in Huojia, Shangqiu and Zhengzhou of the Henan Province, China. In order to achieve the research objectives, interview data obtained from the case studies of multiple sites were transcribed and analyzed. Issues of validity and reliability regarding trustworthiness of data and ethical considerations were also outlined in this chapter. The following chapter will present the research findings and results of the study.

CHAPTER 5: FINDINGS

5.1 Introduction

This chapter presents an overview of the key findings derived from the analysis of thirty-seven open-ended questionnaires, seventeen semi-structured interviews and six training providers. Field observations conducted during the training classes were also analyzed to support the findings. Moreover, relevant official documents from the years 2000 to 2016 about principal selection, training and development were selected for document analysis. The following two sections present the demographic background of the participants, followed by the data analysis which answers the four research questions of this study.

5.2 Demographic Background

School principals' leadership development and demographic background is associated with school principals' career growth, background and past experiences. By investigating school principals' education background, teaching and administrative experiences, it can help the researcher to better understand the process of school principals' leadership formation and development. Therefore, in this section, the school principals' demographic information, qualifications, years of teaching and administrative experiences will be presented.

Table 5.1 Demographic Profile of 37 Principals (Survey Participants)

Demographics	Frequency	Percentage
Gender		
Male	25	68
Female	12	32
Age		
30—39 years	15	40
40—49 years	18	49
Over 50 years	4	11
Highest academic qualification		
Diploma	9	24
Undergraduate	26	71
Postgraduate	2	5
Tenure as principal		
Less than 5 years	10	27
6—10 years	16	43
11—15 years	7	19
16—20 years	4	11
Involvement in principal training preparation		
Yes	28	76
No	9	24

Note: 37 respondents participated in the Survey, n=37.

According to the school principals demography in Table 5.1, 25 (68%) of them were male, and 12 (32%) were female. Based on age groups, 4 (11%) of them were over 50 years old; 15 (40%) principals were between 30—39 years and 18 respondents (49%) were aged between 40—49 years. Based on their academic qualifications, nine principals (24%) have diplomas, 26 principals (71%) have a bachelor degree (71%), and 2 principals (5%) have a master degree. Majority of the respondents (16 principals or 43%) have worked as principals between 6—10 years, 10 principals (27%) have under five years of principalship, 7 principals (19%) have 11—15 years of principalship and 4 principals (11%) have had 16—20 years of principalship. Regarding training to become principals, 28 (76%) of them had participated, while 9 of them did not (24%).

Table 5.2 Demographic Profile of 17 Principal Interviewees

Demographics	Frequency	Percentage
Gender		
Male	12	71
Female	5	29
Age		
under 30 years	1	6
30—39 years	2	12
40—49 years	8	47
Over 50 years	6	35
Highest academic qualification		
Diploma in Vocational Studies	2	11.5
Diploma	4	24
Undergraduate	9	53
Postgraduate	2	11.5
Tenure as principal		
Less than 5 years	1	6
6—10 years	4	24
11—15 years	7	40
16—20 years	3	18
20 years and above	2	12

Continued

Demographics	Frequency	Percentage
Involvement in principal training preparation		
Yes	14	82
No	3	18

Note: 17 principal interviewees, n=17.

As for the 17 principals interviewed, 12 of them were male (71%), and 5 of them were female (29%). Regarding age, only one of them was less than 30 years (6%) and six of them were over 50 years old (35%); two of them were between 30—39 years (12%) and eight (47%) principals were between the age of 40—49 years. Regarding their highest academic qualifications attained, four principals (24%) had diplomas, nine of them (53%) had undergraduate degrees, two of them (11.5%) were master degree holders, and two senior school principals (11.5%) underwent secondary normal school education. Only one principal (6%) held this position for less than five years; four of them (24%) held this position for 6—10 years; seven principals (40%) were in office between 11—15 years, and three others (18%) were in this position for 16—20 years, and two of them (12%) worked as a principal for more than 20 years. Regarding their involvement in principal training preparation, 14 principals (82%) were involved in pre-service trainings and 3 (18%) of them were not trained before taking up the posts.

Table 5.3 Education and Career Profile of 17 Principal Interviewees

Principal Identifier Code	Education, Teaching and Administrative Experiences
I-1	Normal university—physics teacher—class advisor—dean of teaching affairs office—school principal
I-2	Normal college—Chinese teacher—class advisor—secretary of youth league committee—vice school principal—school principal
I-3	Normal university—Chinese teacher—class advisor—grade teacher—dean of teaching affairs office—vice-school principal—school principal

Continued

Principal Identifier Code	Education, Teaching and Administrative Experiences
I-4	Normal university—mathematics teacher—class advisor—vice-dean of teaching affairs office—vice-school secretary—school principal
I-5	Secondary normal school—Chinese teacher—primary school principal—dean of teaching affairs office in secondary school—vice-school principal—school principal
I-6	Normal college—English Teacher—class advisor—secretary of youth league committee—school principal
I-7	Normal university—geography teacher—class advisor—vice-dean of teaching affairs office—dean of teaching affairs office—school principal
I-8	Normal university—Chinese teacher—class advisor—dean of general service office—vice-school secretary—school principal—secretary of youth league committee—school principal
I-9	Secondary normal school—mathematics teacher—class advisor—vice-dean of teaching affairs office—vice-school principal—school principal
I-10	Normal university—mathematics teacher—class advisor—accountant of centre school—vice-school secretary—school principal
I-11	University of science and engineering—chemistry teacher—class advisor—teaching and research group leader—dean of teaching affairs office—school principal
I-12	Normal university—English teacher—class advisor—vice-director of discipline—director of discipline—vice-school secretary—school principal
I-13	Normal university—mathematics teacher—class advisor—dean of teaching affairs office—vice-school secretary—school principal
I-14	Normal college—Chinese teacher—director of discipline—school principal
I-15	Normal college—physics teacher—class advisor—vice-director of discipline—vice-school principal—school principal

Continued

Principal Identifier Code	Education, Teaching and Administrative Experiences
I-16	University of science and engineering—mathematic teachers—director of discipline—vice-school principal—school principal
I-17	Normal university—Chinese teacher—class adviser—vice-dean of teaching affairs office—vice-school principal—school principal

According to Table 5.3, only two of the school principals graduated from universities of science and technology, nine of them graduated from normal universities, two of them graduated from normal colleges and four of them graduated from secondary normal schools. Besides, all the school principals are with teaching experiences and 14 of them worked as a teacher advisor before being appointed as a school principal. This is reflected by the words, *"a good teacher is the foundation of a good school principal"* (Sukhomlynsky, 1999: 1). Moreover, the majority of the school principals had management experiences and worked as school middle-level cadres, such as dean of teaching affairs, secretary of youth league committee, teaching and research group leader and vice-school principal. This also indicates that school principals had rather rich administrative experiences, and that their leadership capacity was due to the accumulation of their work experiences.

In China, most school principals were appointed by education departments based on their excellent work experiences. The demographic information shows that all school principals went through the process of being a teacher and a middle-level leader. None of them appeared to have majored in education management and administration. This provides an opportunity to provide empirical evidence on how are the Chinese school principals prepared for their principal leadership role, whether through formal and informal learning to positively improve their leadership capacity.

Besides the school principals, six training providers were interviewed to obtain their views on principal leadership from a principal trainer's perspective. Table 5.4 illustrates the demographic profile of these six training providers. Among the six of them, there was only one female training provider. The rest were males. In terms of age, one of them was 30—39 years old, three of them were 40—49 years old, and two of them were in the 50 years and older age category. As for their highest attained academic qualifications, two of them had bachelor degrees, another two had master degrees and the remaining two had doctoral degrees. Regarding their working experiences as training providers, three of them had less than 5 years, two of them 6—10 years, and one had 11—15 years' training experience. As for their roles in training institutes, two were training managers and the rest of them were training teachers. Two of them pursued their trainings at county level, municipal level and provincial level training institutes.

Table 5.4 Demographic Profile of Training Providers

Demographics	Frequency	Percentage
Gender		
Male	5	83.3
Female	1	16.7
Age		
30—39 years	1	16.7
40—49 years	3	50
50 years above	2	33.3
Position		
Teacher	4	66.7
Manager	2	33.3
Highest academic qualification		
Degree	2	33.3
Master	2	33.3
Doctorate	2	33.3
Years of experiences		
Less than 5 years	3	50
6—10 years	2	33.3
11—15 years	1	16.7
Level of Institutes		

Continued

Demographics	Frequency	Percentage
County level	2	33.3
Municipal level	2	33.3
Provincial level	2	33.3

Note: 6 Training Providers, n=6.

5.3 Presentation of Research Findings

In this chapter the research findings were obtained through the triangulation of data collection methods namely, document analysis, interviews with principals and training organizers, and observations at schools and principal training institutes. Moreover, official documents, open-ended questionnaires, semi-structured interviews and field observations were used to analyse and answer the four research questions in this study. During the interviews, audio data were digitally recorded, transcribed and coded according to themes. Through a thematic analysis, codes were selected from broad themes such as roles of school principals, principal preparation, professional development of principals, leadership practices and leadership challenges. In line with research ethics and for further confidentiality purposes, the names of principal interviewees were not revealed. Instead, the names of school principals were represented by identifier codes, such as I-1, I-2, etc. (see Table 5.3). Further identifier like "R" that symbolizes data from questionnaires, "I" denotes interview with principals, while "T" represents training organizers. The following subsections present the data analysis based on the four research questions of this study.

5.3.1 Research Question 1: To what extent do the governmental training policies impact the leadership preparation and development of the secondary school principals in Henan Province, China?

This research question seeks to investigate the impact of training policies on the preparation and development of secondary school principals' leadership in Henan. Training policies function as a guide and legislative approach for securing school principals' professional development and to ensure the implementation will be a complementary factor in education reform (Zhou & Zhu, 2007). There are 11 national and provincial policy documents and development plans that were studied and analyzed to examine the structure of the governing order and action plans that appear to have an influence on cultivating and improving the professionalism of the school principals. The document analysis intents to provide a clearer understanding of the relevant training policies that can help the education administrative departments and training organizers to innovate their training systems in order to promote school principals' professional development. Moreover, this investigation helped to provide the theoretical basis and knowledge required for establishing the school principals' professional development system. The following subsections elaborate on the governmental training policies from the perspectives of school principals' selection system, qualification system, training system, evaluation system as well as their incentive system. The researcher has also included a brief historical account about the evolution of training policies.

5.3.1.1 School Principals' Selection System

School principals' capability building and development defines their overall quality. In appointing the leader of a school community, a regulating policy is vital to ensure that the selected leader possesses the appropriate qualifications and professional demeanour of a school principal. According to Yang (2005), a well-regulated principal selection system is the key features required to pledge and sustain the excellence of principals. Conversely, Chen (2010) found that the overall quality of school principals is not usually in line with the educational development needs and that this matter should be addressed.

The national education reform and development plans, as well as the published policies dated 28 years ago, have been emphasizing on the principal selection criteria enforced in the nation. After the issuance of the *"Opinion on Strengthening the Training for the Principals of Primary and Secondary Schools* (MOE, 1989)*"* and *"Opinions of the State Education Commission on Post Training for Headmasters of Primary and Secondary Schools* (SEC, 1990)*"*, the Chinese government started to be aware of the need urge of a regulatory policy in standardizing the principal selection and the position responsibilities. In 1991, the PRC State Education Commission put forward the *"Requirements and Position Requirements of Headmasters of Primary and Secondary Schools in China"* as the answer to the urge (SEC, 1991). The general requirements of selecting and appointing school principals are based on the following criteria which include basic requirements, major responsibilities and job requirements. There are three defining criteria used to stipulate the job requirements of school principals, which are political proficiency, qualification, educational background and physical capability of the recipient (SEC, 1991).

(a)Political Proficiency

Walker et al. (2012) highlighted that adherence to mainstream political ideology is a widely prescribed part of a principal's job, where almost all principals in China are Party members and as such work within the cadre system. They are expected to work hard in delivering moral education and be committed to the socialist ideology, which is reflected in their job requirements stipulated in the *"Opinion on Strengthening the Training for the Principals of Primary and Secondary Schools"* and *"Training Regulations for Primary and Secondary School Principals"* (Feng, 2003a; MOE, 1989; MOE, 1999). Besides that, they are expected to conform to the national laws and the Party policies and implement the national educational guidelines, policies and regulations. They are also supposed to ensure loyalty, maintain unity, prioritize strong collectivistic ideology, and be willing to sacrifice their interests for collectivistic importance (Jia, 2005; MOE, 1989; MOE, 1999). The principal has to be able to manage the school work, create a conducive learning environment for students and build collaborative relationships with parents and other stakeholders. Corrective action in perfecting the principal appointment has never ceased, as the State Council launched the *"Decision of State Council on the Reform and Development of Basic Education"* in 2001 to revise the appointment and selection system of school principals (State Council, 2001).

(b)Qualifications and Educational Background

Education background and qualifications are the key selection criteria that are taken into consideration during the school principal selection process. In December 1999, the Ministry of Education issued the *"Training Regulations for Primary and Secondary School Principals"* . This regulation has legally endorsed the principal qualification training in China (MOE, 1999). It states that the qualifications of a Chinese secondary school principal must not be lower than a college degree holder, and that a qualified senior secondary school principal must possess academic credentials higher than a bachelor degree. Primary and secondary school principals have to attain first class for their secondary and advanced level primary school teacher qualification. According to MOE (1999), candidates are expected to have working experience in the education industry and be certified with professional training credentials. 2 years after the principal training requirement was gazetted, the policy *"Decision of State Council on the Reform and Development of Basic Education"* was issued to improve the principal appointment and selection system.

(c)Physical Capability

While health condition is one of the defining criteria in selecting a school principal, it is crucial that school principals are in good health and are capable of fulfilling their job responsibilities. However, the fact remains that many of the school principals are unable to meet the actual needs of primary and secondary schools, due to their low qualifications. The document *"Requirements and Position Requirements of Headmasters of Primary and Secondary Schools in China"* shows that the qualification of school principals is ranked low. Similarly, SEC (1991) reported that the quality of school principals is slightly weak.

With the continuous reformation of the Chinese education system, the school principal selection process is becoming competitive. In 2001, the *"Decision of the State Council on the Reform and Development of Basic Education"* highlighted that primary and secondary school principals shall be selected and managed by the national education administrative departments (State Council, 2001). The State Council also declared that there is a need to redefine the qualifications of school principals and gradually establish open and fair practices when selecting school principals.

The *"Outline of China's National Plan for Medium and Long-Term Education Reform and Development (2010—2020)"* clearly states that the nation needs to reduce the criteria for school principal selection (CPCC, 2010). Nevertheless, at present there is still no changes made to the standards and rules regarding the selection of school principals. Thus, the *"Decision of State Council on the Reform and Development of Basic Education"* sets out to ensure that the management and contract systems of primary and secondary school principals, is in accordance with the law. It is also needed to further define the qualifications of school principals and gradually establish public recruiting and competition for the position of school principal (State Council, 2001).

Since the establishment of the PRC, primary and secondary school principals were selected and appointed directly by the government or education administrative departments. At present, some regions have started implementing contract systems. However, some operations are still under the control of the local administrative departments. The administrative officer is the main representative body of the selection process, without the involvement of stakeholders like teachers, parents and the community. Therefore, the election of administrative leaders is still traditionally approached, and the selection of school principals requires administrative authorization. Inevitably, the personal preference of government leaders will somehow affect the selection of school principals. Thus, the different employment standards in many regions have resulted in the inequality of school principals throughout the nation.

The selection and hiring of school principals is subject to the candidate' s appraisal and teaching achievements, without considering other criteria like teaching ability, qualifications and academic diplomas. Thus, it can be seen that the school principal employment system in this nation is merely a formality and non-competitive. The government perceives that principalship is just an administrative function. The government emphasizes that the candidates should be more politically obedient to Communist rule instead of being concerned about school leadership and principal professionalism. This situation caused many school principals to become conventional leaders, as they focused their efforts on administrative housekeeping. Many of the school leaders displayed authoritative leadership, which appears to exhibit a lack in professionalism.

At present, the regulation of primary and secondary school principal employment in Henan, is based on the candidate's qualifications, the employment procedure, the job contract and evaluation. The principal rank system emphasizes the occupation of the principal as a profession while the appointment system places emphasis on the principal as a school leader. In summary, it may be concluded that the Henan Province has not yet established a complete school principal selection system.

5.3.1.2 School Principals' Qualification System

In 1999, the *"Training Regulations for Primary and Secondary School Principals"* (MOE, 1999) stipulates that the prerequisite of school principals is to participate in principal trainings within the prescribed time to obtain the relevant certification. Article Five of *"Notice of the Education Department of Henan Province on Further Strengthening the Education Cadre Training in the Province"* also stipulates that all parts (of Henan Province) should strictly implement the post-holding certificate system. It regulates that all new principals, including the kindergarten director, must upscale their qualifications and participate in at least 300 hours of training within half a year, after being appointed as a school principal (Department of Henan, 2010).

A qualified school principal must be certified with the necessary training qualifications, as the prerequisite for employment as a school principal (MOE, 1999: 2). However, a review of Article 5 indicated that there is a contradiction in two of the clauses stipulated in Article 5. One clause highlights that school principals are required to obtain training qualifications before serving as school principals. Within the same article, another clause addressed the prerequisite of 300 hours of training after serving as school principals. This appears as a contradiction and further implies that this government regulation does not provide clear clauses for the school principals' qualification system. If training certification is not one of the essential conditions for school principal selection, and so is pre-service training, then many of the candidates who apply for this post, may not be capable of handling school principals' work.

School principal (I-1) also did not participate in any training programmes prior to her appointment as a school principal:

"I did not take part in any training programme before I was a school principal. I was obliged to take this position. My school's situation is special, due to the establishment of a new campus; the financial debt of my school had more than 50,000,000 CNY (Chinese currency, equivalent to 7,279,821 USD). Under this situation I was forced to be appointed as the school principal by the government. But, later I had participated in national secondary school principal training which was organized by the Ministry of Education." (I-1)

Various studies report about the phenomenon of taking up the position of school principal before undergoing training. This is not only in Henan Province but the whole nation (Dong, 2010; Feng, 2013; Ma, Zhang & Mu, 2009). As a matter of fact, the qualification system of school principals is supposedly a formality. A stringent, professional qualification system has not yet been established, although the State Council has promulgated in 2012, the *"Opinions of the State Council on Strengthening the Construction of Teachers' Ranks"* to upgrade the quality of the education system in this country (State Council, 2012). The document highlighted about the chief assignments to be drawn up for the teaching team in schools. It also proposed a stricter verification and evaluation process to be imposed for the principal qualification system. This is because of the need to further establish and further develop the professionalism of school principals, for both pre-school headmasters and principals of various school ranking. The State Council also emphasizes on raising the quality and reputation of the teaching team and school principals. The Council also encourages the Management to have the autonomy in formulating and creating their teaching and management styles (State Council, 2012).

In reality, this certification is a kind of formal recognition. School principal who possess an all-rounded training qualifications tends to outperformed from his peer and is easily to be appointed by the government (Jia, 2005; Xia, 2011b). This is supported by one of the school principal's (I-14):

"If you can finish all your assignments and with full attendance, you will pass... you can get the certificate." (I-14)

Another school principal added:

"As long as you are involved in the whole process of training, you definitely will get the certificate. Even though you can take leave during the training. In our country, the laws, regulations, as well as policies are non-binding." (I-16)

The fundamental reason of this phenomenon is due to the primary and secondary school principal qualification certificate system that has not been legalized and unified, causing it to be disorganized and not less efficient. Nevertheless, the "*Training Regulations for Primary and Secondary School Principals*" stipulates that serving principals must participate in Improvement Training every five years within the prescribed time, and obtain an "Improvement Training Certificate" as the prerequisite for renewal of post (MOE, 1999: 1).

5.3.1.3 School Principals' Compensation System

The compensation and promotion systems are the evaluative processes that assess the working performance, personal values and professionalism of school principals. This is an incentive scheme to guide and motivate school principals towards enhancing their professional development, and also act as a guide for their future work (Chu & Yang, 2002). According to Hu (2006) and Wu (2009), an unreasonable salary system is not favourable to the professional development of school principals. However, the compensation system for school principals has not been established in this nation yet (Chen & Lv, 2010; Hu, 2006; Yu, 2012). In addition, without establishing specific qualification standards the identities and responsibilities of school principal tend to be ambiguous.

The *"Opinions on Strengthening the Construction of Headmasters of Primary and Secondary Schools"* (SEC, 1992) stipulates that *"primary and secondary school principals are involved in school management, certain amount of teaching, and are required to participate in teacher evaluation of professional and technical posts"* (SEC, 1992: 2). Furthermore, it has also been published in the "*Opinions of the State Council on the Implementation of the Outline of China's Educational Reform and Development*" that all school principals as well as certain school administrative staff are responsible for setting the wage scheme for levels 3—6 (State Council, 1994). The promulgation of these two policies shows the dual roles of the school principal, involving school management and human resource management. Besides that, the promotion scheme for school principals and teachers is identical.

The nature of school management by the principal varies substantially compared with the teaching role of teachers. The current compensation system has somehow ignored the complexities of a school principal's job. It is also quite unreasonable that the salary scheme of school principals is the same as that of teachers. Moreover, school principals who achieved senior title could no longer be promoted. Most of these school principals are lacking of the enthusiasm and motivation, which results in a holdup in their careers and professional development. One of the school principal claimed that the retirement remuneration for the school principals is much lower than teachers, adding that although schools principals earn the reputation of being the school leader, but their job rank and salary is equivalent to that of a teachers post. This is confirmed by the following comment made by school principal I-14 below:

"Principals' responsibility and pressure are bigger than teachers, but their income is no different from teachers..." (I-14)

From the above excerpt, we can see that the school principals are not satisfied with the compensation system. Therefore, this issue about establishing a reasonable compensation system for school principals, needs to be further addressed.

In 2008, the *"Instruction for the Implementation of Performance-based Pay in Compulsory Education Schools"* clearly defined that *"the performance-based salaries of school principals are verified by the personnel and finance departments. It is determined by the overall evaluation results of the school principals."* This post-performance payment system actually includes post wages, salaries, performance pays and allowance subsidies. However, this performance payment system has not been fully implemented. Lv (2004) and Wu (2009) have revealed that school principals are dissatisfied with the existing wage, which they feel does not justify their highly stressed jobs, as commented by one school principal:

"Good work that deserves good pay is not reflected in school principals' pay. The assessment of the education bureau for school principals' performance is less specific, and this does not guarantee the school principals' legitimate rights." (I-8)

Schools with higher student enrolment and monetary resources tend to have better subsidies from the government. In contrast, those schools located in the outskirt areas and small towns have a lower chance to be financially assisted. As a result, school principals rely solely on their monthly income and have no available funding for any value adding initiatives.

In recent years, the government has issued a series of strategies and policies to raise the wages of school principals. However, in comparison to the other public service sector workers, the wage level of school principals remains low. The tremendous contrast in the salary and responsibilities of school principals has dampen their passion towards teaching. In addition, Gong (2000) stated that even with a quality training programme, school principals are still not encouraged to participate in these trainings, if there were no incentives.

5.3.1.4 School Principals' Evaluation

School principals' evaluation is essential for assessing the leadership performance of school principals. A systematic and rigorous application of scientific methods can provide useful feedback for the professional development of school principals and for school improvement. Nevertheless, at present there is no scientific or systematic assessment for the principals' evaluation. In 1992, the *"Opinions on Strengthening the Construction of the Headmasters of Primary and Secondary Schools"* indicates that the school principals evaluation should take into consideration the local context (SEC, 1992). Principals are evaluated based on their working ability and political integrity; they will be assessed comprehensively based on their "德 (Morality)", "能 (Ability)", "勤 (Diligence)" and "绩 (Achievement)" (Jia, 2004; Zhao & Wang, 2007). The evaluation can be further cross referenced with the *"Requirements and Position Requirements of Headmasters of Primary and Secondary Schools in China"* (SEC, 1991). However, there is still no clear and unified evaluation index in place for a fair assessment for all candidates.

Subsequently, after three years, the *"Opinions of the State Education Commission on the Primary and Secondary School Principals Training during the Ninth Five-year Plan"* (SEC, 1995) was issued to implement the *"Opinions of the State Council on the Implementation of China's Educational Reform and Development"* (State Council, 1994). Although there is no clear guidance on the evaluation process for school principals, the policy has highlighted that principals need to undergo principalship training and be certified with the *"Qualification Training Certificate"* before being appointed, following which they will be awarded the *"Improvement Training Certificate"* to be able to continue serving as a principal. This requirement is stricter to ensure the principals and the newly appointed candidates will continue serving and participating in professional development.

Annual appraisals and tenure evaluations are part of the performance evaluation of school principals. Annual appraisals are concerned with the personal summary while tenure evaluation is carried out every five years. Wise and Darling-Hammond (1984) suggests that performance evaluations should be based on the combination of two levels (*Individual and Organizational*) and two purposes (*Improvement and Accountability*), where the four combined outcomes facilitate in the evaluation process. The purpose of the evaluation is to review the duties and performance of school principals, in order to determine promotions, demotions, rewards and penalties. Currently, the principal evaluations involve summative rather than formative evaluation which assesses generally the professional growth of school principals. According to Uren and Tovey (2001), most teachers are not in favour of performance evaluations as evaluations are not effective in appropriately assessing their job performance. The overall quality standards of these evaluations are found to be lacking and not that reliable. Up till now, the nation has not yet established any scientific evaluation standards for school principal leadership evaluation.

5.3.1.5 School Principals Training System

This section presents the findings about the school principals training system and its policies address concern on the training institutes, the sources of training funds and training evaluations. This is to identify the influence of the governmental policies on the training system in three perspectives: (1) training institutes, (2) training funding, and (3) training evaluation.

(a)Training Institutes

In 1989, the *"Opinion on Strengthening the Training for Principals of Primary and Secondary Schools"* (MOE, 1989) was issued by the Ministry of Education. This was the first systematic training policy that serves as a guide for the implementation of trainings for primary and secondary school principals. During this time, school principal trainings were perceived as *"comprehensive and in line with the national education policy and strategy"* (MOE, 1989: 1). However, it was proposed that the provincial, municipal and county level trainings should be implemented by normal universities and colleges, colleges of education, teachers' colleges for vocational studies and other training institutes.

In 1999, the *"Training Regulation for Primary and Secondary School Principals"* confirmed that qualified universities can also provide training for school principals (MOE, 1999). However the *"Opinion of Ministry of Education on Further Strengthening and*

Improving the Training of Primary and Secondary School Principals" (MOE, 2002) wisely suggested the execution of principalship training to be managed under a single education body with "closed" training institute instead of distributing the training service authority to different training centre to ensure a standardized training plan and structure. The opinion was then superseded with a justified view of entrusting cadre training to be executed by the colleges, universities, scientific research institutions and social institutions level to that of a more diversified and professional establishment, proposed in the *"National Eleventh Five - Year Plan for Cadre Training of the Educational System"* in 2007 (MOE, 2007).

Apart from that, the *"Outline of China's National Plan for Medium and Long-Term Education Reform and Development (2010—2020)"* also states that to set up competitive training institutes and provide quality training services, the municipal and country level training institutes should be removed (MOE, 2007). During the document analysis process, the researcher found that training policies do address the ways of improving and developing school principal training institutes. However, the standards of assessment and the accreditation of training institutes have not yet been established. Furthermore, the government does not have enough quality training resources.

(b)Training Funding

Schools need financial support to ensure the normal operation of the schools. According to the *"China Educational Reform and Development Outline"* (CPCC, 1993) and the *"Decision of the Central Committee of the CPC on Several Major Issues Concerning the Building of a Harmonious Socialist Society "* (CPCC, 2006), it is stated that financial education funding constitutes 4% of the Gross Domestic Product. This was to secure government finances allocated for education funding. However, schools at cities and county levels often fail to achieve the target due to many counties not having financial reserves for education. There is a huge gap between targeted funding and actual funding (Chen, 2012; Liang & Zhang, 2010). As a result, the government's financial allocation is inadequate for meeting the needs of school development.

Moreover, school principals are facing the problem of raising funds. Principals need money to improve their school infrastructure, support teaching activities as well as school management. The shortage of fund is caused by many problems, such as school debts, an overall poor quality of teachers and low enthusiasm among teachers and staffs. Currently, schools are entirely funded. The payment of teachers' and school principals salaries are at the disposal of public funds

Training funds are essential for the professional development of school principals. The *"Notice of the Education Department of Henan Province on Further Strengthening the Education Cadre Training in the Province"* (Department of Henan, 2010), declared that the nation should increase the funding investment and enhance the efficient usage of training funds. However, it does not clearly indicate how to improve the efficient usage of training funds, with a feasible plan. It is parallel in the *"Opinions of the State Council on Strengthening the Construction of Teachers' Ranks"* issued by the State Council where the funding of training should be supported to ensure that educators and school principals are able to undergo necessary trainings in order to equip themselves with optimized teaching standards and qualifications. In addition, the financial expenses for training purposes should be enumerated in the annual budget planning, where 5% of the total sum of budget should be used for intensive training (State Council, 2012).

The *"Training Regulations for Primary and Secondary School Principals"* (MOE, 1999) points out that school principal trainings rely on funds from the government and through other multiple channels. Part of the educational funds is utilized in school principals' trainings. However, this regulation does not specify the source of the multiple channels and the authorities responsible for fund collection. This implies that raising funds through multiple channels may be difficult to implement. Besides, specific training expenditures are made by the regional education administrative department. However, due to the regional economic differences, each region does not have a unified standard for training expenditure, and this result in the large regional differences. Moreover, there has not been school principal training fund properly set up. Self-raised fund is a challenge for school principals who come from underdeveloped areas, as this causes many school principals to forgo training due to insufficient training funds.

(c)Training Evaluation

Training assessment and evaluation is an important criterion for school principal professionalization. Training evaluation allows an intensive corrective action to be taken to promote school principals' professional development and to address quality assurance in the areas of training, planning and execution (Chu & Cravens, 2012). Policies issued by the government have never ceased to highlight the importance of training evaluations. In 1994, the *"Opinions of the State Council on the Implementation of the Outline of China's*

Educational Reform and Development", placed emphasis on the job evaluation of school principals (State Council, 1994). In 1999, the *"Decision of the CPC Central Committee and the State Council on Deepening Educational Reform and Promoting Quality Education"* (CPCC, 1999), clearly outlined the criteria of training evaluations. According to this policy, the Education administrative departments of provinces, autonomous regions and municipalities are in charge of primary and secondary school principals' training work. They are responsible for formulating the regions' training plans and supporting policies of primary and secondary school principal trainings. They are also fully responsible for the implementation, inspection and evaluation of primary and secondary principal trainings in the regions (SEC, 1999).

In adherence with the national policy, the *"Notice of the Education Department of Henan Province on Further Strengthening the Education Cadre Training in the Province"* emphasizes on conducting onsite training evaluation, by training participants and other third-party evaluators in order to strengthen the formative evaluation and performance appraisal of education cadres. Evaluation results may be used to attune the training tasks and funds (Department of Henan, 2010). This information shows that training evaluation has been gradually creating awareness that is increasingly being recognized by the government.

With the same ideology, the State Council in their issuance of *"Opinions of the State Council on Strengthening the Construction of Teachers' Ranks"* highlighted the need to establish stricter training evaluations, regardless of the level of the evaluation procedure. The appraisal system is encouraging, as the rewards given are based on the participants' performance assessed throughout the training (State Council, 2012). The evaluation results are announced in order to allow supervision and monitoring of central concerns and to ensure that the necessary measures are put in place. Overall, the training evaluation process looks into the evaluation of the subjects only. It does not clearly denote who the third-party assessors are, and the training evaluation index. This makes it difficult to fully comprehend the training evaluation process completely.

5.3.2 Research Question 2: How the secondary school principals are prepared for their present principal leadership role?

The secondary school principals, prior to their in-service period, are required to complete the pre-service qualification training to get them ready for the new level of obligations (Chu & Yang, 2009). Improvement training and self-directed development strategy are to reinforce their management knowledge and to keep their leadership skills up-to-date and sharpen their research ability to be innovative. Being appointed as the head teacher in the school, specialization and skills require continuous development and learning through the training and institutional teaching (Zhou, 2015).

The data analysis of the interview with the school principals has revealed a variety approach to deliver the training curriculum, for example: face-to-face lectures, group discussions, school visit, internship program and submission of a project paper. Moreover, the study found that, apart from formal learning procedure, the leadership role and abilities that they acquired presently are owing to the informal knowledge gaining ways. Thus, the findings that correspond to the second research question will be presented into two categories of learning mode: formal learning and informal learning.

5.3.2.1 Formal Learning

The preparation and professional development programme is an important means of equipping school principals with the professional competencies and self-consciousness needed for their professional development. The professional development of school principals through formal learning is beneficial for the sustainable development of schools. The following sub-sections expound how school principals were prepared and influenced by formal learning.

(a)School Visits

One of the modules of the training is to visit school with good reputation and outstanding performance.Data revealed that school principals have a deeper understanding regarding the concept of "school culture" through the school visits made to other schools.

Several responds are positive to this knowledge delivery method that:

"School principal training is necessary... We should visit those schools with the similar school context and management mode; it will be more effective." (I-4)

"Both Qualification Training and Improvement Training have too many theories... school principals should involve the whole process of school management during the field visiting. We can spend half a month to study theory, and another half a month to stay in a particular school to participate in their school management." (I -10)

"Trainings brought me the greatest experience. When I went to other schools for visiting, I was always being attracted by their school culture... Especially nowadays, establishing distinctive campus culture has become the new tendency of school running in the nation. Without this knowledge, school principals will be less capable." (I-13)

It is obvious that school principal I-13 was impressed by the school culture of the school he visited and school principal I-4 and I-10 were in favour that school visit is able to add value to their learning. To a large extent, these testimonies also suggested that this school principal gained the knowledge of improving his school culture and this would have inspired him to adopt new ideas of leading his school in a better way.

(b)Acquire Updates on Educational Developments

The development of school principal leadership keeps continually evolving alongside the development of the whole society. Undeniably, trainings expose school principals to the new developments in education, which gives them different perspectives on the formulation of the school mission, administrating schools and planning their school vision. One school principal gives his example as below:

"Previously, our school lacked school vision planning. At least through training, I know it is not just a slogan. Although we learn about professional guidance in theory, I found that training is a way of getting to know the various developments in education. For instance, the awareness created about the effect of exam-oriented education on school effectiveness and quality education in the future." (I-2)

Another school principal further noted that:

"After the training, some of the schools changed their management style in terms of using a more humanistic approach with their teachers and students. So, I think training is necessary. If you always stay in school, your way of your thinking most likely won't change. You have to be open-minded and learn some new theories and management experiences from high-performing schools." (I-8)

School principals also pointed out that training enables them to master the dynamics of education and educational development trends, as expressed by one school principal:

"Through trainings, I learnt to understand more about some current national educational policies, which also improved my theoretical knowledge. I found that it effectively improved my school management ability." (I-6)

In addition, another school principal further explained:

"The trainings helped me carry out the education policies more firmly. I think trainings also guide school principals with their leadership practices, as they are the executors of education policies." (I-9)

According to the principals testimonies, training programmes had a positive effect on school principals, as they learnt to understand the professional concepts of principal leadership development. Trainings equip school principals with the knowledge needed for better planning and accepting new ideas. Training also helps school principals change their out-dated school management methods, and makes them more open-minded to viewing school development from different perspectives.

Moreover, by comparing the advanced theories and concepts gained from training programmes, school principals have been able to discover their shortcomings of their leadership practices to update their professional concept. One school principal expressed:

"Training makes me feel that I need to continuously update my educational concepts. I think the important function of trainings is to improve the theoretical level and expand the knowledge of school principals." (I-14)

The nation has implemented an exam-oriented education for thousands of years. Since the 1990s, quality-oriented education (素 质 教 育) has been introduced as the national education reform initiative for its intended focus on school effectiveness and quality education across China (Chu & Cravens, 2012). It is because of the increasing competition, especially among Asian societies, schools are under societal pressure to inculcate a more holistic approach for student development. This has led them to pay close attention to redesigning their curriculum improved instructional practices. Ideally, curriculum training should be offered as part of the training programmes for school principals. Training programmes should also focus on developing school principals on the new concepts of curriculum reform, as this can help school principals to plan and promote the new school-based curriculum in their schools. The findings suggest that through training programmes, school principals have developed a deeper understanding of the professional concepts of leadership development and application.

The principals interviewed have reached a consensus about how trainings provided the theoretical knowledge that helped them improve their leadership practices. Below is an excerpt taken from an interview conducted with a school principal:

"I was inspired during the training, I think training improves my theoretical level, deepens my understanding of educational policies, educational laws and quality-oriented education. As a school principal, the trainings helped me to enhance my sense of mission and inspired me to do a great job. It also improved my educational teaching management level, strengthen my determination and confidence to continue pursuing an education career. I was able to reflect." (I-17)

Expectation from the authority on the function of training programme in school principals' leadership improvement is still in the development stage. At this stage, the training providers are the resource for theoretical knowledge in leadership growth. Below are the comments from a training organizer regarding the impact of trainings on his participants:

"Currently, there are no leadership degree courses to develop the leadership competencies of school principals in China, and so, school principal trainings are useful for providing principals with the required knowledge and skills needed for school management... for the most part, the training curriculum played a role in the school principals' theoretical attainment." (T-3)

(c)Urge of Role Changing

School principals are the frontlines of education. They are the educators and leaders, who have experience in both teaching and school management. The development in the education sector also requires principals to shift their roles from a transactional management style to a research-based type. Trainings have an influence in urging school principals to change their roles from an ordinary administrative role to an all-rounded leader in coordinating progress and growth of the school community. A school principal also pointed out that training programmes help them understand the essence of curriculum reform:

"Trainings can improve school principals' theoretical level and further improve our understanding about the school-based curriculum, which is very difficult to implement, without theoretical guidance and support." (I-11)

Training also acts as an external stimulus, which plays the role of promoting self-reflection among the school principals. School leaders who are often engaged in unceasing interference often spend time on self-improvement. Some of the school principals commented that training programmes although less extensive, tend to be mainly complimentary. The following are remarks from two school principals:

"Participation in the training programmes enabled me to expand my knowledge about leadership." (I-14)

"The preparation programmes helped me to understand more clearly what I should prepare in line with my work." (I-16)

(d)Leadership Capacity-building

The majority of school principals highlighted the positive side of trainings and said that trainings prepare them better for the job. At the same time, there are also a few principals who commented that trainings provide them the opportunity to compare and contrast their views about leadership with other principals:

"The training was very effective. In particular, it has helped me become more competent. The training has broadened my horizons through my exchanges with other peers." (I-3)

"I valued meeting with colleagues. I know my own strengths and weaknesses and I know how to address the problems I face through my leadership practices." (I-2)

The following school principals also highlighted that trainings enable them to balance their workload more effectively:

"It is difficult to be a school principal as it involves a very heavy workload. During the preparation programme, I now better understand the work of school principals, and this is a great help for my future work." (R-6)

"Trainings had a certain effect on me... it expanded my horizon and I was able to learn about school administration from other advanced school leaders." (I-8)

Another school principal added:

"Training expands my horizon and widens my mind. Meanwhile, I fully understand the qualities of being a good school principal. It has been a profound experience to have gained more insight regarding school principals' leadership." (I-15)

In addition, the preparation and professional development programme also helps school principals to better understand their roles, as remarked by school principal I-13:

"Before participating in Qualification Training, I was not very clear about my roles. I thought I was just a manager, but after having joined the training, the first thing that came to my mind was that I have a lot to catch up on regarding school principal leadership. This training further helped me understand what my school mission and responsibilities are." (I-13)

Two other school principals commented:

"In my opinion, the preparation programmes are effective. They help you to predict issues and seek solutions in advance. It helped me know what I should do when faced with leadership uncertainties. Therefore, in my view, the preparation programmes are effective." (R-20)

"Through the preparation programme, I have gained a deeper understanding about leadership and I feel much more prepared. I can improve my leadership practices. For example, I realized that I should also need to rethink the curriculum and train teachers to have community engagement. This would improve my leadership ability." (R-23)

According to the findings, most of the school principals highlighted that trainings have a positive influence on their professional competencies. As one school principal explained his view:

"Training mainly improves my macro-management ability. Moreover, I can master the art of leadership better... It also provides better strategies for school development. I also had participated in the training programme named School Principals' Leadership Art, at the Capital Normal University. It was effective for improving the skills of school principals' leadership practices." (I-3)

The positive comments from the principals in this study, reinforced that training programmes can improve their professional competency. The other school principals added that:

"The main harvest of training is improving my post competency; it also has a positive influence on school principals' execution." (I-6)

"I had participated in a public management training for two weeks. It helped to improve my abilities in execution and coordination, and I found it very effective for school principals' work." (I-4)

Another school principal remarked:

"I participated in pre-service training when I was a vice-school principal. This taught me about the school principal's roles and mission. During my tenure, I participated in various forms of trainings which have greatly helped me with my school management skills. I think the most important component of school principals' leadership kernel are educational beliefs and concepts. Others include educational philosophy, school spirit and school culture. I also think that the most effective training is internship. You can emulate some measures from other high performing schools." (I-15)

The majority of school principals emphasized that they acquired knowledge and skills through training and this fulfilled their job responsibilities. Furthermore, the training institutes also pointed out that trainings can improve the overall quality of school principals. A few school principals also indicated that the training content can be applied to their leadership practices. One school principal elaborated on how he and his teachers benefited from the professional development programmes that he participated in:

"During the past six years of having participated in training programmes, I found several trainers to be very impressive... Generally, I think that the trainings were very useful. I have used some of the training material in delivering a speech to our teachers, and I found it to be very effective. School principal training is not just limited to teaching school principals

how to implement their work, but also teaches them how to guide their teachers, and how to work well with the class adviser and with other teachers. After delivering the content to teachers, they also felt that they benefited from it." (I-12)

It is apparent that trainings are very helpful for school principals in equipping them for their roles. For example, Qualification Trainings provide theoretical orientation, which can help school principals adjust to their leadership role. Improvement Trainings are perceived to equip principals with the knowledge and skills which they receive generally after they have gained some practical experiences. As for Advanced Trainings, the aim is to cultivate high-performing school principals. This implies that each training stage is set according to its training qualification, with its own different functions and influences.

5.3.2.2 Informal Learning

Informal learning was also a means whereby principals found indirect ways of enhancing their leadership competencies. The analysis of the combined qualitative data obtained from the open-ended questionnaire responses and the interview transcripts revealed that the majority of the school principals, who participated in the study, were actively seeking additional ways to improve and develop their leadership capability. As one principal explained:

"Being a school principal is not easy; this position is not just simply a management role. The school principal's work is very diverse and difficult; I therefore have to adequately prepare myself to meet the job requirements, although there isn't a wide range of trainings and self-development courses provided for me." (I-4)

(a)Learn from other School Principals

The data showed that the main source of informal learning was through guidance and coaching by another experienced principal:

"My previous principal is the main guide for my leadership practice." (I-5)

"When I was a teacher I used to pay attention to my school principal's work and schedule. I also used to communicate with other school principals, to try to understand their thinking." (R-20)

"To be honest, I had learnt a lot from other leaders when I was a teacher...That is, from my former school principals. I always communicated with other school principals, and I learnt how school principals run their schools and engage holistically." (I-11)

The excerpts above highlight that learning how to perform a job well can be via observing principals at work. Social interaction in schools is also a way of sourcing out first-hand realities about school leadership. This also makes them aware of the complexities in an educational institution, where students and teachers interact. Learning informally from other principals is a common approach that serves as a guide:

"By communicating with former school principals, we can learn about their ideology of running their school. By reviewing the school curriculum, I can make my own policies, and learn how to make my school a better environment for the teachers and students." (R-16)

(b)Communication

Communication is nevertheless a daily task for a school leader. Conversation with the authority, teacher colleagues, parents, public and the students is unceasing and the major way to delivery message and indirectly his influence of leadership. In the interview feedback, the school principals believe that communication is a mean to solve issues and problems that principals face as a school leader. Two principals explain this:

"I engaged in discussions and sharing sessions with experts and high performing school principals to learn more about their good management experiences." (R-25)

"I participated in all kinds of activities, and public events where I had to express myself, and in doing so, it builds my confidence in being able to influence others. At the same time, I also learnt through other principals' sharing. In this way I could reflect upon my own self-deficiencies." (I-2)

Conversely, there is a negative side to such open communications among principals, as pointed out by one school principal:

"We have some communications. But such communications are not without reservation and disclosure. We lack open communication. In fact, many of our problems cannot be openly communicated with other schools due to conflict of interest and competition." (I-7)

A few principals have ventured out, beyond China, to explore new perspectives of school leadership from international school leaders:

"I have learnt from successful educators abroad about school leadership and management." (R-23)

"I went to Taiwan, to understand more about the absorption and retention of Chinese culture.*"* (R-31)

(c)Accumulation from Past Experience

In preparing and developing their leadership skills, principals in this study talked a great deal about learning from others:

"I followed high performing school principals to learn good management practices from them." (R-25)

"I designed and built my leadership 'blueprint' upon the influence of others, particularly other experienced school principals." (R-2)

"To improve the level of my personal specialized knowledge, I learnt from the experiences of other successful educators, I expanded my horizon and improved my abilities as a school leader and school manager by learning from others." (R-23)

"In recent years, I have been learning really hard from old school principals, who enabled me to learn some really useful things that could help with my work. Also, some of my classmates are school principals, and so if I encountered problems I called them for consultation." (I-10)

The data showed that principals in China have an ambition to make themselves more aware about the dynamics of their jobs and are willing to learn from others. It was notable that very few principals talked about the direct influence of formal training upon their practices as a school leader.

Undoubtedly, the accumulation of past experiences has a big influence on school principals' roles. As the data revealed, all the principal respondents had teaching experiences or administrative management experiences before they served as school principals. Their past experiences were very helpful for their current leadership roles, according to one school principal:

"I was a substitute teacher for two years before I became a school principal. I was an accountant of a central school... After graduation, I did one year substitution in a primary school, and then shifted to a central school responsible for teaching management affairs. After that I became an accountant of the central school and was promoted as a school principal in 1999. From my viewpoint, my past experiences have a big influence on my current role." (I-10)

In a similar sense, other school principals also shared their views:

"My leadership is mostly demonstrated through my practices at work, which is guided by my accumulated experiences. I also read about how to manage a school and how to improve my personal leadership qualities." (I-9)

"In fact, my biggest professional development is to do with my leadership practices. As I gained in terms of experiences, there were also problems accumulated along the way which I had to deal with. It was a process involving thinking, reflection, conceptualizing and problem solving. I can say that I managed my school based on my personal experiences." (I-7)

"Before being a school principal, I was already prepared for the role. I had experiences as a business controller and vice-president. I had ambition. I was daring to execute my practices. This is how I accumulated my experiences for this role." (R-23)

(d)Reading Books and Self-motivation

Building human relationships and forging strong bonds with others were consistent themes that emerged from the data. This is typical of a Confucian approach to leadership that pays attention to harmonious relations at work (McDonald, 2012). Hence, it is no surprise that a few principals felt that Confucian philosophy influenced them in terms of managing their school. Another salient finding from the data was that many of the principals in the sample relied on self-learning, mostly by reading books, to prepare for their leadership role. For these principals, reading books about educational management, pedagogy and psychology was considered an essential and key aspect of their leadership preparation:

"I read books about leadership and school improvement. I learnt about advanced educational management concepts through reading." (R-22)

"I studied hard to learn the knowledge of pedagogy and psychology." (R-24)

"I mainly rely on self-study and I'm conscientious about reading books. Several times I participated in the Principal Forum and in school principals short training courses, since I became a school principal. In 2004, our education bureau organized a National High-level Forum in Shanghai, which I attended and in 2010, I went to Beijing for a school principal training. During my tenure I have been participating in all kinds of trainings and forums. But, I mainly rely on self-study and learning through reading." (I-10)

According to the principals' comments, some of the school principals read books to gain knowledge on how to solve the problems of school management. As one school principal said:

"After reading, my outlook changes, as I can see the problem from a different perspective. Also by reading I'm able to understand the problem more comprehensively." (I-1)

School principals believe that reading is a good way to improve their theoretical attainment. As one school principal indicates,

"Reading plays an important role in improving school principals' humanistic qualities

and preparedness for a conducive school culture. Also, as a school principal, you must like to study first, then you will enjoy reading." (I-17)

The comments from the principals in this study suggested that learning to be a principal, is about their personal self-development and that the responsibility to learn and prepare for their role, was essentially, their own. In direct contrast, formal training was viewed by the principals in this study, as being the core responsibility of others, at the provincial level. Several principals in this study talked positively about their formal training and its impact upon them. Most commented at length about their informal learning processes and practices.

Self-motivation is another important factor that drives school principals' informal learning. As one school principal remarked:

"Actually, school principals' preparatory work is difficult and diversified. It ranges from having to have theoretical knowledge to professional management; we play both roles as administrator and educator and we are required to know about their responsibilities. Pressure in a way is motivation. Only by pressure am I motivated to make some progress, and that is how I will know what duties I am capable of. So, self-motivation to me is one of the necessary power tools for school principals' preparation." (I-4)

Another one added:

"I mainly rely on my own professional self-growth, which I gain through the Internet, reading and learning from high performing school principals. I feel that training only has a small impact on school principals' leadership practices and self-development has a bigger impact on my professional development compared to trainings." (I-10)

Another view is expressed below:

"In order to meet the post requirements as a school principal, I study hard to equip myself with professional knowledge by looking for all kinds of learning material and participating in trainings. I do believe that a school principal is the fundamental entity of a school, without which a school will not be able to function well. This is a motivation for me to study, enrich and perfect my leadership abilities. Also because the job is not a simple management job, school principals need a lot of experience to be capable of handling their job." (I-14)

In summary, school principals expressed their opinions on how they were prepared for their current leadership roles. The data showed that the principal preparation and leadership development training program achieved its knowledge sharing through "formal learning" and "informal learning" . Formal learning was the training provided locally or as part of a university degree, whereas the informal learning included a variety form of learning that the principals acquired before taking up their post or during their tenure and training program.

5.3.3 Research Question 3: What are the constraints and challenges faced by secondary school principals of Henan Province, China in their preparation and professional development programmes?

Training is an effective method of promoting the professional development of school principals. Therefore, understanding the constraints and challenges faced by school principals, is significant in order to improve the quality of school principal training. According to the principal respondents, the major constraints and challenges they face were to do with the following: training content, training method, training evaluation, quality of training institute, training fund, training time and incentive mechanism.

5.3.3.1 Training Content

Training content refers to the curriculum that is taught to school principals when they undergo principal trainings. A well prepared training content provides participants with knowledge needed for enhancing their leadership competencies. During the training sessions, participants were given handouts and some useful teaching materials, as part of the course materials of their principal training programme.

(a)Unable to Meet Principal Leadership Needs

During the interview, most of the school principals expressed that the training content was unable to meet their actual needs. Moreover, curriculum overlapping is another critical challenge faced by school principals in this province. The following excerpts regarding training content are extracted from the principal interviews:

"The training content is always repeating, and is not targeted... In my view, I think the training organizer should investigate the school principals' training needs in advance, to understand what kind of training we really need and what kind of training can help us manage our school better." (I-2)

"Local trainings sometimes conflict with superior-agency trainings, which is not only a waste of time and resources, but also affects the normal management of schools." (I-4)

"It doesn't help that much sometimes. Most textbooks are unified and compiled by the

Ministry of Education; the content is comprehensive but lacks focus." (I-3)

"I think training should help school principals to solve the most concerned and the most urgent problems during their school management." (I-1)

It is noted that the current training content is somehow unable to meet the professional development needs of school principals. The majority of school principals said that they did not undergo any training needs assessment before beginning their training:

"Training institutes ideally should improve the curriculum...the trainings are not ideal... The training content that they taught in class neither came from textbooks nor self-study. Some of the training content were purely theoretical and even then, some theories are not in keeping with the development of time." (I-7)

The findings reveal that there isn't a unified training course material designed for school principal training. The training teacher (trainer) bases the training content on the course syllabus. The following is an extract from the interview with school principal I-14:

"China does not have training materials. Training teachers were very casual when they were training school principals... Training institutes do not have their own course material." (I-14)

Training organizers were also aware about the reality concerning training content, as expressed by training provider T-2:

"Training content does not just exist in school principal trainings, but for all trainings in China. At present, the National Training Plan has improved it a lot, but the same problem still occurrs... There are provincial-level backbone teachers, and also teachers who just their career. Backbone teachers can be teachers for those who just started to work. This is one of the reasons that caused training ineffective." (T-2)

The research findings seem to suggest that the training content failed to connect with the leadership practices of school principals and this appears to be the main constraints and challenges of school principal trainings.

(b)Inconsistent with Principal Leadership Practices

There is evidence that the training content is arbitrary and not consistent with what is practiced by school principals. The following are testimonies by several school principals about the training content:

"I feel that the training content can rarely be applied in our practices... it is merely theoretical, not practical... To be honest, some training is like a ritual. This kind of trainings is

not as effective. So, I think the impact is not that obvious." (I-9)

"I participated in school principal training for one month. But when I returned to work to face my annual work plan, I found that it actually didn't help much." (R-7)

"Generally, the training institute invited high-performing school principals to give us lectures and some of them were experts in the field. In that way, I learnt ways of improving my leadership competence. However, after the training, I realized that the theories they taught were totally not the same as in the actual situation. Some of the training content like how to manage your school and how to be better prepared for your role. But I wish training institutes would take into consideration the education condition in rural areas and practical problems of school principals." (I-11)

School principals are expected to apply the theoretical knowledge which they learnt from training classes on their individual practices. However, some principals felt that the training content did not satisfy their professional development needs:

"Training content cannot satisfy school principals' professional development needs. Firstly, most of the training curriculum still emphasizes on knowledge and skill training. Secondly, the curriculum is not updated and cannot be applied to the present situation." (I-5)

From the above information provided by the school principals, we can see that the school principals were not optimistic and felt unsatisfied with the trainings they participated in. School principals expected to solve the problems they faced in their actual situation, via these trainings. The following school principal (I-3) expresses his discontent about the training he attended:

"Lots of content was covered, but our practical work needs were neglected. I participated in trainings when I just became a school principal. I was nervous and afraid because I felt that I may not be able to handle my job. At that time, I felt that I need to be trained urgently." (I-3)

The importance of training has been recognized by many school principals. However, they have also reiterated the significance of the training content being applied to the particular context. In this nation, the tasks of school principal trainings are distributed to normal colleges and universities, by the education administrative departments. After the training venues are selected, participating school principals will be sent to the various training institutes. Training institutes devise their own training content according to the training requirements stipulated by the government authorities. However, it was found that the training content lacks sufficient attention to the actual needs of school principals, based on their levels, regions and stages of professional development. Some of them may come from different regions and their schools performance outcomes may vary. For instance, school principals who come from underdeveloped regions may run schools with poor school conditions. Therefore, it is difficult for them to apply advanced theoretical concepts to their own schools, as commented by school principal I-4:

"School principal training is necessary, but what's important is practice. The training should be based on the actual context of schools. The quality of teachers and students is also different. We should visit those schools with similar school context and learn from those principals... it will be more effective." (I-4)

(c)Lack of Practical Sessions

As previously mentioned, the training programmes are knowledge-oriented, but principals are not able to apply their learning in their practices. Some of the training courses seem to be disconnected from the actual practices of school principals. As a result, integrating knowledge into actual practice has been the core factor that restricts the effectiveness of school principal training. "Learn and apply" is the motto that drives school principals for training. It is also evident that school principals are more eager to apply the knowledge and skills they had learnt from trainings, into their leadership practices. One principal expressed his opinion about the training he attended:

"The training was not very effective because in reality, leadership practice is restricted by the teaching environment." (R-23)

It is crucial that school principal trainings should be factored in under the quality-oriented education and educational reform initiatives. The training content should therefore be more targeted and linked closely to the leadership practices of school principals, which is in line with educational reformation, as expressed by school principal R-23 below:

"I think I am quite weak in terms of curriculum leadership, especially as our nation is emphasizing new curriculum reform; I wish the training programme can focus and improve on curriculum leadership and professional skills." (R-23)

From the perspectives of school principals, it is clear that the training content needs to be relooked at and reorganized according to the new on-going education reformation in the nation. Besides, curriculum leadership training is an area that needs improving, as many of the school principals still lack knowledge and practical skills in this area. Another school principal revealed that the training content is still not aligned to the current education reformation, as well as the actual situation. They are more concerned with motivating and guiding teachers so that the academic achievement of students may be improved. One of the principal respondent also claimed that it is difficult to give consideration to both curriculum and the school's reputation on academic results as most of the schools are competitive based on the student's score and the enrolment rate. The open-ended questionnaire respondent R-23 further pointed out that the training content should emphasize more on the new reformation of education.

5.3.3.2 Training Method

The researcher enquired about the training method from the school principals who attended the trainings. The researcher was informed that, they sat still listening to the trainer's prepared presentation. The training providers invited experienced principals to share their knowledge and school leadership experiences with the participants. The knowledge sharing sessions included "Trainer to Trainee" and "Trainee to Trainee" interactive sessions. This is good for the principals who often have many teaching classes every day. It is only when they can have peer communication and informal learning, that they are more encouraged.

Apart from that, it was found that, when there was no group discussion going on, the participants appeared to be disinterested in communicating with each other. Instead, they were found engrossed with their smartphones, browsing and texting while waiting for the session to proceed. One school principal described the training method as follows:

"They invited some high performing school principals to give lectures regarding management skills and developing personal qualities. Some training institutions hired professors from various colleges or universities to give lectures regarding theoretical concepts. We also visited some high-performing schools and observed how they manage their schools. We also communicated with other school principals and exchanged our views on our management experiences. The training we had participated was short… only four days or five days… maximum not more than one week... but generally it focused more on communication." (I-10)

(a)Theoretical Emphasis

There has been a general dissatisfaction experienced by the principal participants regarding the training method adopted in the principal trainings. Some of the school principals complained about the training method used at various institutions, which are theory-based with no practical use:

"The quality of the provincial and municipal trainings is relatively low. There are

several training courses taught by training teacher. I had participated in trainings organized by Henan Normal University and Henan Education Institute. Their original intentions were very good, but the end result was not so good. The training at East China Normal University is very strict, but most of the training method used does not help much." (I-1)

"School principal trainings still mainly emphasizes on education and teaching. Both Qualification Training and Improvement Training cover too many theories. These trainings are mainly lecture-based and lack the practical aspect. From my viewpoint, during the field visits, school principals should be involved in the whole process concerning school management. We spend half a month studying about theories, and another half a month staying in a particular school, just to participate in their school management." (I-10)

"During the training process, the trainers give lectures on the platform, while the school principals passively accept the teachings... It is more of a theory course, with less practical emphasis." (I-8)

(b)Two-way Communication

Many school principals pointed out about the lack of communication between training teachers and trainees. As a result, the training atmosphere is rather depressing, and school principals were always under a passive learning atmosphere that made them feel less motivated when undertaking the training programme. Below is a typical excerpt from one school principal:

"The opportunities for two-way communication were rare... the training times were too short. Moreover, in the limited time, trainers need to complete different disciplines and training tasks, which result in less communication between trainers and trainees." (I-7)

(c) Combined Trainings

School principals pointed out that trainings are currently being conducted for both school principals and vice-school principals. The participants felt that because of the hierarchy that exists between school principals and vice-school principals, the school principals trainings should not be combined with the trainings of vice-school principals. As one school principal said:

"The training institutes placed academic affairs school principals, logistics principals and school principals together. After attending so many trainings, I have still never seen a school principal training exclusively for school principals." (I-11)

"I cannot understand why the training institutes mix school principals, vice-school principals and party secretaries together during the trainings; I do not think we should be put together as our responsibilities are different with one another." (I-4)

This issue has caused many school principals lack the interest to participate in trainings. The following training organizer from a training institute attempts to clarify this issue:

"School principal trainings in Henan Province can be divided into several modules, as arranged for vice-principals, school principals, and school secretaries. The intention for training institutes is to train school principals in batches according to their hierarchical and professional field... However, it is very difficult for training institutes to identify their actual leadership positions as the participants indirectly claim to be school principals, when they register for school principal trainings. We only realize who they are when they show up for trainings. That's when the problems come out." (T-2)

As training institutes continued to conduct targeted trainings with both principals and vice-principals, the school principal participants expressed their opinion regarding this issue:

"But as the training organizer, you should have a different purpose of training school principals and vice-school principals; you should try to avoid the occurrence of this phenomenon. You should know what kind of courses principal training involves, and what kind of courses vice-principal training involves, and after all, there is a huge gap between school principals and vice-school principals." (I-4)

On a positive note, several school principals talked about the effectiveness of the training method used in the trainings:

"It was effective, especially the case study analysis on educational management. It helps me as a school principal to diagnose and solve the problems of school management." (I-5)

"Among all the trainings that I had participated, I think theme-related case studies are very helpful. We shared our experiences and thoughts with other school principals, about school administration and management. We could reflect and compare our real situations. I also liked the topics on education justice, the problems of left-behind children and students' mental health." (I-2)

"I had participated in well-known school principal training. From my view, I personally think that I can gain the most from school field trips, especially through self-reflection and thoughts of high performing schools. However, the time spent was too short." (I-3)

"Shadow training" was another aspect that the school principals favoured:

"In 2013, I had participated in 'shadow training', which was organized by Henan

Province and China Mobile. Throughout the whole journey I shadowed a school leader, and followed whatever the school principal did. I learned a lot ...yes, I really learned a lot. I benefitted a lot from the advanced management module, teaching philosophy and philosophy of schooling. I found this training effective and very good." (I -12)

"I think 'shadow training' was the most effective method, because I could communicate with experts and high-performing school principals and gained ideas about their management experiences and school operations." (I-6)

From the above excerpts, it is obvious that school principals prefer experiential teaching. Their preferences for practical-based courses were part of the "shadow training" sessions which they participated in an actual school environment. School principals had the opportunity to observe other school principals' leadership styles and management behaviors. This helped them understand the philosophy of schooling and management methods. Nevertheless, there were negative sentiments disclosed regarding the training sessions:

"Although we had the chance to visit quality schools, I found that the context of each school is different. Therefore, what I had listened to and observed is difficult to apply and implement in my own school." (I-7)

Although, the intention of practical courses is to provide a real scenario for school principals, it is somehow difficult to obtain the right fitting school, because every school has its own context. Therefore, although school principals visit other high-performing schools, the management methods may not be suitable for their own school due to the different context of each school.

5.3.3.3 Training Evaluation

According to Phillips & Phillips, (2016), training a targeted group of personnel involves the transfer of learning. Therefore, having an effective training evaluation is necessary to maintain training quality and to identify any inadequacies in the training implementation and the programme design. Throughout the trainings, the principals were notified about the end-of-training evaluation on the programme implementation and self-evaluation which includes feedback on the overall training quality. On the last day of training, a questionnaire and a self-evaluation form were distributed for all participants to express their opinion on whether the programme had met the objectives and their own expectations. However, the school principals generally felt that the evaluations conducted by the education administrative department and the training institutes, are not reasonable:

"Before the training finished, they set aside a short while for us to fill up a questionnaire. They will take a short moment to share what we had gained from the training. Some training were organized by training institutes, and some were organized by our local education bureau, but generally the evaluation was not tightly organized." (I-10)

(a)Monitoring and Follow-up

Training evaluation is actually an important means to assess the training effectiveness. The leadership practices of school principals need follow-up diagnosis and guidance from training institutes. However, all the school principals noted that there was no follow-up or monitoring of their leadership practices after trainings were finished. If school principals encountered any problems concerning their school leadership, they would look for solutions by themselves:

"I generally have to think by myself and seek for solutions by myself." (I-7)

"Trainings were conducted but there was no follow up. They just informed us to attend training, after that they gave us some course material, and then started the lectures." (I-9)

A training institute administrator also shared his view about the principal training evaluation:

"There is no specific index for training evaluation in Henan. There is a large difference between the National Training Plan and school principal trainings. If a training institute wants to bid for a training programme, they need to submit a programme proposal, then experts will evaluate the proposal. After being approved, the training institute can implement it. The training evaluation by trainees, is supposed to evaluate the trainers based on quality training." (T-2)

Other trainers shared their opinion about the training evaluations that they participated in:

"There isn't any policy regarding principal training. Without specific execution standards, many things cannot be implemented and carried out... There is also no specific standard to evaluate school principals' training results." (T-4)

"After the training finished, the training institutes conduct the training evaluation, which I did several times by filling up a questionnaire survey online, and also through on my email." (I -12)

"Training evaluation is just a final achievement test, basically in the form of an open book... "They never conduct a training needs analysis before the training." (I-10)

(b)Lack of Rigorous Evaluation

It can be seen that the evaluation process lacks stringent tracking measures that can be beneficial for the professional development of school principal. Without a systematic evaluation system in place, the school principals also felt that participating in trainings would not make much of a difference in their professional development:

"*There is no big difference whether the training effect is good or not.*" (I-11)

However, there was a lot of positive commentary gathered from the training institutes regarding the school principal training. The researcher was intrigued to know why the school principals perceived their principal trainings as not effective, despite the positive commentary found in the training summary, gathered from the training institutes. Here was the response from principal I-4:

"*You cannot say that the training has no effect. The training institutes did ask us to fill some evaluation forms, without revealing our names; I believe this evaluation might be relatively pertinent.*" (I-4)

5.3.3.4 Quality of Training Institutes

Training institutes are responsible for training activities, and for determining training effectiveness at the end of the training. Han & Dong (2014) and Wu (2009) found that school principal trainings in China are moving from the conventional one-way communication to a more scientific and systematic mode of training. Although, training methods underwent improvement after years of progress, diversified training methods are widely implemented to create a dynamic learning method. However, Zhou (2015) discovered that each training method has its restrictions and functional limitations and cannot be compatible with each other. Thus, training institutes have been in search for advancing and perfecting their training methods, but there has been no fundamental breakthrough (Tian et al., 2012).

In this study, there were three levels of training institutes involved in the field observation, namely county level, city level and provincial level. The quality of the training institutes was evaluated based on the training facilities, quality of trainers' and the learning environment in the institutes. At the county level, it was found that the facilities available were not well developed and that there is still room for improvement. The Information Technology related classes, are not computer-aided. Presentation slides were shown throughout the class. Provincial training centres are well developed and equipped with a special computer room for the Information Technology class, whereas the city level training centres are average compared to both county and provincial level.

In term of trainers, provincial and city level training centres provide professional trainers who are experienced to deliver speeches and conduct sharing sessions with the participants. County level trainers performed slightly worse than the other two levels, as the assigned trainers are still at the elementary training level and are yet to be proficient in superior training skills. The learning environment in provincial training centres is conducive and comfortable, as participants found it relaxed and conducive for learning. Since the trainings were often held during summer breaks, the training centres in the city and county levels were often found to be less comfortable as a result of hygienic issues due to the absence of cleaners during the summer holidays.

It is important that training institutes are comfortable for participants who attend the trainings, despite their busy schedule and having to sacrifice their family time to attend these trainings. Thus, it is important that training institutes ensure the continuous improvement of the training programmes and maintain the quality of the training institutes.

(a)Principal Leadership Needs

The profound shortcoming of the institutes is that the quality and quantity of training faculties cannot meet the professional development needs of school principals. This matter was pointed out by the following two school principals:

"Training institutes did not pay enough focus on school principals' actual needs. Also, training experts are rare." (I-4)

"To be honest, the competent teacher trainers at the county level is limited. Actually, they did not have any teaching experiences. After they graduated from colleges and universities, they were assigned to training schools. Some of them were employed there because of connections. In reality, trainings are casually arranged, and many training teachers know nothing about leadership theories." (I-14)

The above comments provided by the school principals suggest that the quality and quantity of training teachers are obviously unable to meet the training needs and the leadership development of school principals. This has resulted in school principals having a very negative impression about training teachers.

(b)Credibility of Trainers

The training teachers do not have practical experience in actual school leadership, as they have not been a school principal before. This was pointed out by one school principal:

"The training staffs are not school principals... they are pseudo-experts... They are dealing with top-level school leadership, without having actual experience as a school leader. Conducting school principal trainings in their own training institute, in my opinion, is not useful." (I-1)

According to the opinion of the principal participant, knowing the actual needs of school principals is important as it can then be useful to look into ways of improving the quality of preparation and professional development for school principals.

Most of the training teachers are just academic staffs from universities or educational scientific research departments who do not have the experience of school leadership. They do not know the real context of principal leadership practices and therefore, their trainings may be disconnected from actual leadership practice. The following are comments from school principals regarding the training teachers' capabilities:

"Some of the training teachers are just ordinary teachers. They are teachers from teacher training schools and colleges of education. They do not have much administrative management and education management experiences." (I-7)

"The training teachers' theoretical knowledge may be high, but because they do not have experience as school principals, therefore, the theory they teach in class cannot be connected to school principals' real practice." (I-11)

"Generally, training teachers of teacher training schools, at the national level are not qualified. School principal training classes should be taught by managers, but we were lectured by ordinary teachers. These are teachers who have never been a school principal for even a day... neither have they managed a school for even a day." (I-15)

Another school principal commented that training institutes should pay attention to the concerns raised by school principals regarding the suitability of the present teacher trainers who do not have actual experiences in school leadership. This principal points out the situation and problems that training teachers may face:

"We may be principal trainees, but training organizations and the relevant departments should listen to our advice and concerns regarding teacher trainers. We as the front-line governors know best about school leadership." (I-1)

Regarding the above information, school principals implicitly emphasize their dominant position in school principal leadership, and further pointed out that training teachers should respect the experiences of school principals. They also feel that the present training teachers are not qualified for their role as trainers. Although some of them were not satisfied with the quality of training teachers, the following school principal gave a positive comment regarding the training teachers:

"To be honest, some of the teachers are very nice in giving the training." (I -10)

(c)Shortage of Trainers with Professional Expertise

Most of the training institutes do not have sufficient training teacher experts. The shortage of training experts has become a bottleneck that restricts the professional development of school principals. The following are comments made by training organizers regarding the training teachers:

"Training institutions lack qualified training resources and training teachers" (T-2)

"Teacher trainers are not strong enough. On the one hand, it is also about quantity... there is a lack of training teachers, which results in work overload; on the other hand, the teachers' quality is not good, ...those who really know about educational leadership are rarely ... Our training teachers do not have the experience as a school manager, so it is difficult to know or grasp school leadership ideology." (T-1)

"The qualification system and evaluation system for teacher trainers have not been properly established, and this is the main reason for the low quality training resources." (T-3)

Even some of the training teachers were developed from former trainees, one training organizer said:

"One of the training teachers worked in many training institutes in Henan Province. He was a much unknown teacher previously... He has worked in our institute since 2007. The effect was very good. We guided him. He also struggled by himself." (T-2)

"Real experts need to have forward-looking ideas and broad visions, but we lack this kind of training teachers in China." (T-6)

The importance of training institutes' capacity and training teachers' specialization was made evident by both school principals and training organizers. They acknowledged the lack of qualified trainers as a concern for the preparation and professional development of school principals. In addition, the excessive number of training institutions is another reason for the mediocre quality of training institutes. Currently, the education administrative department, and

Government Department are the main sponsors of training institutions. According to Dong (2010), the current training institutes and the investment of training funds are not entirely regulated by the system, but it has political influence with the government.

5.3.3.5 Training Fund

The limited training fund is an obstacle and challenge faced across most areas of Henan Province, especially in underdeveloped areas without an adequate educational budget for school principals' trainings. This perspective of challenges is to see in details in two factors: high demand of training fund and lack of government support.

(a)High Demand of Training Fund

There is a greater demand for principal trainings in the Henan Province compared to more developed areas of China. School principals are required to pay a proportion of the training fee, and this has been an added burden for school principals. In some cases, the high costs tend to fade away their enthusiasm for attending principal trainings:

"Generally, the training expense is covered by our school, but the training colleges also have a training fund to support the training expenses ...but we pay most of it. Training expense is mainly our course material fees. The cost of school visits was high... about several thousand dollars...Due to the high cost covered under the public funding of schools, I felt hesitant to go for the school visits." (I-10)

"I do not have the money to participate in trainings, although I have to attend trainings, because the policy stipulates that trainings are linked with job promotion. Moreover, I think that there is an imbalance in the level of trainings offered for school principals. The quota for school principal advanced training in our region is limited and there are even fewer opportunities for us to go to Beijing to attend advanced training." (I-2)

(b)Lack of Governmental Support

In recent years, training funds provisioned by the government have been reduced. There appears to be a contradiction between the increasing training demand by school principals and the shortage of training funds. The following are the different opinions gathered from training organizers regarding training funds:

"Because of the lack of funding for school principal training in Henan Province, I need to hire experts in order to ensure the quality of training. But I need sufficient money to do

this...What I receive from the government and the education administrative department is not enough to support my training programme... this impacts the school principal trainings, especially in underdeveloped areas." (T-2)

"School principal training mainly relies on government funding. These trainings are administered by the Personnel Department of Henan Province. However, in Henan Province, government funding is restricted. It is an embarrassing situation to ask school principals to pay for the training fee. Under the political and economic situation, it is not good to receive money, so as a result, we do not conduct the training." (T-1)

For a long time, school principal training institutes at the national level have limited funds and poor facilities. Under the current system of education, the training fund for school principals actually depends on the local economic development. However, this is not the only reason. Networking and political connection is another important factor that determines the investment of school principal training funds. As one school principal commented:

"The magnitude of training funds depends on how strong your relationship is with the local government and education administrative department. If you know the leader of the local education bureau, definitely you would have more opportunities and funding approved to go for training." (I-2)

This situation implies that the administration of training funds has not been fully established and is regarded as biased. School principals along with training organizers have showed that the shortage of training funds has become a big issue concerning school principal trainings. Firstly, the investment of training funds usually has rigid constraints. There are no specific provisions made for training fund allocation, except for verbal orders from the education administrative departments. The shortage of training funds can impact the professional development of school principals. Moreover, some training institutes do not wish to take over the entire responsibility of running school principals trainings as remarked by one of the training organizers:

"Without enough training funds, we can only reduce the size of the training class and the number of school principal participants." (T-1)

Meanwhile, the restricted training funds have had a negative impact on the recruitment of quality training teachers and the execution of principal trainings on the whole.

5.3.3.6 Training Time

It is evident that efficient school principals are associated with proper time management (Claessens et al., 2007; Grissom et al., 2015; Hall & Hursch, 1982; Jamal, 1984; Hallinger & Heck, 1998; Orpen, 1994). However, it is reported that in China, the principals are challenged by managing their time as their job tasks are preoccupied with administrative management affairs, attending meetings and networking. This leaves them less time to think about their professional development (Chu, 2009; Liang, 2005; Zhang, 2012). The Researcher found that the principals were generally busy, even during their summer breaks. In welcoming a new school term, the school leaders are required to attend meetings and prepare an agenda for school management and teacher management, as instructed by the Ministry of Education. Unfortunately, trainings are often scheduled during summer breaks when school leaders are busy preparing for their new school term and are usually preoccupied with newly added policies by the ministry. Participating in trainings also interrupts their family time and their work schedule.

(a)Principals Busy Routine

Several school principals pointed out that they are very busy with their daily routine work and this is one of the main reasons for not participating in school principal trainings. The following are the comments and reasons provided by various school principals about their busy routines and not being able to participate in principals trainings:

"I need to attend to a mass amount of appraisals and evaluations that makes me very busy at work. I do not have time for training. Sometimes, I participate in training programmes for short periods, but this impacts my routine work." (I-2)

"Nevertheless, there are too many things that need to be done at our school. As a school principal I need to manage everything concerning my school, and so there is no time to consider training. School principals also face problems managing their school and distributing their work, but I do not have time for training." (I-8)

"I define the role of a school principal as a housekeeper. They have to manage everything. Rural schools are too small, and they do not have proper infrastructure and facilities. Some of the primary schools in villages and towns do not even have a vice-principal and that makes the principal not have time for training, to improve our personal management competency." (I-15)

"I have no energy to think about others and cannot even finish my assigned tasks." (I-14)

"Routine school management, plus meetings, and having to deal with all kinds of school inspections. Basically, from the beginning of the semester, my work schedule for the semester is already fully assigned, but in between, there are a lot of ad hoc meetings that I need to attend." (I-5)

"Being a school principal means that your work is never done. It is very difficult to get out of administrative affairs. Moreover, within a short training period, it is impossible to absorb and digest a great deal of information ... considering my energy level and limited time." (I-11)

"It's hard for school principals to participate in trainings due to the limited of time we have. This is a very common problem we face especially in our region... Our leave system is also very strict, regardless of whether it is for official business or for personal reason. If I want to take leave for one week I need to obtain approval from the relevant authorities." (I-10)

From the above interview excerpts, we can see that school principals spend a lot of time with their daily school management affairs and it is difficult for them to find time for training. Some school principals expressed that they looked at other alternatives such as finding another participant to attend the training on their behalf:

"If I do not have time, I will ask my vice-principal to replace me and attend the training. As a school principal I am really busy. It leaves me no choice but to ask my vice-school principal to attend the training on my behalf." (I-7)

"During one of the trainings I attended, I remember witnessing a participant signing under a different name and I asked him why. He told me that his school principal was busy and did not have time to attend the training, so he replaced him." (I-2)

Such practices also indicated that school principals do not always realize the true value and importance of participating in school principal trainings. They consider trainings as a task assigned by their superior which required them to fulfill.

(b)Principal Teaching Duties

Some principals get their subordinates to replace them for training, because of their heavy teaching schedule. This is very common especially in underdeveloped regions, where the working time of school principals conflict with the training schedule:

"I also teach classes at school. If I want to go for training, it is possible during the vacations, but during class time I am occupied with teaching, so I cannot go for training at that time." (I-9)

"The time for intensive trainings should not be too long, especially for school principals who have classes. If I attend training, I will have to cancel my class. This is a big problem. Also, if the training was not compulsory, I will not want to participate." (I-10)

The findings from the principal interviews show that principals teaching schedule and their daily school management duties are the main reasons why they can't always participate in school principals' training. Battling with the lack of energy and time has become a big challenge for them. In addition, effective time management is an area that these school principals need to pay more attention to, as this can affect the efficiency of their leadership practices.

5.3.3.7 Training Incentives

Training incentives should be provided to entice school principals to participate in principal trainings. Salary is the incentive, which plays an important role in improving the work enthusiasm of school principals (Lv, 2004; Yang, 2003). Moreover, the professional status and reputation of school principals are the main pursuit for their professional development.

(a)Poor Incentives

School principals are motivated if there is an incentive mechanism and a reasonable compensation system in place. This can be seen as a motivating factor that drives school principals to be more proactive with their leadership practices. Wu (2009) demonstrates that performance-based remunerations tend to have a value-added effect on school principals' performance. However, under the education reform initiative, school principals are pressured with the heavy workload and poor wages received. Below are some comments by school principals regarding incentive mechanism:

"Without good incentive mechanism, it's just a waste of time." (I-11)

"At present, school principals have big responsibilities and heavy workload, but our salary is not much different from teachers. It has caused many of us to be not willing to work as school principals, especially in our area... Moreover, there are too many inspections that we need to do. We need to work overtime when we do inspections but we don't get paid for working overtime. Our giving and receiving are not in direct proportion, and so many qualified professionals do not want to be school principals." (I-10)

School principals in this province, lack the initiative and motivation to participate in trainings. It could be partly due to the absence of a post training follow-up with participants who may like to know about the effectiveness of the trainings and whether they are getting the most out of the money and time spent at these trainings. This was pointed out by school principal I-11:

"After the training has finished and all the work is done, nobody seems to care about the effectiveness of the training. Actually training institutes should evaluate the training effectiveness. We go for trainings because of the national policy, rather than our willingness." (I-11)

(b)Training Qualifications for Job Promotion

Some school principals expressed that by participating in school principal trainings, they would be awarded with a qualification certificate that entitles them for a job promotion. Some of the school principals felt that this was an incentive for them to participate in principal trainings:

"School principals have to attend all kinds of trainings, in order to get the qualification certificate from the education administrative department. This certificate will be useful for our future promotion." (I-10)

"I do not want to participate in trainings, but I have to do so, because the policy stipulates that trainings are associated with the promotion." (I-16)

The following is a comment made by a training organizer regarding promotions:

"Nowadays all the school principals attend trainings, just for getting a qualification certificate. Everyone needs this certificate." (T-2)

From the above comments, it is clear that some school principals attended trainings to obtain training certificates, rather than to improve their leadership capacity. This shows that some of the school principals do not realize the importance and the need for principal professional development. Their passive participation at trainings, was revealed by one of the school principals:

"Trainings are assigned by superior government officials. Most of the school principals are passive participants at trainings, rather than willing to participate actively." (I-8)

Similarly, a training provider also shared his opinion about the passive involvement of school principals during trainings:

"School principals are not active during the training process... they did not pay much attention to the training." (T-1)

The following are further views of training organizers regarding the attitude of principal participants during the trainings:

"Some of the school principals appeared disinterested in learning and seemed not motivated to actively engage in the training. They don't value the trainings and they seem to lack of critical thinking." (T-3)

"For some participants, they come with the attitude that they do not want training but since they have been asked to come, they show up for the training." (T-2)

It is evident that trainings are based on the administrative orders imposed on selected school principals. Many of them comply to these orders as instructed by the education administrative departments. This tends to demotivate some of the school principals, who feel that they are forced to participate in trainings. Regardless of the training schedule, some may even arrive late, leave early or are absent from the training classes. The following school principal shared his observation of some of the participants at the training sessions he attended:

"When the training class was held in our region, it was common to see school principals in class for two days and then after, they left. School principals who lived near to the training place, would leave immediately after the roll call... I observed that the training teachers had no choice. There were too many trainees for the training teachers to manage. Also they can't be overly strict with the trainees... sometimes they did not even know these school principals." (I-10)

Here are the views of a training organizer, who expressed that trainings for school principals were not highly valued by the government and that it restricted the professional development of school principals:

"Actually, another big challenge is that the government and education administrative leaders do not highly value school principal trainings... It is not like the National Training Plan, which has instructive policies and people to manage it. In Henan Province, only the Henan Education Institute has two school principal training classes per year, and this only began in the recent two years." (T-2)

5.3.4 Research Question 4: What are the constraints and challenges faced by secondary school principals of Henan Province, China regarding their leadership practices?

In order to better understand the leadership practices of school principals in Henan, China, it is crucial to comprehend the constraints and challenges that they faced. The constraints in practising their leadership ability that we are looking at are on identifying the hindering factors that weaken their leadership influence and application. Six aspects of constraints are outlined in the sub-sections below: (1) education reform and new curriculum reform, (2) principals responsibilities, power and benefits, (3) school fund, (4) teacher management, (5) principals busy schedule, and (6) principals innovative capacity.

5.3.4.1 Education Reform and New Curriculum Reform

Quality education has been the focus of the educational reform initiative since 2001. However, the curriculum and education reforms have brought about a series of constraints and challenges that have impacted the leadership practices of school principals. In the following section school principals from varying backgrounds, discussed about the constraints and challenges they faced from various aspects such as student enrolment rate, staff issues, and funding.

(a)Students Enrolment Rate

The majority of school principals pointed out that their student enrolment rate is the biggest challenge that faced:

"The student enrolment rate is an important index which is associated with the quality of a school because a high enrolment rate tells of your leadership ability. Quality leadership is highly recognized by parents, society and our superior leaders. They only care about students' scores... scores are more important than leadership abilities." (I-13)

This idea was also supported by several other school principals, who emphasized the importance of quality education, student recruitment and the student enrolment rate, which determined the overall recognition of principal leadership:

"The government advocates quality education, but once the students' enrolment is out, the local education bureau will announce schools' rankings according to the enrolment rate. Students' enrolment is a very important factor that affects the school's student recruitment." (I-2)

"Currently, the main challenge that school principals are facing is the conflict of exam-oriented education and quality oriented education... At present, the achievement of high school entrance examinations and college entrance examinations are still how people judge the education quality. It acts as the key index to judge whether people are satisfied with the education system or not." (I-14)

"Actually, schools are having cut-throat competition. There is heavy emphasis placed on children's exam scores. Each school wishes to attract qualified students, and so, as a school

principal, you have to let people trust your abilities to run a school effectively. Basically, in the final year of high school, all extracurricular activities are cancelled in order to allow students to fully concentrate on their national exam." (I-5)

The society has very high expectations from school principals. The sustainability and development of schools are reflected in the school's standard operating procedures, with particular emphasis on education quality. This results in stiff competition among schools. Hence, regardless of how the nation advocates quality-oriented education, the student enrolment rate is an important index used to evaluate thc leadership performance of school principals. As a result, school principals are always on the lookout for high achieving students. Improving the enrolment rate is seemingly the top priority and a challenge for school principals. The following school principal spoke of his awareness regarding quality education:

"Actually, as school principals we are all pretty clear what the problem is. We also want to make changes and implement quality education to improve student learning and help reduce work stress for teachers." (I-5)

However, another school principal argued about the lack of attention paid towards students' holistic development:

"Education is too rigid. There's an over emphasis on academic education without paying enough attention to students' balanced development." (I-8)

(b)Exam-Oriented Education

Students, teachers and school principals are very anxious about the exam-oriented education, as the whole society is highly concerned about student exam scores. Besides, school principals are also seeking different ways of improving the enrolment rate of students. Below is the testimony from a school principal who shows concern for his school's low performance:

"Compared to other schools in Shangqiu, our school is relatively weak. In recent years the exam scores and quality of student resources has been low... our school is difficult to manage in terms of administration, management and teaching." (I-12)

During the principal interviews, they were questioned about what they wished to gain professionally by participating in the trainings. Quite a number of school principals provided similar responses about wanting to learn how to lead teachers and students towards the betterment of their schools. At present, the enrolment rate seems to be the only standard used to form judgment about schools and school principals. However, one of the biggest challenges for school principals is how to deal with exam-oriented education emphasis and quality-oriented educational reforms. Moreover, in rural areas school principals are challenged by poor school conditions and the quality of teachers. The following are some of the comments expressed by school principals regarding the challenges they face in leading rural schools:

"For schools in rural areas, without qualified teachers, and without proper infrastructures, how do you insist on quality education? It is beyond my ability. School principals' achievement only relies on boosting students' scores. The enrolment in rural areas is very low, and it is difficult for schools to recruit students who score high marks. Most of the high performing students go to urban cities to further their studies. As a result, the poorer performing students are the ones left behind in rural areas. It's a vicious circle, and school principals can't do much." (I-4)

Another school principal added:

"The problem is we are not happy and satisfied with the Chinese education system, especially the educational policies and curriculum reform which have been implemented in China. Students and teachers are continually burdened, and we have still not solved these issues." (I-2)

Although curriculum and education reforms have been implemented throughout the nation, the education system is still very much exam-oriented. School principals are being pressured into prioritizing societal demands for achieving results. The following school principals shared their views on exam-oriented education:

"Exam-oriented education has been rooted in our society for thousands of years. It is not easy to make changes within a short period of time." (I-13)

"Quality-oriented education is like a health care product, while exam-oriented education is the medicine. In this situation nothing can be changed for a reformation of the entire education system." (I-14)

School principals are generally concerned about exam-oriented education and quality-oriented education, because exam-oriented education has been deeply rooted in this nation. With exam-oriented education, there is heightened competition between schools. School principals are more inclined towards driving quality education, rather than having to focus on high academic scores viewed as a criterion to assess the achievement of school principals.

(c)School-Based Management

The majority of school principals are struggling with the concept of adapting school-based management. As one school principal pointed out that:

"As a school principal, if you do not adopt new educational concepts, you cannot lead teachers and implement education reforms. It is a big challenge for school principals' to develop their leadership capacity." (I-2)

The development of school-based management is an important factor that tests the professional ability of school principals. However, the contradiction between schools' capacities and the requirement of the new curriculum reform has resulted in difficulties faced by principals during the real implementation. Below are some statements that reflect the views of several school principals' regarding curriculum reform:

"The new curriculum reform has both requirements on software and hardware facilities. Our school does not have the money to buy relevant equipment, and we also lack teachers who are experts in this field. New curriculum reform also requires school principals to have connection with curriculum experts, but I can rarely connect with curriculum experts. Moreover, the limited funds we face, as well as teachers' quality, pose challenges that can slow down the progress of curriculum reform." (I-13)

Another school principal also pointed out the root cause that retards curriculum reform:

"The government just gives us orders and tells us to execute the curriculum reform initiatives, without giving us any specific guidance on how to go about the implementation... The system does not reform, so how are we expected to reform the curriculum?" (I-4)

School principals still expressed their desires to make changes towards better development of their schools. However, the fear of change does pose an obstacle for some school principals, as indicated by school principal I-3 below:

"Fear of change, sometimes I really want to apply the advanced theory and education concepts into my practice, but I'm also afraid of bad results. Sometimes, it is difficult to implement, teachers and parents do not support your ideas; they are also afraid of new decision and new changes that will influence their own interests or students' interests. This is why it is very difficult to change the status quo of school principals' leadership ,which restricts school principals' professional development." (I-3)

From the above expressions, curriculum reform is restricted by teacher faculty, teaching facilities, curriculum resources and school principals' capacity. School principals' are required to deal with these contradictions and eventually find ways of strategically promoting curriculum reform under the drive of school-based management.

5.3.4.2 Principals Responsibilities, Power and Benefits

(a)Safety and Security in Schools

During the interview, most of the school principals spoke of the education system and how it is intertwined with their responsibilities, power and interest. School principals generally felt that safety issues are too big a responsibility for them. Usually when an unlikely event occurs, the school principal is the first person to act and take charge of the situation. Below are the comments made by school principal I-13 regarding security in schools:

"Security is one aspect of our work as a school principal. We have taken measure to establish a reliable security system, to prevent any accidents from taking place. As a precautionary measure, we adopt the necessary security protocols in the interest of ensuring the safety of students. Some parents make a fuss over various issues and sometimes take a lawsuit against the school. This is very bad for both the school and school principals' reputation. This is why safety is always a priority." (I-13)

Other school principals also shared similar views regarding the added responsibilities of principals in having to oversee security issues:

"If an accident occurs, the school principal is the person responsible for handling the situation." (I-10)

Other school principals provided their views to explain this as follow:

"If our school participates in any event are organized by the education administrative department, we can be rest assured that students will attend. We always follow whatever the education administrative department instructs us to do, and we do not dare take any other action." (I-2)

"It is not easy to be a school principal, because as a school principal I have to manage the school's administrative operations, and be well-versed with political ideology, otherwise, you might be reprimanded." (I-13)

According to the principal testimonies above, safety is the top priority of school principals. For a long time, school principals have been influenced by Confucian ideals of moderation. Some of them feel safe *"as long as there is no accident that takes place, is enough."* (I-4)

(b)Lack of School Autonomy

The education system is centralized and schools are governed by the Chinese central government. In the actual situation, school principals do not have the autonomy to make school-related decisions without the approval of the relevant government departments. Below are the remarks made by several school principals who complained about the lack of school autonomy:

"It is said that the nation advocates principal autonomy in schools, but in actual situations, particularly for public schools, principals have to report everything to the education bureau and relevant departments. If they do not approve, we cannot do it." (I-2)

"School principals are like a puppet. We do not really have the power to make important decisions concerning our school. The system is not decentralized, so we tend to be over cautious." (I-3)

"A lot of things are controlled by the education departments but the accountability and responsibility of school outcomes are placed on the school principals. I wish the government can make school-based management happens in our education system." (I-2)

"School principals in rural areas do not have rights. They are mere policy executors and do not have the power to make decisions. For example, my school needs two more music teachers, but I do not have the authority to conduct a recruitment interview, or reject the mathematics teacher that the education bureau had sent instead." (I-15)

Currently, the education departments are in control and school principals are required to manage their schools without being given the autonomy to do so. The findings in this study indicate that the education departments are over controlling and schools lack the vigor and vitality needed for an improved school climate. With limited power and subjected to local government authorities, school principals are continually under huge pressure. In China, the government still functions as the governing authority known for their centralized decision-making powers. On the other hand, decentralization and shared decision-making has unfolded in various countries as an international educational trend. However, such is not the case in this nation, where the notion of decentralization and autonomy is perceived as a rhetorical façade, associated with political propaganda.

(c)Principals Remuneration

The school principal's remuneration is allocated according to their position and responsibilities. Moreover, their performance is further assessed through a system of "rewards and punishment" . Some of the school principals are discontented with their current wage level, as they claim that their salaries do not commensurate with their workload and effort. The following are some of their views regarding this issue:

"I am busy from morning till night, but, my pay is way below the effort I've put in." (I-6)

"At present, school principals have big responsibilities and heavy workload, but our salary is no different from teachers. As a result, many school principals do not want to be a school principal." (I-10)

There are educational policies that govern school principals' responsibilities, rights and interests. Policies concerning principals and school heads have been implemented in this nation since 1985. However, in reality, they are not clearly defined.

5.3.4.3 School Fund

The government provides funding for schools. Nevertheless, the shortage of funds is a huge constraint for school principals who need to lead and manage their schools. It can also affect the growth and development of schools.

(a)Shortage of School Funds and Heavy Debts

Shortage of funds and heavy debts are the problems generally faced by school principals. Here are some comments from school principals regarding funding in their respective schools:

"My school condition is quite poor. To change it, we need a lot of money, but raising funds is difficult." (I-13)

"In my school's situation, a new campus has been set up and our financial debt is more than 50,000,000 Yuan(Chinese currency)." (I-1)

Basically, schools need financial support to improve their school conditions, but due to the shortage of the government's financial allocation of education funds, schools are unable to obtain funds for their school development needs. Generally, school principals are challenged by the problem of raising funds, as informed by one of them below:

"The funds needed for running a school are not small. If there's not enough funds, you need to source for it from the government or education administrative departments." (I-2)

(b)Government Financial Allocation

School principals are highly dependent on the government's financial allocation, provisioned in both underdeveloped and developed areas. One school principal shared his experience:

"In my opinion, the biggest challenge schools face in Henan Province, especially Shangqiu, is an economic-related problem concerning school debt. The school pays salary to hundreds of teachers, but the school has a debt of more than sixty million because of a private investment that they need to pay back." (I-11)

Financial debt is one of the most difficult problems faced by most of the school principals. They have expressed that they require money to improve their school's infrastructure, for supporting teaching activities as well as for school management purposes. However, due to the shortage of funds, it somehow affects the overall teaching quality.

5.3.4.4 Teacher Management

Teacher management is one of the constraints and challenges faced by school principals. It will be discussed in the following section, based on three aspects, the shortage, attitude and conflicts of teachers. Since teacher management is the core mission of schools, teaching quality is an important concern.

(a)Shortage of Teachers

Shortage of teachers is a critical issue faced by school principals. The following school principals have pointed out some of the challenges they face due to the shortage of teachers:

"The challenge we are facing is the lack of teachers especially since the implementation of the 'two-children' policy. There have been many teachers taking maternity leave. Some schools have nine or eight teachers, so when one or two take maternity leave or sick leave, what should I do? This is a very serious problem that school principals are facing currently, especially in rural areas." (I-10)

Another school principal added:

"I think the obstacle that I am facing right now is currently an actual situation. Of course, it is difficult to handle! Firstly, there is a serious shortage of teachers. Moreover, our school's condition is not good. The third point is my limited capacity... scarce capacity." (I -11)

During school management, school principals need to solve all kinds of contradictions and conflicts that they are challenged by. Among these conflicts, teacher management is particularly prominent. Two of the following school principals expressed the challenges they face regarding teacher quality and teacher turnover:

"As far as I know, the government has not issued any laws or regulations that govern teachers' appointments. Teachers cannot be promoted, demoted or dismissed based on their performance, which seriously affects the teaching quality. I think, regarding this matter, the government should devolve their power to school principals, and give more importance to school-based management." (I-2)

"We lack funding as well as adequate personnel. Although, there is an appointment hiring system in place, there is no employment bond enforced on the teachers. So if a teacher does not wish to work here, he can leave and work for another school." (I-8)

(b)Dealing with Difficult Teachers

School principals are finding it difficult to manage their teachers. They complained that appointment policies should take into account the problems faced by principals, such as teacher management. There is no emphasis placed on high quality teaching. Teacher teams are very difficult to manage because of their different interests, as pointed out by one school principal:

"Although, a school is a small unit, it can still have a variety of problems we face, such as teacher evaluation. Whom do we select as excellent teachers? Some teachers offer gifts to make you feel obliged to select them. Some even threaten us... I feel very stressed by these issues." (I-6)

Managing teachers is a difficult task for some of the school principals. Some principals are concerned about the evaluation system that is assessed by high-ranking government officials and their teachers. The following school principal remarks about the appraisal process:

"The evaluation system of school principals is conducted by superior education administrative officers, and teachers. Some of the school principals are afraid to criticize or point out the faults of teachers, because they are afraid that the teachers may give them a low appraisal." (I-2)

The findings indicate that school principals are facing the challenge of building teacher teams. Building teacher teams is one of the concerns for most school principals in Henan. Under the new curriculum reform, schools have high requirements for building teachers' capacity, although the number of quality teachers is limited. However, the structure of teacher team is somehow unreasonable, as pointed out by one school principal:

"We have a case where the geography class is taught by an art teacher" (I-13).

The low wages is also another reason why some of the teachers' work enthusiasm is not high, and their job satisfaction is also not good. Some of the teachers are looking for other ways to make money after their school hours. This was pointed out by one principal:

"The majority of teachers have second jobs outside, which makes them not fully focused on their own teaching job. It seems that teaching is their spare job. Everybody is busy trying to make extra money." (I-4)

It is common practice that some teachers have side businesses as an alternative to their lack of professional self-identity. This can be strenuous for the teachers and teacher attrition is another issue that bothers school principals:

"Schools in rural areas, like ours, with poor conditions, find it hard to retain our teachers. Teachers who have connections try to find a way to transfer to county schools. I want to retain my teachers by giving them good remuneration, but this school has no money. Sometimes I want to hold activities to give teachers some subsidy, but everything has to be reported." (I-9)

According to the following school principals, they feel that teachers are more interested in higher salaries:

"Actually, nowadays teachers are not interested if you talk to them about their professional development. They are only interested if you talk to them about how to improve their salary, anything to do with their welfare, or how to solve the problems they care most about." (I-1)

"If other schools can offer higher salary or better working conditions, teachers will usually transfer out to these schools." (I-6)

Teachers, who are more capable, are not willing to stay in poor performing schools, especially when they have a better offer. From the above information provided by the school principals, we can see that salary is an important factor that affects the working enthusiasm of teachers. It is therefore a challenging task for school principals to retain their teachers, especially when they are offered better salary packages.

5.3.4.5 Principals Busy Schedule

When asked about the constraints and challenges faced by school principals, the majority of them strongly opposed the rigid targets enforced by the superior departments (government authorities) which gave them a lot of pressure. Various meetings and inspections that followed, were very time-consuming, and principals did not have time for teaching management. The following school principals share their experiences and concerns regarding their busy schedule and how it impacts them:

"Education bureau gives school principals a series of tasks, which they have to complete. If you don't finish it, they will criticize you, and reveal your name during the meeting." (I-13)

"There are too many meetings to attend... all kinds of meetings that are never-ending." (I-2)

"80% of the time, school principals are involved in their school daily management; 10 to 15 percent of the time, we deal with inspections. School principals' work schedule is booked up since the beginning of the semester, and we also need to conduct a series of safety procedures. Sometimes even these tasks cannot be finished. Moreover, we need the time to suddenly organize some ad hoc school activities that bound to emerge. As a result, school principals are juggling with too many different tasks. I suffered from neurasthenia due to work exhaustion. The present situation of primary and secondary school management can be described as appalling." (I-15)

Schools have to deal with all kinds of assessments, evaluations and tests. As a result, school principals are too busy and are experiencing severe fatigue. Moreover, numerous administrative orders seem to interfere with other aspects of school management. Frequent interferences can make school principals run out of energy to focus on teaching management. These are comments from school principals regarding teaching management:

"After all, the school is a place for teaching, and the school principal as the top leader of a school, should have time for teaching management. However, school principals are always busy. They do not have time to concentrate on teaching management. For instance, you need to evaluate teachers' performance after observing their lessons. School principals have the knowledge base and teaching ability to handle this. As a school principal without this kind of ability, teachers will not be convinced by your leadership." (I-2)

"School principals are very busy, to the point that it does not make sense." (I-13)

Heavily workload takes a toll on school principals. It can even cause stress and cause health problem, as remarked by this school principal:

"Too much pressure...I have been mentally exhausted... Now I'm having neurasthenia and insomnia problems." (I-6)

School principals complain that they hardly have private time to themselves. They need to attend meetings, trainings and have to cope with inspection duties. The school principal below gave voice to his situation:

"When we can relax, we are not so tired! School principals are also human beings, we do get annoyed just like ordinary people. We also have families to take care of, but school principals hardly have private time." (I-13)

From the above expression, it is understandable that school principals also want to have time for themselves and for their relaxation. Thcy are so tired and overly exhausted having to deal with all kinds of school affairs. As a consequence of their hectic work schedule, school principals are too busy to think about their professional development.

5.3.4.6 Principals Innovative Capacity

School principals pointed out that under the current Chinese education system, they lack innovative consciousness and the drive for innovation. Some of the school principals are innovative but because they are subjected to the education system, they are unable to carry out their ideas and this can restrict their innovative abilities. Innovation is one of the important abilities recognized by many school principals, as necessary for school improvement and effectiveness. Moreover, they also generally believe that Chinese school principals lack innovation. However, they are concerned about developing their innovative abilities. As one school principal remarked:

"I think different schools are facing different challenges, but as a whole, the issue of school principals' management and their innovate abilities are a concern. School principals with innovative abilities are really rare. For instance, there are 16 primary and secondary schools in our district, but only two or three of them have demonstrated their innovative abilities." (I-10)

On similar lines, another principal added:

"In my personal view, China education is like dancing, but bound by chains. It lacks innovation. We are subjected to this system. It's like paternalism education, where I am your father, and you must listen to me." (I-2)

For a long time, school systems ignore the component of innovation, and this results in the ambiguous orientation of school principals' profession. The lack of innovative capacity or the courage needed to display innovation may be associated to their tenuous professional consciousness. The following is a strong remark by one of the school principals regarding the issue of innovation in Chinese education:

"Compared to Western countries, our nation has not established an innovative

educational concept ... I haven't found any innovation in education. I have gone to many famous schools in this nation. But none of them escape from the Confucian educational ideology... so, I couldn't agree more. China's education is dead." (I-1)

The above information shows that Confucianism still has profound influence on the Chinese education system. Here is the perspective of creativity shared by a training organizer:

"We have been emphasizing that students should be creative, but actually, even our school principals are less creative. You can observe this from the training activities. I guess this is also one of the constraints we are facing." (T-1)

Another school principal added:

"I think school principals should run their school with innovation and creativity, rather than manage their school mechanically." (I-4)

The general nature of schools principals being conservative and scholastic is associated with their lack of innovation. One school principal described his experience as follows:

"After being a school principal, routine work makes me too busy to deal with school administrative work. I gradually become mechanical, and now I am not doing what I want to do... I am doing what I have to do, I have no time to be creative. At the beginning, I was full of enthusiasm and ambition, but now I have become conventional. I won't think about innovation, even though you want me to be innovative. Also there are so many rules and regulations that restrict you." (I-6)

It is likely that the lack of innovation is a constraint on the leadership capacity of school principal. The lack of innovation found in the leadership practices of school principals was also highlighted by many of the school principals. At the same time, the school principals have also expressed their hope that trainings could be designed in a manner that can stimulate their innovative abilities. As one school principal commented below:

"Management is too rigid. I always feel bound within the framework, and it is very hard to be innovative. Presently, school principals are urgently being trained to prepare them for education reform and school development." (I-4)

Another school principal further explained:

"In my opinion, the school principal trainings need to be bolder and explorative. I think school principals' leadership practices should be based on the motto, 'learn-act-innovate', and trainings just give us such a chance, to study, observe the development of external things, and reflect on how to change their own schools. This is innovation... to be able to apply my own educational philosophy and progressively improving my competency through learning." (I-5)

With the new curriculum reform, innovation has been given renewed attention by school principals. In an era of innovation, school principals should attempt to demonstrate their innovative abilities in their leadership, as this can lead to innovative school outcomes. This may be viewed as a great potential for principals to engage more in their professional development.

5.4 Summary of the Chapter

As a summary, this chapter presented the data analysis and qualitative findings of this study. The findings were based on the testimonies of the total sample size, fifty-four school principals and six training providers who shared their experiences on their leadership preparation, the principal training programmes that they underwent and the challenges they faced in pursuing their professional development.

Research Question 1 concerns on the impact of the governmental policies on the preparation and leadership development of the secondary school in Henan Province. The Ministry of Education has unceasing effort in shaping the principals' quality especially before they are in position to serve in the school (MOE, 1989, State Council, 2012). Leadership development training has started its construction and execution since the issuance of MOE (1989) with the outline of the training curriculum and allocation of the financial education funding for the principal training. However, the findings show weak connections between the guideline and the training execution, especially in the secondary school principal preparation (Dong, 2010; Feng, 2013) and funding of the training (Liang & Zhang, 2010; Chen, 2012). There are manuals that set a starting point and steps for implementation but there is no review process to ensure the continuous improvement of the preparation and development as demanded by the government.

Research Question 2 intends to identify the ways that the principals are prepared for their leadership roles. Interviewing the purposively chosen principals has revealed two major methods to enable their leadership ability to be prepared: formal and informal learning. Formal learning is through the training curriculum modules which comprise of school visits, continuous update on educational developments, training urge, and leadership building. Whereas the informal learning is the indirect way that prepares their leadership development, which is through learning from others, communication, experience and self-development.

The findings for Research Question Three has revealed a wide insight of the constraints that the school principal faced in their preparation and professional development. Seven major constraints are concluded from the interview with the school principals and training providers: (1) impractical training content, (2) monotone and theoretical focused training method, (3) absence of strict training evaluation, (4) running out of high quality and competent trainers, (5) fail to allocate evenly distributed training fund across the nation, (6) inflexible training time for the busy participants and (7) weak incentive mechanism.

Six aspects of challenges in the school principals' leadership practise are identified to answer the Research Question Four: (1) demands of the education and new curriculum reform are overwhelming their ability, (2) leaders that lack of autonomy to exercise they right to give order, (3) heavy financial debt and non-systematic financial allocation from the government, (4) teacher management in the school, (5) busy schedule with added task to attend improvement training, and lastly (6) lacking of innovative ability and drive to be in the educational reform initiative and leadership improvement.

The data collected from the questionnaires and interviews has been analysed to fulfil the research questions. The next chapter will follow with a discussion of these findings to relate the finding to be in line with the research objectives of this study.

CHAPTER 6: DISCUSSION

6.1 Introduction

The preparedness of school principals and their professional development are recognized as the influential factors that shape principals' leadership ability needed to vitalize the education system in China. This chapter discusses how the study is able to meet the research objectives through the interpretation of the findings based on the four main concerns, namely (1) training policies and their implications on the preparation and professional development of school principals, (2) training methods used in preparing and developing school principals leadership abilities, (3) constraints and challenges to the professional development preparation programmes, and (4) constraints and challenges of school leadership practices. The findings are then summarized to propose several practical recommendations for future research on the central idea of this study. The following subsections seeks to interpret the findings based on the research objectives of this study

6.2 Research Objective 1: The Impact of Training Policies on School Principals' Preparation and Professional Development in secondary schools of Henan Province, China

The first objective of this study was to examine the impact of training policies on the preparation and professional development of secondary school principals in Henan, China. This section discusses the analyses of some of the structural policies and its impact on education reforms and principals' professionalism. The reform policy, *"The CPC's Decisions on the Education System Reform* (CPC, 1985)*"* has spurred interest among policymakers in China, and ever since 1991, the Chinese government has promulgated a series of regulations on primary and secondary school principal qualification trainings and standards. This serves as a legislative instrument to ensure that educational policies are on the right track for effective education reform (Zhou & Zhu, 2007). The policy *"Requirements and Position Requirements of Headmasters of Primary and Secondary Schools in China"* was issued to regulate the school principals' selection, appointment, assessment and trainings (SEC, 1991). In reviewing the impact of legislative policies on school principals' preparation and professional development, an analysis was conducted on 11 national and provincial policy documents. The following subsections report on the outcomes of these legislative approaches from the perspectives of school principals' selection system, qualification system, training system, evaluation system and their incentive system.

6.2.1 School Principals' Selection System

A well-regulated principal selection system is viewed as the key feature required to pledge and sustain the competence of principals (Yang, 2005). The analysis of the findings showed two prominent problems found in the school principal nomination and selection processes. Firstly, the procedure and methods used, are ambiguous and intangibly structured. The terms and conditions of the principal selection criteria are stipulated under the *"Requirements and Position Requirements of Headmasters of Primary and Secondary Schools in China* (SEC, 1991)*"*. According to Chen (2010), the overall quality of school principals in this set of regulations, is not given enough emphasis, as propagated by the concept of *"su zhi jiao yu"*, or "quality education" that is the educational ideals of the reform initiatives in China (Dello-Iacovo, 2009).

Secondly, there were apparent contradictions found in the principal selection system. A stringent selection and entry conditions are crucial to ensure that the chosen candidate can fit well into the position (Liu, 2010). In the *"Training Regulations for Primary and Secondary School Principals"* (MOE, 1999), the qualifications and the minimum eligibility requirements conform to a stricter system. This was further reinforced by the *"Decision of State Council on the Reform and Development of Basic Education* (State Council, 2001)*"* with the aim of revising the principals' appointment and selection system. Unfortunately, the *"Outline of China's National Plan for Medium and Long-Term Education Reform and Development*

(2010—2020)" which addresses the nation's needs to reduce the criteria for school principal selection does not feature the required policy orientation of selecting a principal (CPCC, 2010). This raises a question directed to the Ministry of Education regarding the lowering of the entry criteria and the guidance needed for the desired changes.

According to the Notice (*Further Strengthening the Education Cadre Training in the Henan Province),* the school principal employment system does not appear to have any fundamental changes made to it, despite having promoted quality education through quality principalship and teaching (Department of Henan, 2010). Furthermore, the so-called tenure system is only a formality, even though the terms of contract may have expired. There is no well-defined evaluation criterion to assess the leadership competence of a school principal. Usually a simple evaluation is conducted as a formality for the purpose of job renewal for school principals. Previously, school principals were elected in a democratic way through recommendation from schools, followed by the appointment granted by the Central Government. The contract will be further renewed every five years, except in cases where the denial of tenure constitutes a breach of contract. However, in recent years, such practices have stopped. As stated by Chu & Cravens (2012), taking the school as the locus of professionalism, the value of leadership is manifested in the school's vision and mission and in fostering teacher professional communities that can lead to effective school improvement.

6.2.2 School Principals' Qualification System

The school principal qualification requirement is the admittance criterion for a principal candidate to enrol in this profession. These eligibility criteria are aligned with these two policy documents of Article Five:

· *"Notice of the Education Department of Henan Province on Further Strengthening the Education Cadre Training in the Province".*

· *"Opinions of the State Council on Strengthening the Construction of Teachers' Ranks".*

These two documents require school leaders to go through a series of systematic educational trainings to develop professional consciousness to strengthen their leadership competencies, and at the same time to improve leadership skills in schools (Department of Henan, 2010; State Council, 2012).

There is no leadership course that works duly on sharpening principals' leadership skills, except for principal trainings available. Despite the government's efforts in promoting and developing the education system reformation, the *"Training Regulations for Primary and Secondary School Principals* (MOE, 1999)" has not yet been revised until now. The qualifications and the minimum eligibility requirements still remain as the endorsed version since the year 1999. Moreover, the regulations mentioned, has highlighted a situation in which the policy has very general requirements for school principals' qualifications, as the document does not entail the relevant requirements of professional school-based management experiences from the primary and secondary school principals. This can result in leadership incompetence which is likely to hinder the professional development of principals.

According to the findings, the respondents' demographic profile indicated that all principals had teaching experiences. Liu and Li (2012) claimed that most school principals were selected from qualified, experienced teachers. Feng (2003a) further added that this method of selection is a norm and that it still remains as the main and prevalent way of appointing school heads for all local secondary schools. However, this is also regulated by the law that school principals must process teacher qualifications. In the meantime, there is still no specific standard and rule for selecting school leaders from both national and local levels.

The procedure of issuing qualification certificates for school principals is carried out as a formality. According to Chen and Xia (2015), without a strict qualification admittance system, non-stringent policies can diminish the importance of the qualification system, established specifically for endorsing the qualifications of school headmasters. However, it is known that the internal control of issuing qualification certificates is strongly enforced. Only school principals who are already appointed by the government, are issued qualification certificates. Yang (2005) declared that the qualification certificate system is contextualized as part of school principals' professional development.

Fulfilling system requirements and training needs, provides a basis for quality assurance and the evaluation of school principals' quality, for promoting societal reputation and prestige. Those who participate in school principal trainings will eventually become school principals. However, for those who have the "qualification training", this does not guarantee the quality of school principals. The fundamental reason for this phenomenon is because the primary and secondary school principal qualification certificate system has not been legalized and unified. The findings concerning the qualification system also implied that the qualification system is not a sound and suitable system that can effectively regulate aspects of the principal trainings that can benefit the school leaders.

Furthermore, the endorsed qualification certificate does not serve as a compulsory document in the application for principal candidacy. This is also an indication whereby little or less importance is placed on this qualification system. Therefore, it is crucial to re-establish a stricter school principal qualification system, which should include the occupational qualification authentication standard. This is the pre-requisite of professionalism training in principalship, which forms part of the candidacy requirement (Liu, 2010). Most importantly, this effort would regulate the principal qualification system and in future may be recognized as a legal endorsement.

6.2.3 School Principals' Compensation System

There needs to be a reasonable principal's compensation system established in Henan. Various studies have since reported of the absence of a structured compensation system for school principals (Chen & Lv, 2010; Hu, 2006; Yu, 2012). In recent years, the government had issued a series of policies to increase the wage standards of school principals. In comparison to other public servants, school principals have a lower wage range, which is a pole apart, considering the obligations and burdens that school principals are subjected to. The *"Opinions on Strengthening the Construction of Headmasters of Primary and Secondary Schools* (SEC, 1992)" and the *"Opinions of the State Council on the Implementation of the Outline of China's Educational Reform and Development* (State Council, 1994)" are government policy endorsements that recognize the multiple-roles and demands placed on school leaders. It ranges from administrative to financial planning, overseeing school management and having to drive the action plans authorized by the Ministry of Education.

Presently, principals are demotivated and feel demoralized by their unfair wage packages (Hu, 2006). Their excessive workload is not in proportion to their wages and they find that it does not compensate well. Furthermore, Yu (2012) added that principal's remuneration package does not serve as an incentive to encourage principals to pursue opportunities for learning and their professional development. With the complexities of their job and position, Lv (2004) reveals that some principals feel that they are not appreciated, in terms of not being compensated for their stressful job responsibilities. Chu & Yang (2002) also confers to similar reasons behind principals fading enthusiasm in their workplace. So do the research findings of Lv (2004) and Wu (2009), that elaborate on the testimonies of school principals being displeased with the existing compensation system, as their wages are not fairly compensated according to their highly stressed level of duties.

School principals in Henan are increasingly being challenged to handle different circumstances that arise in their schools and are required to multi-task, juggle with different responsibilities on hand while ensuring that their school management duties are met. Hence, a set of policies should be formulated as a supportive guide, and used as a basis for improving the overall quality of the principals' compensation system. The diversity of training policies should be extended across both national and local levels. Mapping the terrain of polices that support both local and national levels, Fullan (2001) and Sumintono (2006), argue that the lack of relevant and hypothetical supporting policies would delineate the problems faced by school principals. Instead, compensation policies should recognize ways of providing a structured and fair compensation system for school principals; one that reflects the demands of their position, and is consistent with market rates of remuneration.

The Chinese government had introduced the *"Principal Ranking System"* and *"Annual Salary System"* with the intention of formulating a fair incentive mechanism for school principals. However, the findings in Hu (2006) revealed that these two systems have not been widely practiced in Henan Province. There also has not been any evidence to suggest that these two systems have had a positive effect on the principals' job satisfaction. The allocated monetary appreciation provisioned for principals, does not only reflect the government's gratitude for their service and contributions, but principals need to ensure that their ultimate aim is to progress according to the national education directives and towards their school set goals.

Apart from that, Wu (2009) draws attention to the principal's compensation scheme and hints that the government and related bodies are not aware of this cause-and-effect relationship. It was revealed that there were discrepancies found in principals' monthly payroll that did not coincide with their management duties. This led to some confusion in principals professional roles. As for the leadership performance evaluation, there was neither a clear performance evaluation index nor appraisal objectives to indicate the minimum requirements for evaluation. Instead, there are only general items used in the evaluation, to assess principals' achievements.

6.2.4 School Principals' Evaluation System

School principals' evaluation system should be based on a unified and explicit set of criteria and an index to facilitate the leadership performance evaluation system. The evaluation system in these recent decades is no longer compatible to be compared with the general evaluation dimensions of "morality (德), ability (能), diligence (勤), achievement (绩)", used to assess principals' job performance (Jia, 2005; SEC, 1991; Zhao & Wang, 2007). Additionally, the evaluation emphasizes more on cumulative rather than a formative evaluation of operational measures (Hu & Wang, 2009; Zhang, 2012). This method of assessment is regarded as impractical, unformulated and superficial. Up till now, China has not established any scientific evaluation standards for principalship evaluation, apart from the document, *"Opinions on Strengthening the Construction of the Headmasters of Primary and Secondary Schools* (SEC, 1992)*"*. As a result, the training evaluation system faces obstacles that hinder the progress of advancing and developing professionalism among the school principals.

The performance evaluation system should be based on a formative assessment, especially when applied to professional development growth and assessing the performance index of school principals, within a stipulated period of evaluation. As such, training evaluations will play a more significant role in revealing opportunities for improvement in areas like task management and manpower organization. According to Uren & Tovey (2001), the evaluation system has to be well rounded and tailored according to the working nature of the subject being appraised. This would help overcome the weaknesses apparent in a general summative evaluation (Uren & Tovey, 2001).

The *"Opinions of the State Council on Strengthening the Construction of Teachers' Ranks"*was gazetted in 2012. It highlighted suggestions to improve the school principals and teaching teams' professional development, the training qualifications and training facilities. These "Opinions" also suggest that, the trainings should help enhance the leadership skills of school principals so that they comply with the education policies and standards enforced by the Ministry of Education, for the purpose of meeting educational reforms (State Council, 2012).

6.2.5 School Principals Training System

This study revealed that the training policies governing the principals training system, have not made a gainful impact, in the interest of school principals' professional needs. The *"Training Regulations for Primary and Secondary School Principals* (MOE, 1999)*"* was found to be lacking in overall quality concerning school principals' professional development. However, the *"National Eleventh Five-Year Plan for Cadre Training of the Educational System", introduced in 2007*, provided guidance for all training systems (MOE, 2007). The diversity of China' s multiracial country with different regions, histories and cultures, should be taken into consideration, when devising policies. As a result, single policy implementation, may not be appropriate for the whole nation. Instead, policymaking should take into consideration both national and local levels.

According to Chu (2003) and Zhou (2015), every school leader needs to advance and develop their specialization through the trainings and institutional teaching. However, the findings of this study found that the policies governing school principals' training system, do not outline precise and definite standards regardless of national or provincial levels. The documents or regulations are not mandated due to the absence of obligatory institutions and authority regulations or policies to control and standardize the school principal training in China. Nevertheless, solving these problems requires policy document guidance and sound legal protection. In the case of Henan Province, although, the government has implemented local policies to support school principals' professional development, the impact of policies on improving principalship development is rather low. To a certain extent, the policies fail to support school principals in terms of advancing their professional development.

According to Yang (2005), Sun and Qi (2014) and Zhang (2015), there are many deficiencies in the professional development training system for the school headmasters. Some of the prominent issues are the lack of a formal structure, inadequate supporting policies and the lack of legal protection in conducting trainings. Thus, it is obvious that, the downside of the principal training system is its hindrance to principalship development. Therefore, in order to ensure school principals' professional development, there should be appropriate training policies established at both national and local levels, in line with the national agenda of education development.

(a)Training Institutes

The *"Opinion on Strengthening the Training for Principals of Primary and Secondary Schools"* (MOE, 1989) and *"Training Regulation for Primary and Secondary School Principals"* (MOE, 1999), served as a guide for principalship trainings. However, the standards of assessment and accreditation are still under construction (Chu & Cravens, 2012; Zhang, 2012). Looking at the effect of the training scheme and the resultant principalship professional development, it shows that the scheme does not include comprehensive job requirements and descriptions.

Although, the objective of the *"Outline of China's National Plan for Medium and Long-Term Education Reform and Development (2010—2020)"*, was to initiate "high quality" training abilities, however in reality, it has failed to do so (MOE, 2007). The government and educational administrative departments have no clear standard operating procedures for teacher training preparation programmes. It was discovered that there is a lack of consistency with the mechanisms adopted and institutional assurance given for conducting management trainings and evaluations at both national and local levels (Xia, 2011b). At these training institutes, training teachers are responsible for the training methodology and training content (Liu, 2011). The Education Administrative Department only carries out some routine checks but this is not considered as a professional training evaluation. Most of the training programmes conducted by training institutes emphasize on summative assessment rather than formative assessment (Yuan, 2008; Zhao & Wang, 2007; Wu et al., 2015). Moreover, there is no particular concern over the trainer's competency and neither is there any indicator for trainers to conduct performance assessments. This calls for a thorough and systematic planning of principalship trainings that can enhance principalship among school leaders of primary and secondary schools in Henan.

Enhancing the quality and professional competencies of training teachers is the critical factor that can improve quality of trainings. Article 13 of the *"Training Regulations for Primary and Secondary School Principals"* (MOE, 1999) states that there are full-time and part-time training teachers. Training institutes should be equipped with qualified training teachers, specialists and outsourced scholars, who can fulfill the requirements of delivering quality trainings. Leaders from education administrative departments and excellent school principals from primary and secondary schools may be appointed as part-time training teachers. Furthermore, the *"Notice of the Education Department of Henan Province on Further Strengthening the Education Cadre Training in the Province"* (Department of Henan, 2010) stipulates that all of Henan Province complies to the trainer's professional standards formulated by the Ministry of Education. Likewise, the nation also needs to expand their team of trainers and give more importance to hiring education management cadres, renowned specialists and scholars who have the expertise needed and are familiar with the education law. Unfortunately, in reality, there are no clear job specifications for training teachers. It is also reported that there is an inadequate number of training teachers to provide for the professional development needs of school principals.

(b)Training Funding

The *"Compulsory Education Law of the People's Republic of China"* stipulates that the compulsory education fund is the responsibility of the government departments (MOE, 2006). Nevertheless, the limited training budget is another obstacle that poses a challenge for most areas in the Henan Province, especially, training institutes at the county level, who are faced with limited funds and poor conditions. The empirical findings of Han et al., (2014) indicated that only 21.1% of the 171 principal respondents perceived that the training funds were sufficient, 32.2% respondents selected "barely enough", 36.3% respondents deemed training funds were not enough, while 10.4% respondents felt that the training funds were "not enough at all". Chang (2005) also indicated that the lack of funding is the leading cause of school principals' unwillingness to participate in trainings. In recent years, there has been a debate over the increasing training demand of school principals and the shortage of training funds.

Several studies (Shen, 2009; Wu, 2009) indicated that without clearly drawn-up policies, it is very difficult to justify the investment of school principals' training fund. The national policy has pointed out that specific training expenditures are planned by regional education administrative departments. Han, Guo and Liu (2014) reported that the regional economic differences caused large differences in the training funds, which sometimes resulted in chaos. Moreover, the policies regarding school principals' evaluation, only highlighted clauses regarding the evaluation subjects and it does not clearly indicate who the third-party is, and about the training evaluation index, in which case, the training effect cannot be comprehensively understood.

For a long time, school principal training institutes at the national level were limited with funds and poor conditions. Under the current system of education finance, the training fund for school principals actually depends on the local economic development. However, this is not the only reason. "Relationship" is another important factor that affects the investment of school principal training funds. The amount of training funds depends on how close is your relationship is with the local government and education administrative department.

In summary, the testimonies provided by the school principals and training organizers showed that the shortage of training funds has become a big issue in school principal trainings. The amount of training funds received is not specified, except through verbal communication from the education administrative departments. The availability of training funds also determines the class size and the allocation of training participants. Uneven distribution of funding will greatly affect the implementation of the training and is unable to conduct as regulated due to insufficient monetary resource.

(c)Training Evaluation

China has not established systematic training evaluation standards for school principal trainings (Hu & Wang, 2009; Xia, 2011b; Zhang, 2012). The training evaluation is not based on the training objectives. In fact, Xiao (2011b) and Tian et al. (2012) reveal that the training evaluations are based on the school principals' subjective feelings and their personal impressions of their individual training experience. To identify the effectiveness of the trainings, evaluation report forms, completed training plans and training summaries are used to draw conclusions (Tian et al., 2012; Xiao, 2011b). According to Wei and Jiang (2011), training evaluations mostly are superficial, localized and simplistic.

Since the training evaluation process is not of scientific quality, the outcome of the training results may not be as credible (Chen & Lv, 2012). This is due to the lack of explicit evaluation criteria and standards for assessing the efficacy of the trainings. The effectiveness of the training evaluation also depends on the ability of the trainers to deliver the course outline and be able to enhance the participants training experience. Generally, the principal participants feel that the training evaluations conducted by the education administrative department and training institute, are not reasonable, added no evaluation standards exist to monitor and assess the performance of training teachers.

Since China has been facing a shortage of excellent professionals and trainers, as stated in Chu (2009) and Song (2014), more emphasis should be placed on trainings and the evaluation system at both local and national levels. In the framework of principalship training, Wang (2014) disclosed that there is no training review initiative taken and neither is there a long-term tracking system to monitor the training performance and evaluations thereafter. As a result, the training evaluation appears to be rather formalized and superficial and this poses a challenge in promoting school principals' professional development.

In 2010, the *"Notice of the Education Department of Henan Province on Further Strengthening the Education Cadre Training in the Province"* addressed this issue, by providing more detailed notes on conducting training evaluation, such as: engaging experts for evaluations, conducting "student-anonymous" evaluations and having third-party evaluations. This would strengthen the formative evaluation and performance appraisal of education cadres. Evaluation results are important for identifying areas of improvement concerning training tasks and funds (Department of Henan, 2010).Moreover, the national policy, *"Opinions of the State Council on Strengthening the Construction of Teachers' Ranks"* has highlighted the necessity of training evaluation, while Article 56 of the *"Cadres Education Training Regulation"* in 2015, stresses on the objectives to improve the cadre training evaluation system and strengthen its programmes and curriculum.This information shows that training evaluations have been gradually recognized by the government and efforts are being taken to create more awareness in the importance of training evaluation.

6.3 Research Objective 2: Preparation for Principal Leadership

Several studies have indicated that authorized training providers have been provisioned to equip principal participants with the knowledge and skills required for their school improvement needs (Chen, 2010; Wilson & Xue, 2013; Yan & Ehrich, 2009). In addition, Feng (2003a) and Zheng et al. (2012) reported about the principal trainings in China and how it has benefitted the thousands of school principals who participated in the wide range of training programmes offered for principals professional guidance and support.

According to Li (2008), the impact of any formal preparation programme is measured by its effect. Similarly, Wang (2013) conferred that the effectiveness of principalship trainings depends on whether principals learning needs and preparation requirements have been fully met. From a total of 54 principals who participated in this study, 49 of them (91%) had participated in trainings at either a provincial training centre or a local university. However, in this study, the school principals commented that the formal training programmes, focused mainly on the professional concepts and on theoretical concepts.

6.3.1 Formal Training

The majority of the school principals in this study, pointed out that the formal training they underwent, has equipped them with theoretical knowledge. Recent studies have also indicated that trainings provide theoretical knowledge and serve as guidance for school principals' leadership practices (Chen, 2015; Sun & Qi, 2014; Zhuang, 2014). Other studies have highlighted the positive effects of *Shadow Training* that is highly appreciated by school principals in China (Chao, 2016; He, 2011; Liu & Zhang, 2012; Tu, 2014; Zhang, 2013). *Shadow Training* is to be very useful and gainful for their leadership learning experience. However, some of the school principals indicated that through trainings, they are able to master some basic theories of educational management, and also receive updates on their existing educational concepts and perceptions.

Likewise, several studies (Chen, 2011; Qian, 2007; Rao, 2015) have indicated that trainings can actually improve the ability of thinking in an all-round way, and that it can help school principals improve their strategic thinking and management abilities. The majority of school principals emphasize that principalship through training has opened their eyes on the required knowledge and skills needed to fulfill their job responsibilities.

Training is a learning process that enables participants to master certain skills. In this research, school principals expressed that trainings equipped them with the professional knowledge and skills required to develop effective leadership practices. A number of studies conducted (Bush & Chew, 1999; Cai, 2010; Chen & Liu, 2012; Jia, 2012; Ma, 2015) show evidence that training enables school principals to keep pace with the changing world. Yet there are other studies that report about trainings having a positive effect on enhancing school principals' professional development (Chen & Ji, 2009; Chen & Liu, 2012; Fan, 2009; Huang, Liang & Lin, 2010). The present principals may be busy with their daily school management routines and have no time to focus on their professional development needs. However, it is important for principal trainings to be continually offered for principals throughout Henan and for the training programmes to be reviewed periodically for improvement and quality purposes.

6.3.2 Informal Training

The training participants of this study also commented at length about their informal learning processes and practices, which include learning from more experienced principals, engaging in communicative sharing sessions with other principals and self-learning through reading. It was also discovered that ten of the principal participants, which make up 27% of the sample, stated that they continue to actively look to other principals as a guide. Another facet that appears in this social-informal learning context is the emergence of "principal leadership communities" who share expertise for the professional development of school leaders.

Experienced principals, who share about their success and failures, can be a learning lesson for others. The evidential data has shown that principals in Henan province are ambitious to create a shift in their job dynamics and are seeking opportunities to actively learn more from other experts in the field. There are also various empirical studies, which show that Chinese principals are actively seeking additional ways to extend their leadership expertise (Han, 2008; Harris & Jones, 2015; Jones et al., 2015; Shang, 2007; Tang et al., 2014; Wang & Yang, 2011; Wilson & Xue, 2013). This kind of self-development strategies offer an "informal training" platform for school principals to better understand their school context and help solve their school problems by learning from other principals. Such "informal trainings" cannot be gained from formal training programmes as they lack specific focus on a particular context (Zhang & Brundrett, 2010).

In this study, it was noted that very few principals talked about the direct influence of formal training upon their practices as a school leader. The findings in the subsection 5.3.3.1 support this statement and is also consistent with the conclusions arising from the 7 System Leadership Study which shows that from the perspective of the principals, formal training does not necessarily or automatically impact upon their practice (Harris & Jones, 2015; Jones et al., 2015). Similarly, Wang et al. (2011) also reported that 90% of knowledge and skills that principals gained were through informal learning and only 10% are gained through formal learning.

It is evident that many of the school principals have a strong appeal for informal learning. According to Han (2008), informal learning can enable people to draw stronger emotional support from one another. Furthermore, building human relationships and forging strong bonds with others is typical of a Confucian approach to leadership (Walker & Qian, 2015). Furthermore, Sun (2009) claimed that school principals' personal working experiences can have an added advantage on their professional development. In this study, the respondents' demographic information indicates that the school principals who were involved in this study had very rich teaching and administrative experiences, which shows their credibility to take up the position as school principal. On the contrary, Chen and Ji (2009) argues that it is impossible for school principals to develop their leadership competence and professional needs based on their past work experiences and conventional leadership practices used to lead their schools.

The comment by the I-10 on Page 104 is the qualitative evidence extracted from the principal interviews that suggested that the self-directed strategy of the principals gave them the opportunity to learn from other principals and this helped them refine their own approaches and strategies to boost their leadership skills. Indisputably, training provides a platform and opportunity to trainees to learn from each other's experiences in an interactive and informal way within an experiential learning environment. Another salient finding from this study is that many of the principals relied on self-learning, mostly by reading books, to prepare for their leadership role. According to the views of R-22 and R-24 on Page 104, reading books on educational management, pedagogy and psychology was an essential aspect of their leadership preparation. Jia (2012) pointed out that reading is the most effective method of learning and that reading is an efficient way of acquiring professional theoretical knowledge needed for developing self-leadership competencies. Zhou (2008) also pointed out that reading is an important channel to improve school principals' theoretical attainment and promote school principals' professional development.

In summary, there were many positive comments about the formal and informal channels of training that principals received, although the comments about formal training were far fewer than those about the informal training. Formal trainings helped principals cope with their job as a school leader and raised awareness of their need for continuous professional development. In this study, it can be seen that the practical knowledge acquired by school principals was also obtained through "informal trainings" gained from other experienced principals, through reading, as well as from their accumulated past experiences. Further comments from some of the principals in this study implied that learning to be an effective principal, was about personal self-development, and that formal and informal trainings are essentially important for their career and professional development.

6.4 Research Objective 3: Constraints and Challenges in Principals Preparation and Professional Development Programmes

The principal has always been the role model for the school community. The essentials of effective principal leadership are to provide school leaders with quality professional learning experiences. However, the quality of school leadership may be heightened, by enabling principals to select programmes based on their professional development needs. School principals' professional development programmes are designed to help the principals reinforce their knowledge of effective leadership practices that can provide instructional coherence and support. However, as the time and social demands change, the current development training is insufficient to satisfy the participants' desire in self-development (Han & Dong, 2014; Wei & Jiang; 2011). The findings that correspond to the Research Objective 3 will be discussed in six aspects: (1) training content, (2) training context and practicability, (3) training methodology, (4) training evaluation, (5) training programme quality assurance and funding, and (6) training programme and participants.

6.4.1 Training Content

Most of the training programmes in China are knowledge-oriented (Feng, 2003a; Han 2014; Wang, 2013; Wang et al., 2011). According to Gu (2011) the training content of primary and secondary school principal trainings, should reflect the integrated processes of learning and practice, which is result-oriented. School management and leadership is complex and challenging, and as a result, there is an increased demand for highly capable school leaders. The professional demands of school leaders are to improve their leadership practices. However, the literature shows that the training content of principal training programmes appears to be detached from actual leadership practices (Han & Dong, 2014; Wang, 2011). The findings of this present study have established that this is a common phenomenon found to exist in the training content: unable to satisfy principal leadership needs (repeating or impractical training content (comment by I-1, I-2, I-3, I-4, Page 106,107), training resource difference (comment by I-3, I-5, I-9, I-11, R-7, Page 108), and lack of practical sessions (R-23, Page 109). These principals' testimonies imply that the current training content does not meet the expectations of the principal participants.

The training content should be relevant and focused on meeting the actual needs of school principals. Hu and Walker (2012) pointed out that even if school principals' benefit from attending trainings, there will be no impact on their leadership competencies, because the training content is not relevant to their school leadership needs. Moreover, the immediate effect of participating in trainings will fade off. Thus, training providers should seriously consider revising the training content so that it would be more beneficial to school principals and worth devoting their time for these training sessions.

6.4.2 Training Context and Practicability

The school principals of this study also highlighted the issue that some of the innovative theories that they had learnt from the trainings, were unfitting with their school context and local background. Moreover, Qian (2007) claimed that the theories taught during the training have always been a bottleneck in the effort of improving their professional development. Training context is constructed based on the "National Eleventh Five-Year Plan for Cadre Training of the Educational System (MOE, 2007)", which serves as the basic structure of the training curriculum. However, Hallinger (2006) acknowledged that there is gap between the training content and the reality that school principals are confronted with in their daily routines. Zhang (2008) and Wilson and Xue (2013) emphasized the importance of contextualized training as a way of developing principals' leadership skills and proficiency in leading schools more effectively. Gao (2016) proposes a simple fact that the up-to-date Western leadership theories, such as instructional or distributed leadership, do not resonate at all with traditional Chinese values or leadership practices. The implication is that the field of educational leadership does not necessarily reflect, or indeed describe, the leadership practices in provinces and educational settings outside the West (Feng, 2012).

In their work, Qian and Walker, (2014) point to a challenge on the added pressure faced by Chinese principals in trying to navigate their relationships with various stakeholders alongside the need to respond to "upward accountability" (Tang et al., 2014). Respondents I-2 on Page 106 specified that the training curriculum and content are overlapping. It is supported by a study by Militello and Berger (2010) that indicated the inconsistency and repetitive mode of training topics. In addition, training period and duration that are conflicting with their work load and time has triggered their dissatisfaction. As Song (2014) mentioned, the national training plan is conflict with provincial training plan whereas provincial training plan clashes with city level training or county level training with the principalship training program.

6.4.3 Training Methodology

The principal participants underwent a series of conventional training methods, consisting of lecturing, reporting, field visiting and course presentation. Although the training methods used seem diverse, in fact, the training effectiveness showed little to no impact (Liu, 2010; Ma, Zhang & Mu, 2009; Zhou 2015). The training methods used were mainly lecture-based, with minimum communication and interaction between trainers and trainees. Many school principals pointed out that the training methods still prioritize classroom teaching methods and that there is a lack of communication between teachers and trainees. According to the observations conducted by the researcher at the training sites, it was reported that the participants were seemingly passive with hardly any interaction between the trainer and the principal trainees.

Studies such as Dong (2014) and Lu (2014) have pointed out that classroom lecture delivery still plays a dominant role in developing the quality of teaching responsibilities required of school principals. Nevertheless, the findings from Chang (2005) reported on the preferred training methods and out of 182 school principals, "case study" constitutes of a 98.9% affinity and 54.4% of the principals preferred "discussions and analyses of the cases" . Less than half of school principals chosen "expert report" and only 21.05% of the school principals went with "method of lecture" . This shows that lecturing the training curriculum receive the least affinity from the school principals.

In other studies, there are claims that the design of training methods does not take into consideration the school context and principals' background. As a result, training methods seem to deviate from principals' actual leadership needs (Han & Dong, 2014; Militello & Bergers , 2010; Wei & Cai, 2012; Wei & Jiang, 2011). As for the present research findings, school principals indicated their preference for training methods in which they can better relate to and apply in their respective leadership practices.

Various studies have reported that training methods used in Chinese training institutes conform to a formal hierarchical structure, whereby the methods adopted are intended to improve school principals' leadership competencies (Han, Guo & Liu, 2014; Wang, 2014). However, the findings in the present study indicate that both principals and training providers revealed that the participants of the school principal trainings comprised of both principals and vice-school principals. This indicates that the notion of "hierarchy" was not taken into consideration.

This study examined the training methods used during principal trainings and have raised the suggestion that school principal trainings in China should encompass more scientific and diversified training methods, as suggested in Wu (2009) and Han and Dong (2014). However, considering that lecture-based training methods have evidently shown a positive impact on improving the quality of teaching, trainer and trainees are inevitably subjected to the consequence of poor interaction and lack of communication that was observed at the training venues. In addition, each training method has its functional limitations and is incompatible with other methods (Zhou, 2015). Furthermore, Tian et al. (2012) has highlighted that even the training institutes are looking for ways to improve their training methods. On the other hand, Zhao (2005)have reported that some training institutes that are not assuming responsibility and accountability for the training outcomes and this has resulted in ineffective training programmes and poor outcomes. This issue has further caused many school principals to lose interest in participating in principal trainings, although trainings were initially established for the purpose of developing principals' professional development.

6.4.4 Training Evaluation

Training evaluations are conducted to determine the impact and effectiveness of trainings. Evaluations are meant to assist the training institutes identify participants' training needs and any other weaknesses of the training programmes that need improving. At the training venue, where the researcher was present, it was reported that towards the end of the training programme, participants completed a questionnaire survey and were given a brief overview by the trainer, regarding what will be covered throughout the training. A number of studies have indicated that China has not established proper, scientific training evaluation standards and a specific evaluation index system for school principal trainings (Liu, 2014; Xia, 2011b; Zhang, 2012). This was also found in the qualitative evidence of the training provider T-2 on Page 114 testimony regarding the evaluation index system.

Several other research studies have also pointed out that training evaluations were not based on the training objectives but rather on the school principals' subjective feelings and their personal impressions of their overall training experience (Tian et al., 2012; Xiao, 2008). Other studies viewed training evaluations as a mere formality that is generally inclined towards a summative evaluation (Liu, 2014; Wu et al., 2015, Yuan, 2008; Zhao & Wang, 2007). In the present study, the researcher observed that evaluation reports, training plans and training summaries were used to draw conclusions about their participants learning experience and trainer effectiveness. However, some of the training participants of this study revealed that the training evaluations conducted, only assessed the knowledge and skills gained by school principals, without paying any regard for trainees' work environment, their expectations and professional needs, or their school routine schedule.

Ideally, training evaluations should have specific and detailed evaluation indicators. According to Liu (2010) and Xiao (2011), the effectiveness of a training evaluation should be benchmarked against the principals' professional development needs. However, there is evidence to suggest that training evaluation targets were sometimes found to be misaligned (Xiao, 2011b; Yuan, 2008). Therefore, it is important to ensure that participants are evaluated based on the objectives of the trainings. The other area of concern is the lack of qualified training teachers, recognized by both training providers and school principal participants. In this study, the principal participants shared their concerns about training teachers not having principalship experience. They felt that there may be a disconnection between the teaching content and school principals' actual leadership practices. This concern may be associated to the research findings revealed in Fan (2009), where some of the training teachers demonstrated a lack of knowledge and skills required for training purposes, as well as being not familiar with education rules. According to Bai (2006), the lack of training expertise may create dissatisfaction among the participants and the quality of trainings may be compromised.

6.4.5 Training Program Quality Assurance and Funding

In China, training institutes are the major training providers of professional preparation and continuous development programmes for school principals. Their programmes are aimed at providing a pathway for school principals to develop their leadership capacities. As a result, a framework of quality standards and assurance should serve as a key point of reference and conceptual guidance, potentially for increasing the effectiveness of professional preparation and development for school principals.

In this study, training providers have expressed concerns about the inadequate number of training teachers that have increased the workload on the existing batch of training teachers and putting off some of the teaching activities that could not be implemented. Such issues can affect the professional learning development of school principals and not satisfy their training needs. There is also the concern that trainers from underdeveloped areas of Henan Province may not know and understand the core essentials of principal leadership practices at the county level. As a result, the training delivery may not meet the expectations of principal participants, who are there to learn ways of improving their leadership practices. The insufficient number of training teachers, commonly challenged by training institutes, is a phenomena highlighted in various studies (Chu, 2009; He, 2008; Song, 2014). This implies that there is a large possibility that the quality of training standards for principals' professional preparation and development programmes be compromised.

He (2008) also traces the main reasons associated with this phenomenon, such as the deficiency of full-time training teachers, high turnover rate among part-time training teachers, and most importantly, the lack of continuing education opportunities and support for school principal training programmes. Such are the constraints and challenges faced by principals that can affect their profession-wide standards, meant to strengthen principals' commitment for gaining greater professional capacity in their leadership practices.

The training fund set-up to drive the initiatives of quality standard assurance is another area of challenge, as the findings show that school principals are under the burden to bear their respective training expenses. This has resulted in some of the school principals feel reluctant to participate in principal trainings. Various studies have highlighted this issue among the challenges faced by training institutes, who are tasked with the responsibility of driving the principals' professional development initiative, in line with quality standards compliance (Chang, 2005; Dong, 2010; Han, Guo & Liu, 2014). There has been evidence in this research to suggest that a scientific and stringent training funding system has yet to be established in Henan Province, due to training fund constraints, which depends largely on the local economic development . As a result, the principals' training funds investment in different regions of

Henan Province is unevenly distributed.

Following the evidence of this study, the administrative controls and budget constraint are among the major reasons that result in the disorderly management of the training fund. In addition, the training organizers have given voice to the bureaucratic procedures involved in obtaining training funds, to the extent where training organizers may even consider the possibility of discontinuing the school principals' training programmes. However, the testimony of T-2 on Page 120 proposes a solution concerning the provision of training funds that the guarantee of funds will really be helpful to the school principal training, especially in underdeveloped areas.

It is clear that the provision of funding is crucial for the successful implementation of principals training programmes. The findings of this study will reveal the constraints and challenges faced by both school principals and training institutes, for further action to be taken by the relevant authorities who are interested in sustaining principals' preparation and development programmes in Henan Province, China.

6.4.6 Training Programme and Participants

The purpose of conducting principal training programmes is to provide preparatory support for new principals as well as to support continuing professional learning for existing practicing principals. These programmes are designed with the aim of preparing principals for their leadership roles and to encourage them to continue their professional development. In this research, it was found that the principal participants were more interested in enrolling in the trainings because of the training certificate that they will receive upon completion of the programme . The qualification certificate is a professional certification that increases the opportunity for the qualified candidates to be promoted in grade and wages. In this study, obtaining professional certification was considered valuable for principals' professional development and career advancement. The findings also indicated that most of the participants paid little emphasis for the actual desire to learn and improve their leadership competence, as mentioned by the response T-2 on Page 124. According to Chu and Yang (2002), the professional certification and the promising promotion for certified principals, was found to be an effective way of nurturing interest among these principals to enrol in principal training programmes.

Principalship is an intensely demanding job and school principals are known to be incredibly busy with a myriad of things to accomplish in their daily routines. Sadly, the importance of principal trainings is not highly valued by a number of principals in this study. These principals have reported about being laden with heavy workload, including management and teaching tasks, that there is relatively little or no time for them to focus on their professional growth. Thus, it is really a challenge for training providers to stimulate principals' interest, and reinforce their commitment to principal trainings. The comments by respondents of I-10 and I-12 on Page 125 are echoed in various studies that highlight about the principals' busy routine work, and the constraints they face in trying to focus their attention on the trainings, while they have more pressing issues to deal with at work (Liang, 2005; Zhang, 2012; Zhu, 2009).

Other empirical studies (Chang, 2005; Sun, Cheng & Deng, 2015) also indicated that time issue had become an important factor that affected school principals' initiative to participate in training. Moreover, intensive learning is the central practice of school principal training, due to school principals are laden with heavy management and teaching tasks, inevitably, training has conflict with their own work. As the data of this study reveal that school principals are carrying many roles in their work, where they are not just leaders, but also educators and managers, despite giving them time to release from work, the added training program also caused the busy schedules to be a major contradiction between their work and their professional development.

However, training sometimes is an inflexible task delivered from the government, and in this situation, it yields another bad phenomenon where vice-principals are replacing the school principals while they were sent for training. In addition, unreasonable training time arrangements are one of the factors that discourage the school principals to participate in training. Some of the school principals expressed that even they are being in the training program, their focus and concerns still be with the school-related matters and dilemmas, especially trainings are conducted during the school mid-terms. There is no supporting finding found in line with this statement yet.

On another note, Yu (2012) has highlighted that the government does not place great importance to school principal trainings. Program participants have shown a low motivation and sometimes demotivated to be enrolled in the course, said by the training providers. School principals also complained that the government does not value the training and has created another reason that disinterests them to participate in the program (comment I-10 & I-11 on Page 125). However, the Chinese government has introduced the *"Principal Ranking System"*and *"Annual Salary System"* in an effort to form a fair incentive mechanism that can draw more principal participation (Hu, 2006). Conversely, the findings of this study reveal that these two principal incentives have not been widely leveraged upon, in the Henan Province.

6.5 Research Objective 4: Constraints and Challenges in Principal Leadership Practices

The quest for a quality-oriented education has placed significant demands on school principals in China. Another major educational reform initiative (Professional Development for One Million Principals) in 1990 represented the government's effort to introduce training policies and programmes to benchmark the advancement of principal development in China. Even though schools are in pursuit of a quality-oriented education, the current education practice still remains very much exam-oriented, whereby school principals are challenged by the increasing expectations for quality education with improvements in learning processes and outcomes. As a result, the challenge is on how to support and develop principals' leadership practices that emphasize principals' responsibilities for improving instructional quality in response to the new emphasis on quality-oriented education.

6.5.1 Resistance to Innovative Reforms

Promoting and practicing a quality-oriented education has become a consensus and a dilemma to all school principals. In the context of school reforms and the implementation of change, school principals of this study pointed out that the Chinese principals generally lack innovative abilities needed to drive educational system reforms . The lack of innovation could stem from their reluctance to try out innovative approaches. Various studies have showed evidence that Chinese principals are more willing to stick to their conventional habits and traditional practices and are rather hostile towards accepting innovation (Jiang & Li, 2011; Xu, 2008; Yang, 2000; Zhang, 2009). Studies have added supporting proof that majority of the schools are yet manage to transform the conventional way of delivering knowledge and the custom in the educational stage (Chen, 2009; Ye, 2011; Wang & Wang, 2015).

Other studies indicate that teachers, students and parents are not confident in implementing new changes mainly due to their concerns about whether the changes are viable and whether these could have an adverse effect on the core operations of school systems (Jiang & Li, 2011; Xu, 2008; Yang, 2000). Thus, the education reform has become a center of gravity for the school principals to exercise their leadership skills. The finding has pointed to the major constraints that they are facing now is in exercising their principalship to implement the desired education orientation. Another important factor that suppresses educational innovation is the hesitation of some principals to present their innovative ideas, as they are afraid to be discredited or judged by their suggestions. These hesitations and uncertainties tend to stifle the execution of planned innovative changes.

6.5.2 Principal Accountabilities and Autonomy

School principals are responsible for the overall operation of their schools. In an era of increased accountabilities placed on school leaders, they are increasingly being held accountable to establish school-wide vision of academic success. While principals are facing accountability demands from the government and stakeholders for school-wide improvement, they are beleaguered with having to handle a plethora of administrative and management issues on a daily basis, to the point it can become overwhelming. Coping with added accountabilities as a school leader, increased paperwork was found to increase higher levels of stress, leaving principals feeling mentally and physically exhausted. It may be the case where the majority of school principals do not know how to efficiently manage their time. This could be one of the factors that affect the efficiency of their leadership practices.

The findings also revealed that the pressure and heavy workload had caused some of the school principals to develop health problems, such as fatigue, mental strain, neurasthenia and insomnia . Some of them also complained about not having personal time for themselves and their families. As the accountability movement gained momentum in the Henan Province, the emphasis of their leadership roles started to be associated with the duties and responsibilities mandated by state policies. In this study, the majority of school principals were uncertain about their functional rights, with regards to their leadership practices and school development.

In this study, a training organizer revealed that a number of school principal trainings held in Henan Province were only about one out of dozens. It was also reported that since two years back, only one training institute in Henan held two training classes per year. According to Lu (2003), Li (2011) and Wang (2014), there isn't a "principal in-charge" system that has been put in place within the Chinese education system, to regulate principal leadership practices. In this study, principals felt a lack of authority in exercising their managerial powers among their teachers . The reason for this could be associated with the absence of authority that empowers school principals to have the right to recruit and dismiss staff.

Furthermore, the *"People's Republic of China Compulsory Education Law Article 28"*stipulates that principals have the autonomy to appoint teachers and other staff, as well as have a say in the implementation of rewards and punishment. However, according to Xiong (2010), principals' autonomy cannot be truly exercised and that it is limited to the internal management of school affairs. Principals are not authorized to determine any of the schools running expenditure like teachers' salaries, infrastructure renovation costs and purchase of equipment, as these are controlled costs that require approval from higher authorities in the educational administrative departments. Likewise, in this study, there is evidence to suggest the bureaucracy involved when school principals have to report everything to the education bureau in order to obtain their consent and approval before executing any school-based projects.

6.5.3 Curriculum Reforms, Exam-Oriented Education and Quality-Oriented Education

Various studies highlighted that the majority of school principals in China are currently struggling with the curriculum reform initiative, piloted in 2001 (Chu, 2009; Harris et al., 2012; Walker & Qian, 2015; Yin & Lee, 2011; Yin et al., 2014). The new curriculum requires the school principal to be an instructional leader and to focus more on the teaching and learning processes, rather than their managerial responsibilities (Chu & Cravens, 2012). However, Tang et al. (2014) argued that if a school leader only focuses on administrative roles, he or she will be lacking of instructional leadership abilities which in turn slows down the progress of promoting and delivering the new curriculum reform.

The principals face the challenge of knowing how to assimilate the new reforms into curriculum processes and structures that can redefine school success and leadership effectiveness (To face the challenges in implementing curriculum reform, Qian (2017) suggests that school principals should enact student-centric, instructional leadership practices that can contribute towards schools proficiency assessments, while adhering to nationally imposed curriculum reforms. This may explain why school principals "prefer traditional teaching management practices than the external control-oriented and less attention to the interior instructional leadership behavior (Chen, 2009)" .

Another challenge that school principals are facing is the conflict between exam-oriented education and quality-oriented education, as mentioned by I-2 and I-3 on Page 128. With the basic 12-year education span in China, high school and college entrance examinations are still the mainstay and the main benchmark for school performance (Hu & West, 2015). In China, education is highly valued and children are encouraged to attain top scores in their examinations. The other bearing for high scores has also to do with the career prospects of school principals, who are rewarded and promoted in the likely event of their school's academic excellence. According to Hu and West (2015), principals who attain excellent or good in their assessments, are rewarded with extra bonuses and praised publicly in recognition of the school's reputation. On the other hand, principals with low assessment scores would be subjected to bonus cuts and sometimes economic and administrative sanctions.

Principals were also rewarded based on measures of student enrolment. The students' enrolment rate is considered as the school performance indicator which is used to determine principals' performance. As a result of this, schools were constantly in competition to outperform each other, in the attempt to excel above the rest.

Hence, regardless of how the nation advocates quality-oriented education, the student enrolment rate appears to be the most important index to evaluate the leadership performance of school principals. As a result, school principals are constantly trying to draw high quality students that can make a significant contribution to their school academic rankings. Thus, this study finds that principals are required to innovatively improve their leadership practices to find ways of attracting high achieving students and raising the quality of their present student intake, in order to meet the challenges of student enrolment rate.

6.5.4 Funding

The shortage of funds and resources appears to be a big constraint and challenge faced by most of the school principals. Some of the schools are also heavy in debt due to loans taken to establish new campuses. Poor condition in the school seeks neither help from the government nor fund raising from the public. Studies like Lu (2002) and Liang and Zhang (2010) highlight that the school principals are faced with the challenge of securing adequate funds needed for up-keeping and maintaining their school operations. However, in the present study, the finding also demonstrated that school principals throughout the Henan Province are highly dependent on government financial provisions. Moreover, it is a case where most of the Henan Province school principals are in a passive position and do not have the political connection with government officials to be able to secure funds more easily.

6.5.5 School Principals and Teachers

In China's long educational history, teachers are the fundamental educators highly respected by society. With teaching being viewed as a highly respectable profession, 10th September has been designated "Teachers' Day" in Chin1a, as a day when people show their appreciation and respect to teachers for their valuable contributions to society. In terms of achieving excellent school outcomes and preparing the nation for international competition, China has been recognized for having undergone reform efforts to improve on its curriculum and teacher education needed for realizing their goals for globalization. However, there have been reports of teachers facing major challenges regarding their roles and expectations in exercising their influence together with principal leadership practices for promoting school effectiveness.

Challenges and constraints that teachers are being faced with, vary from teacher management issues to teacher attrition and the findings of this study show that these challenges can affect school outcomes, as principals continue to battle with teacher management issues , serious shortage of teachers, poor school conditions , teacher migration from low performing rural schools to high-performing urban schools and the increase in medical and maternity leave which coincides with the government's two-child policy. These are among the current constraints and challenges faced by the teachers in Henan Province that have had an impact on school management and leadership practices.

Teacher exhaustion is another issue of concern revealed in this study. According to the findings, some teachers are signed up for part-time jobs to get additional remuneration. By overworking and having multiple responsibilities, teachers tend to be distracted from their routine teaching jobs and this can seriously compromise on the standard and quality of their teaching. Any negative impact on their teaching profession can cause teachers to eventually feel less motivated and enthusiastic about their teaching job. This can further cause teachers to be disinterested in backing up their school principal in actualizing their school goals.

The importance of maintaining a professional interpersonal relationship between principals and teachers is echoed in Price (2012). There is also evidence to suggest that the shortage of teachers can have a serious effect on the discourse of education. In the present study, principals have also pointed out that they are facing the challenge of developing and mobilizing teacher teams under the drive of new curriculum reform . Under the call of the government, the new curriculum reform has placed high demands on teachers who are expected to be the executors of the new curriculum implementation. However, the finding of this study has indicated that the majority of teachers are deficient in knowledge and are unable to accomplish the requirements of developing a school-based curriculum .

There is also a prevailing situation documented in various studies that compare the teaching quality of teachers from urban and rural areas. It was made known that those who live in the city and county demonstrate higher and better competence in teaching, compared to the teachers living in rural areas (An, 2013; Ma, 2015; Wang, 2007; Zhang, 2005). Similarly, there were the testimonies from the school principals in this study, who also shared common views about the quality of teaching being a concern in the more underdeveloped areas of Henan Province compared to the county.

6.6 Summary of Findings

The core of this research study concerns the school principals' preparation and professional development trainings in Henan Province of China, and the findings have reinforced the role of the principal, as being uniquely positioned to provide a clear vision for teaching and learning and the means to realize their school goals. Principalship training, in China, has been introduced as a strategy to improve the leadership practices of school principals and to encourage their interest and participation in professional development trainings. Thus, the concern of school principals' initial preparation and professional development trainings have been the highlight of this study, in ensuring that school principals are provided with professional trainings that can equip them with sound leadership knowledge regarding effective leadership practices that can guide these school leaders to accomplish their set goals.

The findings from this study have also identified the constraints and challenges faced by training providers in attempting to provide more effective training programmes that can suit the objectives and preferences of the school principal training participants. The current shortage of training funds and the non-rigorous post training evaluation procedures were found to stifle the aims and objectives of implementing preparatory and professional development training programmes for school principals. These were the areas that need resolving for improved training effectiveness.

The qualitative findings also showed evidence of formal and informal trainings that provide theoretical guidance for improving school principals practical know-hows and their knowledge in adopting professional practices for school effectiveness. It also has been highlighted that an innovative mindset needs to be cultivated among the school principals of Henan Province, to facilitate their creative problem handling of school matters. The professional development training programmes are held for school principals to learn ways of leading teachers through the new curriculum reform and cater for the needs of students by providing a conducive environment for attaining school excellence.

The strength and weakness of these training programmes have been highlighted with the hope that the findings are able to provide targeted and instructional cues for school principals to act on. They also highlight the positive influence that preparation and professional development programmes have on school principals' leadership Practices. These are useful for further recommendations on future studies concerning the preparation and professional development of school principals' leadership in Henan Province, China. The concluding chapter and its recommendations are discussed in the following chapter.

CHAPTER 7: CONCLUSION AND RECOMMENDATIONS

7.1 Introduction

This final chapter presents the recommendations for future research, the limitations of the study and concludes with the contribution this research study has made to the body of knowledge. The recommendations put forth are directed towards policy implications on school principals' professional development, some overall suggestions concerning formal and informal learning and some constructive remedies in support of principal leadership practices and their professional development.

7.2 Brief Overview of Discussion

Following from the Chapter 6, the chief four research objectives have been discussed based on the data collected from document analysis, interview, questionnaire, and observation. Research Objective 1 concerns on the impact of the policies issued by the government in initiating and constructing the preparation and development of principal leadership programme. It was found that the policies generally outline the guideline but not pragmatically guide the execution and no evaluation made specifically to allow assessment of training providers and the participants. The document analysis has outlined 5 key areas of impacts: (1) vague principal selection system, (2) loosely regulated qualification system, (3) unfair compensation system, (4) incomplete evaluation system, and (5) not well established training system.

The second research objective identifies the way the principals are prepared for their leadership roles. Among the aspects that can be drawn from the response can be concluded into two major ways of acquiring the leadership ability: (1) formal and (2) informal learning process. Formal learning is inclusive of training classes, urge of roles changing, and school visits, whereas informal learning is through learning from others, communication, accumulation of experience and self-motivation. It is found that informal learning contributes more to the leadership acquiring ways among the respondents. This should be an evidence to include more interactive session in the training programme to enable learning process to be active and brightly conducted.

The third research objective has revealed six major constraints from the leadership preparation and development programme: (1) training content unable to satisfy the participants' demands and needs, (2) impractical training context and too much focus on theoretical approach, (3) monotone knowledge delivery method without much interaction in the class, (4) poorly established evaluation system for training programme and participants, (5) absence of quality assurance on training providers and uneven distribution of funding and compensation, and (6) heavy work loaded participants that can be demotivate easily.

The last research objectives can meet its requirement with 5 challenges in the leadership practise of the school principals. Firstly, busy schedule at school has demotivate the leaders in enriching themselves to be innovative and upgrading themselves to be competent under education reform. Secondly, poorly delegated authority in certain decision making has disinterest them to do more for the community as they have no autonomy in initiating any programme for the sake of education reform. The new curriculum requires the school principal to urge the focus changing from an instructional leader to focus more on the teaching and learning processes,which has left a heavier burden for them. Lastly, teacher colleagues can be a stepping stone in the school management when the school leaders have to deal with difficult teachers and teacher migration that is common in the rural areas.

The recommendations in the subtopics are suggested based on the findings and discussion based on the key issues of each research objective. It is with the hope that the recommendations made from the study can be a constructive idea for further research and for the policymakers to be acknowledged of the constraints that actually exist throughout the programme implementation.

7.3 Recommendations

Since the policy planning has its confidentiality and is under the government authority, hence, the thesis will only suggest some overall suggestions in this respect. Secondly, the recommendations for school principals' formal learning and informal learning will be elaborated to strengthen their learning and the knowledge acquiring. Thirdly, the challenges and constraints of school principals' preparation and professional development will be given suggestions and constructive remedies. Last of all, the recommendations for the challenges and constraints of school principals' leadership practice will be presented, with the hope that the efforts given are in support of the education reform and create a better study ground for the children and a better workplace for the teachers.

7.3.1 School Principals' Professional Development and Training Policy

This research had shown that there is no clear policy framework governing school principals' preparation and professional development training programmes. This study recommends that a professional development and training policy should be introduced to offer explicit guidelines and eligibility criteria regarding the school principals' selection process. Such a policy should also cover other qualifying criteria related to principals' preparation and professional development training programmes, such as qualification system, training system, compensation system, evaluation system and incentive system. Presently, the set of standards and rules for school principal's selection, recruitment and training are not well defined due to its ambiguous and unclear regulations. Regarding the selection of school principals, more stringent procedures and methods need to be established at both national and local levels. The school principals' selection should not just focus on principals' teaching achievements and their professional rankings, but more importantly about their professional needs in relation to acquiring leadership concepts and competencies. It is also recommended that the central government should reinforce the planning process concerning the school principals' selection system, by urging timely updates on the job requirements of school principals under the new education development affinity. Moreover, the education administrative departments should standardize the principal selection procedure, according to the current stipulated laws and regulations while considering the nation's drive for education reform. Reward and punishment system should be applied if necessary to ensure strict execution of principals' preparation process, from selection, pre-service training, on-the-job evaluation, and the continuous development of leadership and management ability. Reward of recognition award, performance bonus and promotion can be applied to motivate the desire of self-improvement and the interest to be a better leader to achieve school excellence and hitting education reform target.

7.3.2 Principals Qualification Trainings

In Henan Province, pre-service trainings are made compulsory for pre-service principal candidates to attend. However, this research study revealed that the participants who registered at the Qualification Training programmes were actually in-service principals. The principal qualification system needs to be strictly reviewed in its implementation of a proper and relevant post-holding certificate system. Audit for the training quality is essential to closely monitor the training curriculum, teaching materials, trainers' qualifications and the participants' feedback can be a value adding factor. Moreover, school principals should be urged to attend trainings continuously especially when the training certificate has its own period of validity. Continuous professional development should be a priority especially with school principals in service, who should strive for up scaling themselves with higher qualifications. More importantly, the education administrative departments should be responsible for formulating the set of criteria that defines principals' requirements, their performance index and appraisal procedures that could standardize the principal qualification system.

7.3.3 Principals Remuneration Incentive

The current compensation system offered to school principals who participate in principalship trainings, is not favourable to the majority of school principals who participated in this research study. The principal compensation system, with regards to their remuneration package and other performance incentives, should ideally reflect their professionalism as school leaders, rather than equating them to the level of teachers. Under no cost should the average salary of principals be lower than that of teachers, considering the hierarchy of their professions. Appropriate and reasonable incentive rewarded to the high performing school leaders will surely generate fruitful results when the multi-tasking leaders receive recognition and appreciation for what they are doing. Also, consideration is needed for the principals' remuneration package which should be protected by the legislative *"Teachers Law"*. This is psychologically motivating as they have work hard and at their best to achieve what the stakeholders are demanding. Furthermore, the government should consider increasing their investment on principalship development for all school leaders throughout the nation, and making the Qualification Training programmes compulsory for all school leaders, in which the participation needs strict monitoring to ensure what is offered is not taking for granted. When these recommendations can be made into real run, the school leaders will have no doubt to perform better than what they should because they are doing it better for the society, the students and at the same time for themselves as they are given what they are deserved for their hard work.

7.3.4 Trainer Selection

The selection of qualified trainers for school principals' trainings needs to be based on stringent criteria and carefully assessed. The study has pinpointed on the need of trainers : knowing what is needed to satisfy the hunger of knowledge of the participants and they are more experienced in terms of principalship and leadership to be able to cope with the school leaders' enquiry and request. The government authorities involved in the trainer selection process need to formulate an appropriate set of criteria based on education level, related experience and qualifications that can be used to cross-verify the selection of potential trainers for principal training programmes. The candidacy requirements should consider candidates who have a strong conceptual understanding of the job and can demonstrate competency in delivering the training content in a conducive learning environment. The target audience of these trainings should be given due consideration since the majority of the participants occupy high positions in the school hierarchy. Moreover, trainers should be able to exhibit the ability to establish rapport with the participants and show respect for principals' status. The findings of this study have clearly revealed the expectations of principal participants who wish to be recognized for their reputed status as school leaders and to be dealt with respect, especially by the trainers. As and when the situation warrants, the ideal trainer should be able to respond non-defensively and not be judgmental. Most importantly, the chosen trainers will have to show commitment to their role as trainer and are willing to support the training providers' initiatives in fulfilling the objectives of principal professional training programmes.

7.3.5 Training Evaluation

Following the roll-out of principal training programmes at training institutes at Henan

Province, this study proposes a training evaluation to be established, as it would be useful to identify if the overall training programmes meet the expectations of the principal participants. The suggestion for a formative evaluation would essentially measure the principal participants learning experience, and perceived practicability for replicating leadership practices. Based on specific standards and criteria, establishing an effective evaluation mechanism or a periodical audit on the training curriculum, teaching methodology, participants' performance assessment and the peer evaluation among the trainers would place greater emphasis on good practices and quality assurance and help evaluate the effectiveness of the principal training programmes. Training evaluations would suitably identify effective strategies that can enable improved training design and delivery and would be supportive for the building of greater leadership capacities of the training participants and satisfactory from the participants as well.

7.3.6 Formal and Informal Learning

The evidence from this study illustrates that some of the formal and informal trainings have been helpful and instrumental in providing continuous professional learning that coincides with the leadership needs of principals. This study recommends that principals be provided the means to gain access to a resource centre or an officially subscribed online database of magazines and journals on educational leadership, as well as books related to their leadership careers. In this manner, principals would keep abreast with the educational trends and developments in the field of educational leadership. This study also suggests that the Education Departments should stay committed to the advancement of learning by implementing learning initiatives such as setting up a "Learning Week", a "Learning Exchange House" or a "Work and Learn Fellowship", that would provide principals a network of learning resources and a platform for information exchange. The other proposition is to explore the possibility of setting up China's most popular social media application, 'WeChat', to enable a privately hosted communication channel for principals to share career development-related information and their leadership experiences to enhance their professional consciousness.

7.3.7 Training Institutes

This study proposes that the training institutes in Henan Province, as the authorized training providers of principal preparatory and professional development programmes, should consider the lucrative investment in setting up a resource centre, library and subscribe to online journal academic databases, equipped with an archive of academic scholarly information. This would be a breakthrough for training institutions as they would be recognized as the exclusive owners of officially subscribed academic databases, introduced for trainers as well as principal participants, who will gain password-enabled access to a reservoir of pertinent information that can be highly useful for fulfilling their training needs as well as for enhancing their knowledge in their areas of expertise. Moreover, with the increase in demand for principal preparatory and continuous professional development trainings, the government should establish more training institutes in Henan Province. Training institutes could take advantage of the increase in demand and tailor training programmes with a better quality according to the principal's needs. Enlarging the number of training institutes will constitute a competitive environment where training institutes will need to give importance to provide quality enhanced training programmes specially catered for school principals' needs. Besides, the government can initiate research on the training design that will deliver an international standard skill advancement programme. The existing programmes that are implementing in other countries can be a guidance to upgrade the present training. Wide spreading the institutes especially for the underdeveloped areas will ensure unified control and execution of training program to solve the dilemma in training centre and resource deficiency which will demotivate the participation from the rural areas.

7.3.8 Training Schedule

This research had indicated that many of the school principals were not willing to participate in the trainings offered for their continuous professional development, mainly because of their work commitments, and the difficulties they face in having to make alternative arrangements for their teaching and school management affairs to be handled in their absence. It is recommended that short-term, intensive training programmes should be scheduled during the weekends, instead of during the middle of the semester. Preferably, the training schedule should be arranged with due consideration given to the availability of school principals. If trainings were scheduled at suitable times during the year, more principals would be encouraged to participate in them and this would increase the participation rate and meet the objectives of the training providers. Apart from that, time and task management should be one of the modules to enable school principals to handle their overloaded task effectively and at the same time a session with the government authorities and policy makers is a better way to allow bottom-up communication that mutual understanding can be established and ways to reach the common goals can be made acknowledged when the authorities get to know what is happening beyond their knowledge and real situation observation.

7.3.9 Training Fund and Incentive Mechanism

An exclusive principal training fund should be established, separately from the education fund allocated specifically for school principals' professional development in Henan Province. This would ensure the proper use of funds to be apportioned for principals preparatory programmes as well as programmes for the professional development of school principals in Henan Province. As for the incentive mechanism, a more attractive and reasonable incentive mechanism needs to be established, in order to extend that reach and inspire school principals to participate in principal trainings. An attractive incentive mechanism could draw the interest of school principals especially when the incentives are linked to principal's appointment, evaluation, promotion and welfare package. An appropriate incentive mechanism can enhance the attractiveness of principal trainings and stimulate principals' interest for wanting to build their self-development capacity. In addition, the active engagement in principal trainings should be a determining criterion in recognizing school principals' promotion. It would also increase the awareness among school principals in realizing the importance of these trainings. Incentives for the training institutes will in return enable the institutes to be competitive in providing a better programmes and the best institutes will be given recognition and promote nationally on their performance.

7.3.10 Principal Autonomy

This study proposes that principals be granted more autonomy in managing their schools. This exercise of autonomy suggests a greater decision-making authority for school principals, particularly in key areas concerning school budget, staffing and teacher selection as well as curriculum planning. With school principals in Henan Province assuming more responsibility for school outcomes and students' results, some degree of autonomy and greater involvement of principals in decisions about school resources, curriculum and instructions may create the opportunity for schools to innovate and excel. Leaders without authority are like a power generator without fuel to operate. Thus, allocating specific field of right for the school leaders is essential to let the leader be a leader. However, the designated rights should be well monitored as well to avoid abuse of the power that they own in some decision-making protocol.

7.3.11 Teacher Recruitment and Retention

There is a need for highly skilled teachers in the Henan Province of China. The scarcity of teachers and teacher retention is more acute in the rural areas of Henan Province. The government should implement teacher quality and retention programmes that are designed to recruit, train and retain high quality teachers who can have an impact on the future generation of student learners in Henan Province, China. Increasing the teacher workforce and curbing teacher turnover also require strong principal leadership. For principals to be capable of addressing issues like teacher shortage and retaining competent teachers, effective preparation and professional development programmes for principals could provide near-term solutions to address these pressing problems. However, short-term fixes may not be effective for retaining a high quality, sustainable teaching workforce. This study thus recommends that policies be aligned to support systemic change, build the teaching profession and improve the retention of new teachers in Henan Province, China. Ultimately, by addressing the issues of teacher recruitment and retention, it would empower learning for all students and promote gains in student learning.

7.4 Suggestions for Future Research

This research had successfully addressed the research questions of this study. These research questions fall in line with the research objectives that underpin this study. However, there are areas of this study that may be further explored, for purposes of future research. Research on policy regulations, their implications and applications for the preparation and professional development of school principals' leadership trainings, may be an area that is worth exploring. Currently, school principal training regulations are largely dependent on two broad national policies that cover principals' qualification and their leadership evaluation. This study therefore suggests the implementation of new policies and regulations that should take into consideration the local context of Henan Province before standardizing the regulations for principal trainings in this province.

Henan Province is just one of the thirty-four provincial administrative regions in China. Similar studies should be undertaken in other provinces as this can offer comparative insights of principal training programmes offered across a number of other provinces. The other suggestion is to further extend the area of research to cover a nationwide study of principal preparation and professional development training programmes across Mainland China, as research of the entire nation would identify meaningful perspectives and in-depth exploration to this research. A nationwide study could also lead to a cross cultural multinational research project that compares school principals' training programmes in nations across the region. Future research could also explore the possibility of conducting a longitudinal study which may offer further insight into tracing the development and the progress made with principals training programmes catered for their professional development.

7.5 Implications of the Study

The findings of this study will have the attention of policymakers who are strongly connected to the Chinese government and the relevant education administrative departments. To drive systemic change, policymakers will need to take into consideration the importance of policy construction, and define strong standards that can secure the interests of school principals' preparation and professional development in the Henan Province. The findings of this study are also beneficial to the larger community of research scholars, in-service principal practitioners and training institutes, who share common interests in the area of school principals' preparation and professional development. Ultimately, the joint efforts of all parties would contribute towards the sustainable development of school principals' professional growth and leadership practices in Henan Province, China.

7.6 Limitations of the Study

In the course of this study, there were several limitations of the study that need to be declared. The primary source of data for this study was gathered from a purposeful sample of school principals and training providers. It is therefore assumed that the comments and opinions shared by the respondents are truthful, unbiased and valid. This study had adopted a qualitative approach to investigate school principals' preparation and professional development training programmes in Henan Province, China. Despite the credibility of the findings obtained through interviews, surveys and field visit observations, a mixed methodological approach by integrating a quantitative methodology could have resulted in further methodological triangulation that may have further reinforced the validity of the findings. In addition, reflecting upon the integral part the researcher played as the prime investigator of this study, all attempts were considered carefully wherever applicable to minimize and if possible eliminate researcher bias that would obscure the credibility of the overall findings. As a result, this qualitative research study does not seek to generalize the findings but serves as a guide for other researchers who are interested in further exploring the course of this study.

Other inevitable shortcomings that arose during the course of this study that had led to the extended duration of this research study include constraints like having to accommodate to the busy schedules of school principals, and the difficulty in obtaining willing respondents to participate in this study. Moreover, there were instances where some participants were not willing to divulge information for fear of any repercussions on their jobs. As a result, the researcher had to take additional time in order to source for other participants who were willing to be interviewed for the purpose of this research study. Besides, during the data collection process, interviews were frequently interrupted by the sudden announcement of visits to be made by the education administrative departments, which disrupted the attention of the principals being interviewed. Such incidences tended to disrupt the interview sessions, and the interviews had to be rescheduled.

7.7 Conclusion

In its entirety, the purpose of this study was to apprehend the phenomenon of the preparation and professional development of secondary school principals' leadership in Henan Province, China. The primary objective of this study was to investigate the current issues, obstacles, challenges and paradoxes that secondary school principals in Henan Province face, concerning their leadership preparation and professional development goals. It is evident that the results of this study potentially offer new and effective ways of supporting an environment where school principals can grow and develop professionally and would be able to better facilitate instructional matters to enhance the quality of teaching and student performance in their school environment. Ultimately, the findings of this study has provided empirical evidence that supports its intended goals to encourage the implementation of policies that can govern school principals' preparation and professional development, the ways they are prepared for their leadership roles, the challenges and constraints they face concerning their leadership practices and to support school principals in their ongoing professional growth.

REFERENCES

[1] An X H. 2013. The different allocation of teachers between urban and rural schools within county and policy suggestions[J]. National Center for Education Research, 8:50-56. (In Chinese)

[2] ANON. 2011. "Sample Size: How Many Survey Participants Do I Need?" Accessed on 20 June 2011.

[3] Avolio B J, Bass B M. 1995. Individual consideration viewed at multiple levels of analysis: A multi-level framework for examining the diffusion of transformational leadership[J]. The Leadership Quarterly, 6(2), 199-218.

[4] Bai T. 2006. A study on the validity of principals in primary and secondary schools. (Unpublished master's thesis)[D]. Faculty of Education, Northwest Normal University, China. (In Chinese)

[5] Bailey J. 2008. First Steps in Qualitative Data Analysis: Transcribing[J]. Family Practice, 25(2): 127-131.

[6] Baker G P, Jensen M C, Murphy K J. 1988. Compensation and incentives: practice vs theory[J]. The Journal of Finance, 43(3): 593-616.

[7] Bass B M 1985. Leadership and performance beyond Expectations[M]. New York, NY: Free Press.

[8] Bass B M. 1997. Does the transactional-transformational leadership paradigm transcend organizational and national boundaries? [J].American Psychologist, 52(2): 130.

[9] Bass B M. 1999. Two decades of research and development in transformational leadership[J]. European Journal of Work and Organizational Psychology, 8(1): 9-32.

[10] Bass B M. 1990. Bass and Stogdill's handbook of leadership[M]. New York: The Free Press.

[11] Bass B M, Stogdill R M. 1990. Bass & Stogdill's handbook of leadership: Theory, research, and managerial applications[M]. Simon and Schuster.

[12] Bao C Y. 2004. The powers and its statute under the Principal Responsibility System[J]. Education Science, 20 (4): 51-53. (In Chinese)

[13] Bazeley P. 2013. Qualitative data analysis, practical strategies[M]. Los Angeles: Sage.

[14] Berg B L, Lune H. 2004. Qualitative research methods for the social sciences[M]. Pearson Boston.

[15] Blanchard K H, Zigarmi D, Zigarmi P.1985. Leadership and the one-minute manager: increasing effectiveness through situational leadership[M]. Huang Chia Book Company.

[16] Blase J, Blase J. 1999. Principals' instructional leadership and teacher development: teachers' perspectives[J]. Educational Administration Quarterly, 35(3): 349-78.

[17] Bloom M, Milkovich G T. 1998. Relationships among risk, incentive pay, and organizational performance[J]. Academy of Management journal, 41(3): 283-297.

[18] Bolman L G, Deal T E. 1991. Reframing Organizations[M]. San Francisco: Jossey-Bass.

[19] Bowen G A. 2009. Document analysis as a qualitative research method[J]. Qualitative Research Journal, 9(2): 27-40.

[20] Bratton J, Gold J. 2012. Human resource management: theory and practice[M]. Palgrave Macmillan.

[21] Burns J M. 1978. Leadership[M]. New York: Harper & Row.

[22] Bush T. 2011. Theories of educational leadership and management (4th edition)[M]. Los Angeles: Sage.

[23] Bush T. 2012. International perspectives on leadership development: making a difference[J]. Professional Development in Education, 38(4): 663-678.

[24] Bush T, Chew J. 1999. Developing human capital: training and mentoring for Principals[J]. Compare, 29(1): 41-52.

[25] Bush T, Jackson, D. 2002. A preparation for school leadership international perspectives[J]. Educational Management Administration and Leadership, 30(4): 417-429.

[26] Cai F, Du Y. 2003. Destructive effects of cultural revelation on physical and human capital[J]. Chinese Academic of Social Science, 2:795-860. (In Chinese)

[27] Cai L G. 2010. Study on the effectiveness improvement of the training of headmasters in secondary vocational school[J]. Journal of Fujian Radio and TV University, 2010(81):69-71. (In Chinese)

[28] Camburn E, Rowan B, Taylor J E. 2003. Distributed leadership in schools: The case of elementary schools adopting comprehensive school reform models[J]. Educational Evaluation and Policy Analysis, 25(4): 347–373.

[29] Chang L P. 2005. A study on the present situation, problems and countermeasures of the secondary school principal training in Handan (Unpublished master's thesis)[D]. Hebei Normal University, Hebei, China. (In Chinese)

[30] Chao D X. 2016. Discuss on the method of "Shadow Training"—A case study of Shadow Training for headmasters of primary and secondary schools in Anhui Province[J]. Chinese Journal of Education, 2016 (6): 3-6. (In Chinese)

[31] Chen C, Xia X W. 2015. A comparative study of principal qualification training between China and the UK—base on the comparison of training objects, content, program, assessment and so on[J]. Journal of Zhejiang Business Technology Institute, 14(3): 80-84. (In Chinese)

[32] Chen F P. 2015. Analysis on the specialized construction of headmasters training in primary and secondary schools[J]. Journal of Anqing Teachers College (Social Science Edition), 34(5): 163-166. (In Chinese)

[33] Chen L, Chai C Q, Fang Z X, Lv L. 2011. Establishing exoteric, diversified and professional primary and secondary school principal training institute patterns[J]. School Principal Training, 302(9): 28-31. (In Chinese)

[34] Chen L, Lv L. 2010. Research review on the professional training of primary and secondary school principals: From a professional perspective of trainers[J]. Management of Primary and Secondary Schools, 2(4): 4-7. (In Chinese)

[35] Chen N N. 2015. Analysis of the constraints of primary and secondary school principal training with Chongqing as example[J]. Empirical Research, 6(92): 186-187. (In Chinese)

[36] Chen W Y, Hong Z C. 2007. After the 17 years of establishment of PRC: the judgment and enlightenment of higher education development in China[M]. (In Chinese)

[37] Chen X X. 2009. The thinking and practical conception of the core competence construction of headmaster training institutions[J]. Journal of Guangxi Education Institute, 103 (5): 17-19. (In Chinese)

[38] Chen Y. 2009. Implementation of instructional leadership: predicament and countermeasures[J]. The Journal of Inner Mongolia Normal University, 22(1): 53-57. (In Chinese)

[39] Chen Y M. 2010. Educational Leadership[M]. Peking: Peking University Press. (In Chinese)

[40] Chen Y M, Xu S. 2010. Study on primary and secondary school principals' professional standards[J]. Education Development Research. (In Chinese)

[41] Chen Y M. 2011. Unscramble on Professional Strands for Primary and Secondary School Principal[M]. Peking: Peking University Press. (In Chinese)

[42] Chen Y M, Liu Y H. 2012. Modern education leadership training[M]. Peking: Peking University Press. (In Chinese)

[43] Chen Y M, Tian A L. 2006. Research on further improving the principals in primary and secondary schools[J]. Journal of Jimei University, 7(1): 3-10. (In Chinese)

[44] Chen Z S, Gao L S, Zhou Y B. 2009. The Establishment of socialist market economy system with Chinese characteristics[J]. Journal of Tianjin Social Science, 2009(2):73-93. (In Chinese)

[45] Cheng C F. 2001. Authority and usage of educational administrator[J]. Teaching and Management, 2001 (1): 21. (In Chinese)

[46] Cheng T J. 2012. Transformation of education reform and educational policy adjustment: views based on the educational reform experiences in P.R. China[J]. Peking University Education Review, 10(4): 33-49. (In Chinese)

[47] Cheng Z X, Ji C M. 2009. Connotation of principals' developmental training and conception of training specialization[J]. Education Development Research, 20(6): 23-27. (In Chinese)

[48] Cheng Z X. 2004. The professional development of primary and secondary school principals: its major characteristics and strategic consideration[J]. Journal of Jiangsu Institute of Education, 20(5): 1-5. (In Chinese)

[49] Chemers M. 2014. An integrative theory of leadership[M]. Psychology Press.

[50] Chu H Q, Cravens X C. 2012. Principal professional development in China: challenges, opportunities, and strategies[J]. Peabody Journal of Education, 87(2): 178-199.

[51] Chu H Q. 2008. The glory and the dream: establish the new educational order for equality and efficiency: the review of 30 years of Chinese educational policy[J]. Chinese Educational Journal, 2008 (10): 1-7. (In Chinese)

[52] Chu H Q. 2009. The reform path of the training curriculum for primary and secondary school principals[J]. Teacher Education Research, 21(6): 41-46. (In Chinese)

[53] Chu H Q, Lv L, Liu J. 2009. The construction of the training institutes and reformation of training system of primary and secondary school principals[J]. Journal of China Education, 2009(12): 1-6. (In Chinese)

[54] Chu H Q, Yang H Y. 2009. Towards principals' specialization[M]. Shanghai Education Press. (In Chinese)

[55] Chu H Q, Yang H Y. 2002. The principals' specialization and system guarantee[J]. Theory and Practice of Education, 22(11): 20-26. (In Chinese)

[56] Chen Y M, Xu S. 2009. The exploration of Chinese primary and secondary school principal evaluation index system[J]. Modern School Leadership and Management, 01: 41-44. (In Chinese)

[57] China Statistical Year Book. 2015. Number of schools, educational personnel and full-time teachers by type and level[R/OL]. Retrieved from http://www.stats.gov.cn/tjsj/ndsj/2015/indexch.htm. (In Chinese)

[58] China Statistical Year Book. 2015. Number of students of formal education by type and level[R/OL]. Retrieved from http://www.stats.gov.cn/tjsj/ndsj/2015/indexch.htm. (In Chinese)

[59] China Statistical Year Book. 2015. Household, population, sex ratio, and household size by region[R/OL]. Retrieved from http://www.stats.gov.cn/tjsj/ndsj/2015/indexch.htm. (In Chinese)

[60] Chirichello M. 2010. The principal as educational leader: What makes the difference [M]// School leadership. International perspectives. Springer Netherlands: 79-100.

[61] Claessens B J C, Eerde W V, Rutte C G, Roe R A. 2007. A review of the time management literature[J]. Personnel Review, 36 (2): 255-276.

[62] Clark D R. 2011. Transformational Leadership[EB/OL]. Retrieved from http://nwlink.com/~donclark/leader/transformational_leadership.html.

[63] Coleman M, Low G T, Bush T, Chew O A J. 1996. Rethinking training for principals: The role of mentoring[C]. Paper presented at the annual meeting of the American Educational Research Association, New York, NY.

[64] Costellow T D. 2011. The preferred principal: leadership traits, behaviors, and gender characteristics school teachers desire in a building leader[D]. Published dissertation, Western Kentucky University, Kentucky, United States.

[65] CPC. 1985. The CPC’ s decisions on the education system reform[EB/OL]. Retrieved 20th November, 2014 from http://www.moe.edu.cn/publicfiles/business/htmlfiles/moe/moe_177/200407/2482.html. (In Chinese)

[66] CPCC. 2006. Decision of the Central Committee of the CPC on several major issues concerning the building of a harmonious socialist society[EB/OL]. Retrieved in 15th January, 2015 http://cpc.people.com.cn/GB/64162/64168/64569/72347/6347991.html. (In Chinese)

[67] CPCC. 2010. Outline of China’ s national plan for medium- and long-term education reform and development *(2010—2020)*[EB/OL]. Retrieved 6 December, 2014 from http://planipolis.iiep.unesco.org/upload/China/China_National_Long_Term_Educational_Reform_Development_2010-2020_eng.pdf. (In Chinese)

[68] CPC. 2015. Cadres education training regulation[EB/OL]. Retrieved 21 February, 2016 from http://news.12371.cn/2015/10/18/ARTI1445170465334477.shtml. (In Chinese)

[69] Creswell J W. 2012. Qualitative inquiry and research design: Choosing among five approaches[M]. Sage publications.

[70] Creswell J W. 2013. Research design: qualitative, quantitative, and mixed methods approaches[M]. Los Angeles: Sage.

[71] Crossley M, Watson K. 2003. Comparative and international research in education: globalization, context and difference[M]. London: Routledge.

[72] Davis S, Darling-Hammond L, LaPointe M, Meyerson D. 2005. School leadership study: developing successful principals[M]. Stanford Educational Leadership Institute.

[73] Deng X P. 1978. The speech of Deng Xiaoping on National Education Conference.

[74] Denzin N K, Lincoln Y S. 1998. The landscape of qualitative research: theories and issues[M]. Thousand Oaks, Sage.

[75] Denzin N K, Lincoln Y S. 2011. The SAGE handbook of qualitative research[M]. Los Angeles: Sage.

[76] Dello-Iacovo B. 2009. Curriculum reform and Quality Education in China: an overview[J]. International Journal of Educational Development, 29(3): 241-249.

[77] Department of Henan. 2010. Notice of the education department of Henan Province on further strengthening the education cadre training in the province[EB/OL]. Retrieved 6 December, 2014 from http://www.9299.net/read/kli88269011ig300g6i390l9.html. (In Chinese)

[78] Di C G. 2014. Theory of MAO's "Four Modernizations" [J] Journal of Mao Zedong Research, 2014 (2): 52-60. (In Chinese)
[79] Dinham S, Aubusson P, Brady L. 2008. Distributed leadership as a factor in and outcome of teacher action learning[J]. International Electronic Journal for Leadership in Learning, 12(4): 4.
[80] Dong H H. 2014. A comparative study of primary and secondary school principal training in China[J]. Teachers Training of Middle and Primary Schools, 332(3): 32-34. (In Chinese)
[81] Dong Z W. 2010. The study on the current situation, problems and countermeasures (Unpublished master's thesis)[D]. Hebei Normal University, Hebei, China. (In Chinese)
[82] Downton J V. 1973. Rebel leadership: Commitment and charisma in the revolutionary process[M]. Free Press.
[83] Eisenhardt K M. 1989. Agency theory: An assessment and review[J]. Academy of Management Review, 14(1): 57-74.
[84] Encyclopedia of China, 2009. Encyclopedia of China[M]. Publishing House.
[85] Evans M G. 2002. Path-goal theory of leadership[J]. Leadership. 115-138.
[86] Fan J. 2013. Focus on school leadership construction, promote the development of education reform[J]. Journal of World Education, 335 (23): 41. (In Chinese)
[87] Fan Y K. 2009. Way out for the secondary school principal training: Reflections on the core competence of the new oriental group[J]. Journal of Hebei University, 11 (8): 38-41. (In Chinese)
[88] Fai W Y, Wang J. 2008. Giving priority to development and laying a foundation for future: Chinese education in the 30 years of reform and opening up[J]. Educational Research, 343(8): 3-14. (In Chinese)
[89] Feng D M. 2003a. Principal training in the People's Republic of China: retrospect and prospect. Reshaping the landscape of school leadership development: A global perspective[J]. Business & Economics, 205-216.
[90] Feng D M. 2003b. Restructuring and reinventing the principal responsibility system[J]. Theory and Practice of Education, 23(1): 34-37. (In Chinese)
[91] Feng D M. 2006. China's recent curriculum reform: progress and problems[J]. Planning and Changing, 2006(37): 131-144. (In Chinese)
[92] Feng D M. 1996. On competence-based principal training[J]. Journal of Shanghai Institute of Education, 54(4): 89-95. (In Chinese)

[93] Feng D M. 2012. Distributed leadership in China[J]. Exploring Education Development, 12: 31-35.
[94] Feng H M. 2013. Researches on professional growth problems of school principals and coping strategies based on researches in M city of Hubei province. (Unpublished master' s thesis)[D]. Faculty of Education, Central China Normal University, China. (In Chinese)
[95] Fiedler F E. 1964. A contingency model of leadership effectiveness[J]. Advances in Experimental Social Psychology, 1(1): 149-190.
[96] Fullan M. 2001. The new meaning of education change (3rd ed)[M]. New York: Teacher College Press.
[97] Gao H. 2016. The plights and outlets of leadership studies in China from the perspective of globalization[J]. Exploration and Contention, *2016*(12): 34-37.
[98] Gardner J W. 1990. On Leadership[M]. New York: Free Press.
[99] Ge X B. 2003. A legal and systematic Analysis on the system of headmasters' accountability of primary and secondary school in China[J]. Journal of Beijing Normal University (Social Science Edition), 180(6): 48-55.
[100] Gillham B. 2008. Developing a questionnaire[M]. A & C Black.
[101] Goksoy S. 2015. Distributed Leadership in Educational Institutions[J]. Journal of Education and Training Studies, 3(4): 110-118.
[102] Gu J F. 2011. Primary and secondary school principals' training needs analysis in Ningbo[J]. School Principal Training, 294(1): 31-33. (In Chinese)
[103] Guan P J , Song Y G. 2000. Chinese primary and secondary school principal training and team building at the turn of the century[J]. Exploring Education Development, 2000(11): 43-47. (In Chinese)
[104] Guo Q Y. 2013. Balanced development of compulsory education and construction of rural weak schools[J]. Journal of Central China Normal University (Humanities and Social Science), 52(1): 161-168.
[105] Guo S L. 2007. The professionalism and training of primary and secondary school principal. (Unpublished master's thesis)[D]. Hubei University of Education, Hebei, China. (In Chinese)
[106] Guo S L. 2009. The main problems in the specialization of primary and secondary school principal and cause analyses[J]. Journal of Hubei University of Education, 24(4): 95-97. (In Chinese)

[107] Gong L. 2012. Grasping the training policy, defining the objectives of training, improving the training content and emphasizing the key to the training.—reflections on the training of school principals in Jilin Province[J]. Journal of Education Institutes of Jilin Province, 286(28): 1-10.

[108] Gong M. 2000. Reconsideration of the Incentive of Principals' Training[J]. Journal of Hunan Educational Institute, 18(4): 78-80.

[109] Goode W, Hatt P. 1952. Methods in Social Research [M].New York: McGraw-Hill Book Co.

[110] Graeff C L. 1997. Evolution of situational leadership theory: A critical review[J]. The Leadership Quarterly, 8(2): 153-170.

[111] Grissom J A, Loeb S, Mitani H. 2015 Principal time management skills： Explaining patterns in principals' time use, job stress, and perceived effectiveness[J]. Journal of Educational Administration, 53(6): 773-793.

[112] Gronn P. 2002. Distributed leadership as a unit of analysis[J]. The Leadership Quarterly, 13(4): 423-451.

[113] Gronn P. 2009. From distributed to hybrid leadership practice[M]. Springer.

[114] Gu J F. 2011. Primary and secondary school principals' training needs analysis in Ningbo[J]. School Principal Training, 294(1): 31-33. (In Chinese)

[115] Hall B L, Hursch D E. 1982. An evaluation of the effects of a time management training program on work efficiency[J]. Journal of Organizational Behavior Management, 3(4): 73-96.

[116] Hallinger P. 2003. Leading educational change: Reflections on the practice of instructional and transformational leadership[J]. Cambridge Journal of Education, 33(3): 329-352.

[117] Hallinger P. 2006. Scholarship in school leadership preparation: the unaccepted challenge[J]. Journal of Research on Leadership Education, 1(1).

[118] Hallinger P. 2011a. Leadership for learning: lessons from 40 years of empirical research[J]. Journal of Educational Administration, 49(2): 125-142.

[119] Hallinger P. 2011b. Developing a knowledge base for educational leadership and management in East Asia[J]. School Leadership and Management, 31(4): 305-320.

[120] Hallinger P, Bryant D A. 2013. Review of research publications on educational leadership and management in Asia: A comparative analysis of three regions[J]. Oxford Review of Education, 39(3): 307-328.

[121] Hallinger P, Heck R H. 1996. Reassessing the principal's role in school effectiveness: A review of empirical research, 1980—1995. Educational administration quarterly, 32(1): 5-44.

[122] Hallinger P, Heck R H. 1998. Exploring the principal's contribution to school effectiveness: 1980—1995[J]. School Effectiveness and School Improvement, 9(2): 157-191.

[123] Hallinger P, Heck R H. 2009. Distributed leadership in schools: does system policy make a difference? [M]. Springer.

[124] Han Y Y. 2008. Informal Learning in Workplace: A case study of a human resource team. (Unpublished master's thesis)[D]. East China Normal University, Shanghai, China. (In Chinese)

[125] Han F B, Dong J M. 2014. A new exploration of the teaching mode of principal training courses[J]. Education and Teaching Research, 28(4): 43-45. (In Chinese)

[126] Han F B, Guo H Z, Liu X M. 2014. Investigation of the effect factors of primary and secondary school principals' cultivation[J]. Journal of Baoding University, 27(2): 102-106. (In Chinese)

[127] Harris A. 2008. Distributed leadership in schools: developing the leaders of tomorrow[M]. London: Routlege Falmer.

[128] Harris A, Chapman C. 2002. Leadership in schools facing challenging circumstances[J]. Management in Education, 16(1): 10-13.

[129] Harris A, Jones M. 2015. Transforming education systems: comparative and critical perspectives on school leadership[J]. Asia Pacific Journal of Education, 35(3): 311-318.

[130] Harris J, Zhao Y, Caldwell B J. 2012. Conditions for successful reforms: characteristics of the organization and culture in Chinese schools in a global context [M]// Yin H B ,Lee C K (Eds). Curriculum Reform in China: Changes and Challenges (pp. 61-77). New York: Nova Science Publishers.

[131] Hatcher R. 2005. The distribution of leadership and power in schools[J]. British Journal of Sociology of Education, 26: 253–267.

[132] He J. 2011. Discuss on the "Shadow Training" of the "National Training Program" [J]. Mentai Higher Education, 29(5): 87-89. (In Chinese)

[133] He L F et. al. 1997. The report on the appraisal of principal training[M]. Beijing Educational Publishing House. (In Chinese)

[134] He S W. 2008. Current principal training and its countermeasures[J]. Journal of Guangdong Education Institute, 28(2): 67-71. (In Chinese)

[135] Hemphill J K, Coons A E. 1957. Development of the leader behavior description questionnaire [M]// Stogdill R M, Coons A E (Eds.). Leader behavior: Its description and measurement (pp. 6-38). Columbus: Bureau of Business Research, Ohio State University.

[136] Henan Statistical Year Book. 2013. Basic statistics on primary schools by city[R/OL]. Retrieved 11th October, 2016 from http://www.ha.stats.gov.cn/hntj/lib/tjnj/2014/indexch.htm. (In Chinese)

[137] Henan Province Bureau of Statistics 2016. Statistical communique of Henan Province on national economic and social development in 2015[R/OL]. Retrieved 20, January, 2015 from http://www.ha.stats.gov.cn/hntj/tjfw/tjgb/qstjgb/webinfo/2016/02/1455680060827752.htm. (In Chinese)

[138] Henan Province Education Department. 2010. Henan Province Medium and Long-term Education Reform and Development Plan Outline 2010—2020[EB/OL]. Retrieved 6th December, 2014 from http://www.henan.gov.cn/jrhn/system/2010/09/26/010214106.shtml. (In Chinese)

[139] Hersey P. 1985. The situational leader[M]. Center for Leadership Studies.

[140] Hersey P, Blanchard K H. 1969. Management of organizational behavior: Utilizing human resources[M]. New Jersey: Prentice Hall.

[141] Higgs M. 2003. How can we make sense of leadership in the 21st century?[J]. Leadership and Organization Development Journal, 24(5): 273-284.

[142] Horner M. 1997. Leadership theory: Past, present and future[J]. Team Performance Management, 3(4): 270-287.

[143] Hou H S. 2012. The study of selection system of primary and secondary school principal (Unpublished master's thesis)[D]. Southwest University, Chongqing, China. (In Chinese)

[144] House R J. 1971. A Path Goal Theory of Leader Effectiveness[J]. Administrative Science Quarterly, 16(3): 321-339.

[145] House R J. 1996. Path-goal theory of leadership: Lessons, legacy, and a reformulated theory[J]. The Leadership Quarterly, 7(3): 323-352.

[146] House R J, Mitchell T R. 1974. Path-goal theory of leadership[J]. Journal of Contemporary Business, 3: 81-97.

[147] Hu B, West A. 2015. Exam-oriented education and implementation of education policy for migrant children in urban China[J]. Educational Studies, 1-19. Doi: 10.1080/03055698.2014.977780

[148] Hu J. 1991. Letting education serve the interests of reinvigorating local economies is a basis for rectifying the concept of education[J]. Chinese Education: A Journal of Translations, 23(4): 52-74. (In Chinese)

[149] Hu T Y. 2013. Education and training institutes in China: regulations and governance[J]. Education Research Monthly, 7(14): 14-19. (In Chinese)

[150] Hu R K, Walker A. 2012. An analysis of the effectiveness of the new curriculum development of school leaders—take the blue sky plan of the Hong Kong special administrative region as an example[J]. Continuing Education Research, 2012 (11): 17-19. (In Chinese)

[151] Hu Y L. 2006. Research on the motivation of school principals in secondary schools (Unpublished master's thesis)[D]. Hunan Normal University, Hunan, China. (In Chinese)

[152] Hu Z F, Wang H. 2009. The evaluation of school principals regarding school principal evaluation: The voice of 30 primary school principals come from Guangzhou, Guangdong Province[J]. Education Evaluation, 2009 (2): 18-21. (In Chinese)

[153] Huang H H. 2014. Discuss on school-based management and the professional development of principals[J]. Life Education, 2014(14): 7-8. (In Chinese)

[154] Huang J Y. 2013. Towards professional training of principals[J]. Researches on Basic Education of Fujian, 14-16. (In Chinese)

[155] Huang X Q, Liang R H, Lin G J. 2010. The literature review on primary and secondary school principals' leadership development[J]. The Southern Publication, 2010(11): 81-84. (In Chinese)

[156] Ibukun W O, Oyewole B K, Abe T O. 2011. Personality characteristics and principal leadership effectiveness in Ekiti State, Nigeria[J]. International Journal of Leadership Studies, 6(2): 246–262.

[157] Jackson B L, Kelley C. 2002. Exceptional and innovative programs in educational leadership[J]. Educational administration quarterly, 38(2): 192-212.

[158] Jamal M. 1984. Job stress and job performance controversy: An empirical assessment[J]. Organizational Behavior and Human Performance, 33(1): 1-21.

[159] Jia H L. 2005. A comparison of credentials system and standard of primary and middle school principals between America and China[J]. Journal of Guangzhou Education Institute, 25(1): 81-85. (In Chinese)

[160] Jia L. 2012. The study of school principal team construction and self-professional development strategy from a professional perspective (Unpublished master's thesis) [D]. Sichuan Normal University, Sichuan, China. (In Chinese)

[161] Jiang J. 2006. The change of headmaster' s role under curriculum reform: case study of a primary school principal (Unpublished master's thesis)[D]. Northeast Normal University, Jilin, China. (In Chinese)

[162] Jin Y. 2007. The theory of distributed leadership plays a game of the principal's responsibilities system in Chinese high schools[J]. Journal of Beijing Institute of Education, 21(2): 75-78. (In Chinese)

[163] Jiang J H, Li Y C. 2011. The cultivation of school principals' innovation capacity[J]. Journal of Education Institute of Henan Province. (In Chinese)

[164] Jones M, Adams D, Tan M H J, Vasu M, Perera C J, Harris A. (2015). Contemporary challenges and changes: Principals' leadership Practices in Malaysia[J]. Asia Pacific Journal of Education, 35(3): 353-365.

[165] Judge T A, Bono J E, Ilies R, Gerhardt M W. 2002. Personality and Leadership: A Qualitative and Quantitative Review[J]. Journal of Applied Psychology, 87(4): 765-780.

[166] Kirkpatick S A, Locke E A. (1991). Leadership: do traits matter?[J]. The Executive, 5(2): 48-60.

[167] Kwan P. 2011. Development of school leaders in Hong Kong: Contextual changes and future challenges[J]. School Leadership and Management, 31(2): 165-177.

[168] Kwong J. 1988. Cultural Revolution in China' s Schools: May 1966–April 1969[M]. Hoover Press.

[169] Lattuca P. 2012. The principalship in transition: The educational forum[J]. Taylor & Francis, 76(2): 224-233.

[170] Lee C K, Pang S K. 2011. Educational leadership in China: Contexts and issues[J]. Frontiers of Education in China, 6(3): 331-341.

[171] Leithwood K. 1994. Leadership for school restructuring[J]. Educational Administration Quarterly, 30(4): 498-518.

[172] Leithwood K. 1996. Preparing school leaders: what works?[J]. Journal of School Leadership, 6(3): 316-342.

[173] Leithwood K A, Poplin M S. 1992. Transformational Leadership[J]. Educational Leadership, 49(5): 8-12.

[174] Lepak D P, Snell S A. 1999. The human resource architecture: Toward a theory of human capital allocation and development[J]. Academy of management review, 24(1): 31-48.

[175] Li B Z. 2014. On the institutional shortage and improvement route of educational funds expenditure in China[J]. Educational Research, 417(10): 42-47. (In Chinese)

[176] Li E ,Wen J ,Liu L. 2008. The economic analysis of educational innovation[J]. Modern Enterprise Education, 2008(8): 208-209. (In Chinese)

[177] Li Q W. 2011. Discuss on the connotation, questions and improvement countermeasures of the responsibility system of primary and secondary school principals[J]. Research in Teaching, 34(1): 67-91. (In Chinese)

[178] Li S, Zhao X. 2006. New curriculum reform appeals to school principals be effective instructional leaders[M]. People's Education Press, China: The fifth national curriculum academic papers. (In Chinese)

[179] Li W K. 2005. On the professional development of principal of primary and secondary schools and specialized training work[J]. Journal of Education Science of Hunan Normal University, 4(2): 89-92. (In Chinese)

[180] Li Z C. 2013. The research of power operation of the three level managerial system of curriculum (Unpublished PhD's thesis)[D]. Southwest University, Chongqing, China. (In Chinese)

[181] Liang H S, Zhang Y. 2010. Situation analysis and countermeasure of the state education funding[J]. Heilongjiang Education (Higher Education Research & Appraisal), 2: 14-16. (In Chinese)

[182] Liang Y X. 2005. What roles do the headmasters play? A study of the daily work of the two secondary school principals[J]. New Education, 2(8): 7-8. (In Chinese)

[183] Liao X Y. 1999. The multi-value expectations of education innovation[J]. Educational Review. (6): 14-17. (In Chinese)

[184] Liu D M. 2011. A research of need-based model of principal training[J]. The Modern Education Journal, 4(178): 17-19. (In Chinese)

[185] Liu E W. 2014. Construction of multi-mode of education in training primary and secondary school principal[J]. Journal of Educational Institute of Taiyuan University, 32(1): 41-43. (In Chinese)

[186] Lin J. 1993. Education in Post-Mao China[M]. New York: Praeger Publishers. (In Chinese)

[187] Liu J. 2010. Investigation on the qualifications of headmasters of primary and secondary schools in Beijing[J]. Primary and secondary school principals, (1): 64-67. (In Chinese)

[188] Liu J, Li A H. 2012. The way to promote the conversion of role of the new school principals. reconsideration on the objectives of qualification training for principals[J]. Primary and Secondary School Teacher Training, 313(8): 31-33. (In Chinese)

[189] Li J X, Xu M Z, Li R Z. 2006. Investigation by questionnaire into the contingent of primary and secondary school principals in China[J].Theory and Practice of Education, 26(3): 59-64. (In Chinese).

[190] Liu J Y, Zhang X Y. 2012. The origin, content and value of the shadow training. Primary and Secondary Teacher Training[J]. Primary and Secondary Teacher Training, 307(2): 3-6. (In Chinese)

[191] Lu J. 2014. A study on the content and method of training of principals: A case study of Changchun City[J]. Journal of Changchun Education Institute, 5(30): 164-165. (In Chinese)

[192] Lu N G, Chen S Y, Zheng Y L. 2010. The description and analysis of changes and continuities in the policy documents issued from 1989 to 2009[J]. Tsinghua Journal of Education, 31(5): 95-102. (In Chinese)

[193] Lu W X. 2003. The research on the obligation, scope of power and benefits of China’s headmaster against the background of the system of the headmaster job responsibility (Unpublished master’s thesis)[D]. Central China Normal University. Hubei, China. (In Chinese)

[194] Lattuca P. 2012. The principalship in transition[J]. In The Educational Forum, 76(2): 224-233.

[195] Lv L. 2004. Reflections on the salary system of primary and secondary school principals[J]. Contemporary Educational and Science, 2004(19): 17-19. (In Chinese)

[196] Lv L. 2011. Specialized study on primary and secondary school principal training[M]. Beijing Normal University Publication. (In Chinese)

[197] Malloy J P. 2012. Effects of Distributed Leadership on Teachers’ Academic Optimism and Student Achievement (Doctoral dissertation in Education, Institute for Studies in Education, University of Toronto)[EB/OL]. Retrieved from http://hdl.handle.net/1807/34799.

[198] Maxwell J C. 1993. Developing the leader within you[M]. Nashville: Thomas Nelson Publishers.

[199] Mays N, Pope C. 2000. Assessing quality in qualitative research[J]. British Medical Journal, 320: 50-52.

[200] Ma P N. 2015. The research on the system of the balanced teacher resources allocation of the country: in H County as an example (Unpublished master's thesis)[D]. Henan Normal University, Henan, China. (In Chinese)

[201] Ma X H. 2005. School principal training: issues, foundations and innovation[J]. Journal of Urumqi Adult Education Institute, 13(4): 67-70. (In Chinese)

[202] Ma X Y, Zhang D, Mu X C. 2009. Several issues should be noted for principal training[J]. Journal of Xianyang Normal University, (6): 118-119. (In Chinese)

[203] Ma Y. 2015. An investigation of primary school principal training[J]. Journal of Changchun Education Institute, 31(21): 119-120. (In Chinese)

[204] MacBeath J E, Dempster N. 2009. Connecting leadership and learning: Principles for practice[M]. Routledge, 32-52.

[205] McGuire D. 2014. Human Resource Development: Theory and Practice(2nd Ed)[M]. London: Sage.

[206] Merriam S B. 1988. Case study research in education: a qualitative approach[M]. San Francisco: Jossey-Bass,Inc.

[207] Merriam S B. 1998. Qualitative research and case study applications in education[M]. San Francisco: Jossey-Bass, Inc.

[208] Merriam S B. 2009. Qualitative research: a guide to design and implementation[M]. San Francisco: Jossey-Bass.

[209] Miles M B, Huberman A M. 1994. Qualitative data analysis: An expanded sourcebook[M]. Los Angeles: Sage.

[210] Militello M, Berger J B. 2010. Understanding educational leadership in northwest China[J]. International Journal of Leadership in Education, 13(2): 185-202.

[211] MOE. 1989. Opinion on Strengthening the Training for the Principals of Primary and Secondary Schools[EB/OL]. Retrieved 3th December, 2014 from http://www.moe.gov.cn/publicfiles/business/htmlfiles/moe/s7148/201303/148717.html. (In Chinese)

[212] MOE. 1999. Training Regulations for Primary and Secondary School Principals [EB/OL]. Retrieved 3th December, 2014 from http://www.moe.edu.cn/publicfiles/business/htmlfiles/moe/moe_621/201005/88483.html. (In Chinese)

[213] MOE. 2002. Opinion of Ministry of Education on Further Strengthening and Improving the Training of Primary and Secondary School Principals[EB/OL]. Retrieved 3th December, 2014 from http://www.moe.gov.cn/publicfiles/business/htmlfiles/moe/moe_106/200407/939.html. (In Chinese)

[214] MOE. 2006. Compulsory Education Law of the People's Republic of China[EB/OL]. Retrieved 12th December, 2014 from http://www.moe.edu.cn/publicfiles/business/htmlfiles/moe/moe_2803/200907/49979.html. (In Chinese)

[215] MOE. 2007. National Eleventh Five - Year Plan for Cadre Training of the Educational System[EB/OL]. Retrieved 12th December, 2014 from http://www.naea.edu.cn/gjjyxzxy/17479/17665/10369/index.html .(In Chinese)

[216] MOE. 2013. Professional Standards for School Principals of Compulsory Education[EB/OL]. Retrieved 11th December, 2014 from http://www.moe.edu.cn/publicfiles/business/htmlfiles/moe/s7148/201302/147899.html. (In Chinese)

[217] MOE , MOF. 2014. Notice on the Unified Standard of Authorized Strength of Urban and Rural Schools[EB/OL]. Retrieved 2th December, 2015 from http://www.moe.edu.cn/publicfiles/business/htmlfiles/moe/s8471/201412/181014.html. (In Chinese)

[218] Moorhead G, Griffin R W. 1998. Organizational behavior: managing people and organization (5th ed.). Boston: Houghton Mifflin Company.

[219] Morse J M. 1989. Strategies for sampling [M]// J M Morse (Ed.), Qualitative nursing research: A contemporary dialogue (pp. 117-131). Rockville, MD: Aspen.

[220] Ngai N P, Cheung C K, Ngai S S Y, To S M. 2012. Youth leadership training in Hong Kong: current developments and the way ahead[J]. International Journal of Adolescence and Youth, 17(23): 165-179.

[221] Northouse P G. 2012. Leadership: theory and practice[M]. London:Sage Publications.

[222] Northouse P G. 2016. Leadership theory and practice (7th ed.)[M]. Thousand Oaks, CA: Sage Publications.

[223] Ogawa R T, Bossert S T. 1995. Leadership as an organizational quality[J]. Educational Administration Quarterly, 31(2): 224-243.

[224] Orpen C. 1994. The effect of time-management training on employee attitudes and behavior: A field experiment[J]. Journal of Psychology, 128(4): 393-396.

[225] Patton M Q. 1990. Qualitative evaluation and research methods (2nd ed)[M]. Newbury Park, CA: Sage.

[226] Peterson K. 2002. The professional development of principals: Innovations and opportunities[J]. Educational Administration Quarterly, 38(2): 213-232.

[227] Phillips J J, Phillips P P. 2016. Handbook of Training Evaluation and Measurement Methods (4th ed)[M]. New York: Routledge.

[228] Price H E. 2012. Principal–teacher interactions how affective relationships shape principal and teacher attitudes[J]. Educational Administration Quarterly, 48(1): 39-85.

[229] Punch K F. 2009. Introduction to research methods in education[M]. Los Angeles: Sage.

[230] Qian L Q. 2004. The Construction of assurance system of primary and secondary school principal training at New Era[J].Primary and Secondary School Teacher Training, 2004(6): 20-22. (In Chinese)

[231] Qian L Q. 2007. Developmental thinking on primary and secondary school principals' training mechanism innovation[J]. Management Forum, 2007(4): 53-59. (In Chinese)

[232] Qin L X. 2003. The history and inspiration of elementary educational curriculum reform in China in recent 20 Years (Unpublished master's thesis)[D]. Shanxi Normal University, Xi'an, China. (In Chinese)

[233] Rao W. 2015. The evolution and reflections of primary and secondary school principals' training curriculum[J]. Journal of Chongqing University of Education, 28(4): 111-114. (In Chinese)

[234] Robbins S P, Judge T A, Odendaal A, Roodt G. 2009. Organizational behavior: Global and South African perspectives[M]. Pearson Higher Education AU.

[235] Robbins S P, Judge T A. 2012. Organizational Behavior/ Örgütsel Davranış (Translation Editor, İnci Erdem), 4. Edition[M], Ankara, Nobel Yayıncılık.

[236] Schein E H. 2010. Organizational culture and leadership[M]. San Francisco: Jossey-Bass, Inc.

[237] Schriesheim C A, Neider L L. 1996. Path-goal leadership theory: The long and winding road[J]. The Leadership Quarterly, 7(3): 317-321.

[238] SEC. 1982. The Opinion on Strengthening the Training Work for The Opinion on Strengthening the Training Work for Ordinary Education Administrative cadres[J]. People's Education, 45. (In Chinese)

[239] SEC. 1990. Opinions of the State Education Commission on Post Training for Headmasters of Primary and Secondary Schools[EB/OL]. Retrieved 4th December, 2014 from http://www.gdjyw.com/jyfg/13/law_13_1089.htm. (In Chinese)

[240] SEC. 1991. Requirements and Position Requirements of Headmasters of Primary and Secondary Schools in China (Trial Implementation)[EB/OL].Retrieved 4th December, 2014 fromhttp://www.qtedu.net/jygl/glzd/200504/9904.html. (In Chinese)

[241] SEC. 1992. Opinions on Strengthening the Construction of the Headmasters of Primary and Secondary Schools[EB/OL]. Retrieved 4th December, 2014 from http://www.moe.gov.cn/publicfiles/business/htmlfiles/moe/s7148/201303/148717.html. (In Chinese)

[242] SEC. 1995. Opinions of the State Education Commission on the Primary and Secondary School Principals Training during the Ninth Five-year Plan period [EB/OL]. Retrieved 4th December, 2014 from http://laws.66law.cn/law-15433.aspx. (In Chinese.

[243] Sandelowski M. 1995. Sample size in qualitative research[J]. Research in Nursing and Health, 18: 179–183. (Retrieved from http://www.ncbi.nlm.nih.gov/entrez/query.fcgi?cmd=Retrieve&;db=PubMed&dopt=Citation&list_uids=7899572 Google Scholar)

[244] Sergiovanni T J. 1991. Value-added leadership: How to get extraordinary results in schools[J]. NASSP Bulletin, 75(533): 118-119.

[245] Shang R. 2007. Informal learning and the development of teachers in primary and secondary schools (Unpublished master's thesis)[D]. Henan Normal University, Henan, China. (In Chinese)

[246] Shen J. 2009. Discussion on how to make good use of training fees by headmasters after the reform of funds guarantee mechanism for compulsory education[J]. Primary and Secondary School Principals, 2009(3): 37-39. (In Chinese)

[247] Shenton A K. 2004. Strategies for ensuring trustworthiness in qualitative research projects[J]. Education for Information, 22(2): 63-75. (In Chinese)

[248] Shi D D. 2003. A study on the assurance system of primary and secondary school principal training[J]. Primary and Secondary Teacher Training, 2008(8): 26-28. (In Chinese)

[249] Skowronek S. 1993.The politics presidents make: leadership from John Adams to Bill Clinton[M]. Boston: Harvard University Press.

[250] Song Z H. 2014. The issues and countermeasures of primary and Secondary school principals' training[J]. Education Exploration, 282(12): 60-61. (In Chinese)

[251] State Council. 1995. Decision about hastening scientific and technological progress [EB/OL]. Retrieved 4 th December, 2014 from http://www.most.gov.cn/ztzl/jqzzcx/zzcxcxzzo/zzcxcxzz/zzcxgncxzz/200512/t20051230_27321.htm. (In Chinese)

[252] State Council. 1994. Opinions of the State Council on the Implementation of *the* Outline of China' s Educational Reform and Development[EB/OL]. Retrieved 4th December, 2014 from http://www.moe.edu.cn/publicfiles/business/htmlfiles/moe/moe_177/200407/2483.html. (In Chinese)

[253] State Council. 2001. Decision of State Council on the Reform and Development of Basic Education[EB/OL]. Retrieved 3th December, 2014 from http://zwgk.gd.gov.cn/006939748/200909/t20090915_8710.html. (In Chinese)

[254] State Council. 2012. Opinions of the State Council on Strengthening the Construction of Teachers' Ranks[EB/OL]. Retrieved 17th December, 2014 from http://www.gov.cn/zwgk/2012-09/07/content_2218778.htm. (In Chinese)

[255] Stogdill R M. 1948. Personal factors associated with leadership: A survey of the literature[J]. The Journal of Psychology, 25(1): 35-71.

[256] Stogdill R M. 1974. Handbook of leadership: A survey of theory and research[M]. New York: The Free Press.

[257] Strauss A, Corbin J M. 1990. Basics of qualitative research: grounded theory procedures and techniques[M]. London: Sage Publications.

[258] Stuart C S, Philip K P. 1997. School leadership handbook for excellence[M]. San Francisco: Jossey-Bass, Inc.

[259] Sui Z H. 2012. Beijing primary and secondary school education under the guidance of "the proletariat politics" (1949—1966)[M]. Beijing: Capital Normal University. (In Chinese)

[260] Sukhomlynsky V. 1999. Bovleksh secondary school[M]. Beijing Science and Education Press. (Translated in Chinese).

[261] Sumintono B. 2006. Decentralized centralism: school based management policies and practice at state secondary schools Mataram, Lombok, Indonesia. (PhD's thesis)[D]. Victoria University of Wellington, New Zealand.

[262] Sumintono B, Sheyoputri E Y A, Jiang N, Misbach I H, Jumintono N V. 2015. Becoming a principal in Indonesia: Possibility, pitfalls and potential[M]. Asia Pacific Journal of Education. DOI: 10.1080/02188791.2015.1056595

[263] Sun J M. 2009. Research on secondary school principal leadership (Unpublished EdD's thesis)[D]. Faculty of Educational Administration, East China Normal University, Shanghai, China. (In Chinese)

[264] Sun J, Cheng J K, Deng Z. 2015. Survey and analysis of principals' time allotment[J]. Jiangsu Educational Research, 2015: 30-35. (In Chinese)

[265] Sun Z H, Qi J. 2014. The dilemma and the ways of rural primary and secondary school principals' professional development under the background of urbanization[J]. Modern Education Management, 2014(6): 23-28. (In Chinese)

[266] Swanson R A. 1995. Human resource development: performance is the key[J]. Human Resource Development Quarterly, 6(2): 207-213.

[267] Swanson R A. 2001. Human resource development and its underlying theory[J]. Human Resource Development International, 4(3): 299-312.

[268] Tang S L, Xu H D. 2000. An analysis of the teacher's quality[J]. Teacher Education Research, 12(6): 34-39.

[269] Terry G R. 1960. Principle of Management[M]. Homewood: Richard D. Irwin, Inc.

[270] Thogersen S. 1990. Secondary education in China after Mao: reform and social conflict[M]. Denmark: Aarhus University Press.

[271] Tang S, Lu J Hallinger P. 2014. Leading school change in China: A review of related literature and preliminary investigation[J]. International Journal of Educational Management, 28(6): 655-675.

[272] Ten H P. 2007. Doing conversation analysis[M]. Sage.

[273] Tian H Z, Meng F H, Fu S J. 2012. Personalized training of principals: innovative exploration from theory to practice[J]. Educational Science Research, 12(24): 24-29.

[274] Trost J E. 1986. Statistically nonrepresentative stratified sampling: A sampling technique for qualitative studies[J]. Qualitative Sociology, 9: 54-57.

[275] Tsang M C. 2000. Education and national development in China since 1949: Oscillating policies and enduring dilemmas[J]. China Review, 579-618.

[276] Tsang M C, Ding Y. 2005. Resource utilization and disparities in compulsory education in China[J]. China Review, 1-31.

[277] Tu S G. 2014. The "Shadow Principal" training: A self-directed professional development model of the principal[J]. Vocational and Technical Education, 35 (25): 43-47. (In Chinese)

[278] Uren M L, Tovey M D. 2001. Part B: Performance Management[J]. Managing Performance Improvement,57.

[279] Wahlstrom K L, Louis K S. 2008. How teachers experience principal leadership: The roles of professional community, trust, efficacy, and shared responsibility[J]. Educational Administration Quarterly, 44(4): 458-495.

[280] Walker A, Hu R, Qian H Y. 2012. Principal leadership in China: An initial review[J]. School Effectiveness and School Improvement, 23(4): 369-399.

[281] Walker A ,Qian H Y. 2015. Review of research on school principal leadership in Mainland China, 1998—2013[J]. Journal of Educational Administration, 53(4): 467-491.

[282] Wang C. 2014. A study on the implement and countermeasure of principal responsibility in primary and secondary school. (Unpublished master's thesis)[D]. Ludong University, Shandong, China. (In Chinese)

[283] Wang F. 2010. The frameworks of early leadership development (Unpublished master's thesis)[D]. Faculty of Education, East China Normal University, Shanghai, China. (In Chinese)

[284] Wang J. 2008. The reasons and countermeasures of fund shortage of compulsory education in rural areas, China[J]. China Agricultural Education, 2008(6): 1-18.

[285] Wang L G. 2007. A study on teacher quality standard: The perspective of teacher professional development (Unpublished master's thesis)[D]. Northwest Normal University, Lanzhou, China.

[286] Wang S M. 1994. The educational reform under the socialist market economy[J]. Beijing Normal University Journal. (In Chinese)

[287] Wang T J. 1999. Modern school principal training: concept, operation and experiences[M]. Nanjing Normal University Press. (In Chinese)

[288] Wang X. 2002. Education in China since 1976[M]. McFarland. (In Chinese)

[289] Wang T. 2007. Understanding Chinese educational leaders' conceptions in an international education context[J]. International Journal of Leadership in Education, 10(1): 71-88. (In Chinese)

[290] Wang J P, Wang L J. 2015. The investigation and evaluation of instructional leadership of school principals[J]. Modern Primary and Secondary Education, 31(2): 1-6. (In Chinese)

[291] Wang T Y. 2013. The reflection of primary and secondary school principals' training in China from global perspectives[J]. China Education Innovation, 2013(22): 96-97. (In Chinese)
[292] Wang Y L, Yang G X, Wang J ,Yang R J. 2011. The content analysis of the domestic research on informal learning[J]. Journal of Distance Education, (4): 71-76. (In Chinese)
[293] Wang Z. 2011. The problem and improvement strategies to training courses for primary and secondary school principals[J]. Educational Administration, 2011(12): 180-181. (In Chinese)
[294] Wang Z R. 2013. The needs based construction of training content system for primary and secondary school principals[J]. The In-service Education and Training of School Teachers, 6(323): 30-33. (In Chinese)
[295] Wang W H. 2014. The Problems, countermeasures, and self-examination framework of countries primary and secondary school principal training[J]. Teacher Education Forum. 27(6): 56-60. (In Chinese)
[296] Wei H. 2015. Evaluation of principals' qualification training results based on Kirkpatrick's model[J]. Journal of Ningbo Institute of Education, 17(4): 92-95. (In Chinese)
[297] Wei L Y, Cai Q Y. 2012. The principles of training curriculum for primary and secondary school principals[J]. Continuing Education,3: 100-102. (In Chinese)
[298] Wei L Y, Jiang L Q. 2011. Specialization of principals and course system of training of elementary and secondary schools. Journal of Chongqing Education College, 24(5): 157-159. (In Chinese)
[299] Werner J M, DeSimone R L. 2011. Human resource development[M]. Cengage Learning.
[300] Winston B E, Patterson K. 2006. An integrative definition of leadership[J]. International journal of leadership studies, 1(2), 6-66.
[301] Wilson M ,Xue X. 2013. School leader perspectives on leadership learning preparation and continuing professional development in the Chinese province of Fujian: An exploratory study[J]. Educational Management Administration and Leadership, 41(6): 800-818.
[302] Wise A E, Darling-Hammond L. 1984. Teacher evaluation and teacher professionalism[J]. Educational leadership, 28-31.

[303] Wen H F. 2006. Leadership and management of educational innovation organization[M]. Beijing Educational Science Press.

[304] World Bank. 2016. Purchasing Power Parity of China[EB/OL]. Retrieved on 16th, November, 2016 from http://data.worldbank.org/data-catalog/GDP-PPP-based-table. (In Chinese)

[305] World Bank. 2016. Gross domestic product[EB/OL]. Retrieved on 16th, November, 2016 from http://cn.knoema.com/nwnfkne/world-gdp-ranking-2016-data-and-charts-forecast.

[306] Wu X D. 2009. Research on principal training of elementary and high schools for 30 Years (Unpublished master's thesis)[D]. Faculty of Education, Hunan Normal University, Hunan, China. (In Chinese)

[307] Wu X W, Gong L, Liu J, Chen Y. 2015. Implementing and thinking of the training program for primary and secondary school principals[J]. Journal of Changchun Normal University, 13(4): 127-130. (In Chinese)

[308] Wu Y D. 2009. Research on the salary system of primary and secondary school principals: A case study of central county in China (Unpublished master's thesis)[D]. Faculty of Education, Ningbo University, Zhejiang, China. (In Chinese)

[309] Xia F. 2011a. Practical exploration of primary and secondary school principal training method[J]. School Principal Training, 298(5): 27-29. (In Chinese)

[310] Xia F. 2011b. A comparative study of the training pattern for headmasters of primary and secondary schools[J]. Journal of Liaoning Normal University (Social Science Edition), 34(3): 62-65. (In Chinese)

[311] Xiao B F. 2011. Systematic study on primary and secondary school principals' training evaluation professional development: nearly 20 years' literature review on primary and secondary school principals' training evaluation[J]. Journal of Beijing Institute of Education, 25(5): 24 -28. (In Chinese)

[312] Xiao X H. 2008. The current issues and countermeasures of education cadre training[J]. Journal of Shandong Agricultural Management Cadre Institute, (23): 184-185. (In Chinese)

[313] Xiao Z L, Yu B. 2001. New school management[M]. Southeast Normal University Press.

[314] Xie Y, Ma Y P, Zhang Z P. 2013. Is it true that the curriculum reform has been really carried out for eight times in new China?[J]. Educational Research, 2013 (2): 125-132. (In Chinese)

[315] Xiong W. 2010. Discussion on the imbalance of the responsibility, power and interests of school headmasters in compulsory education[J]. The Primary and Secondary School Principal, 2010(1): 40-43. (In Chinese)
[316] Xu W L. 2011. The analysis of primary and secondary school principal training curriculum settings after the establishment of People's Republic of China[J]. Journal of Adult Education of Hebei University, 13(3): 76-78. (In Chinese)
[317] Xu Y B. 2008. The research on the problems and improvement strategies of school education innovation execution[D]. Beijing Normal University. (In Chinese)
[318] Yan W, Ehrich L C. 2009. Principal preparation and training: A look at China and its issues[J]. International Journal of Educational Management, 23(1): 51-64. (In Chinese)
[319] Yang X H. 2000. Countermeasures and problems of innovation education in primary and secondary schools (Unpublished master's thesis)[D]. Southeast Normal University, Jiangsu, China. (In Chinese)
[320] Yang H Y. 2003. The impact factor of primary and secondary school principals' professional development[J]. Theory and Practice of Education, 23(3): 14-19. (In Chinese)
[321] Yang H Y. 2005. The establishment and perfection of primary and secondary school principals' management system in China[J]. Theory and Practice of Education, 25(1): 17-21. (In Chinese)
[322] Yang X M. 2011. Training methods of primary and secondary school principals: from classification to systematic construction[J]. Journal of Beijing Institute of Education, 25(5): 20-23. (In Chinese)
[323] Ye L. 2011. The status and reasons of quality education promotion, Educational Development Research[J]. 2011(4): 3-5. (In Chinese)
[324] Yin H B, Lee C K. 2011. Curriculum reform in China: changes and challenges[M]. New York: Nova Science Publishers. (In Chinese)
[325] Yin H B, Lee C K, Wang W L. 2014. Dilemmas of leading national curriculum reform in a global era: A Chinese perspective[J]. Educational Management Administration and Leadership, 42(2): 293-311. (In Chinese)
[326] Yin R K. 2013. Case study research: design and methods[M]. London: Sage publications.
[327] Ying J F, He J. 2005. Research on training method: The growth pattern of famous headmaster[J]. Educational Development Research, 2005(5): 77-80. (In Chinese)

[328] Youngs P, King M B. 2002. Principal leadership for professional development to build school capacity[J]. Educational Administration Quarterly, 38(5): 643-670.

[329] Yu B. 1999. What kind of power of school principals should have?[J].Primary and Secondary School Management, 10: 3-5. (In Chinese)

[330] Yukl G A. 2002. *Leadership in organizations* (5th ed.)[M]. Englewood Cliffs: Prentice-Hall.

[331] Yu X H. 2012. Out of bondage, from good to excellent: research on incentive effective strategy of famous principals[J]. Forum on Contemporary Education, 248 (2): 60-63. (In Chinese)

[332] Yuan X L. 2008. The exploration on primary and secondary school principals' training evaluation quality[J]. Forum on Contemporary Education, 2008(8): 30-32. (In Chinese)

[333] Zeng G P, Li Z F. 1999. The world's innovation system - knowledge production, proliferation and utilization[M]. Shandong Education Press. (In Chinese)

[334] Zhang H. 2011. Training curriculum of primary and secondary school principals: historical review and relevant reflections[J]. Journal of Beijing Institute of Education, 25(5): 15-19. (In Chinese)

[335] Zhang K M. 2005. Research on the teachers' quality and training: under the view of constructivism (Unpublished PhD's thesis)[D]. East China Normal University, Shanghai, China.

[336] Zhang J. 2012. On the problems and countermeasures in the training and evaluation of primary and secondary school principals[J]. Journal of Liaoning Normal University, 35(6): 808-811. (In Chinese)

[337] Zhang S P. 2013. Thoughts on the practice of "Shadow Training" of school principals[J]. Journal of Dalian University, 29(2): 1-3. (In Chinese)

[338] Zhang W, Brundrett M. 2010. School leaders' perspectives on leadership learning: the case for informal and experiential learning[J]. Management in Education, 24(4): 154-158. (In Chinese)

[339] Zhang X M. 2008. Effectively enhance the contextualized training of school principal leadership[J]. Journal of Fujian Institute of Education, 2008(6): 6-7. (In Chinese)

[340] Zhang Y. 2013. Political culture dimension and the choice of political system: an interpretation of contemporary Chinese political system (1954-2012) (Unpublished PhD's thesis)[D]. East China Normal University, Shanghai, China. (In Chinese)

[341] Zhao H T. 2005. Exploration of problem-based principal training (Unpublished PhD's thesis)[D]. East China Normal University, Shanghai, China. (In Chinese)

[342] Zhao F C, Wei X X. 2000. Innovative thinking of principals[J]. Journal of Hanshan College, 2000(3): 80-86. (In Chinese)

[343] Zhao Q, Wang M. 2007. Construction of performance appraisal system for primary and secondary school principals: A case study in Beijing[J]. Educational Administration Review, 2007(4): 194–244. (In Chinese)

[344] Zheng H Q. 2003. China' s education management review[M]. Beijing: Science Education Press. (In Chinese)

[345] Zheng Y L, Chen S Y, Lu N G. 2012. The competency building of principal training institutes: study on the types of the institutions and the natures of the strategy[J]. Education Development Research, 2012(18): 65-79. (In Chinese)

[346] Zheng Y L, Chen S Y, Lu N G. 2010. From developing leader to developing leadership: shift in the ways of looking at principal training[J]. Education Science, 26(6): 1-5. (In Chinese)

[347] Zhou B. 2015. The principal specialization: dilemma, path and system guarantee[J]. Teacher Education Research, 27(5): 34-40. (In Chinese)

[348] Zhou J G. 2008. Reading: An important channel of school principals' professional development[J]. Primary and Secondary School Principals, 2008(7): 55-56. (In Chinese)

[349] Zhu X Y. 2009. An investigation report on time management behavior of secondary school principals, 2009(30): 118-119. (In Chinese)

[350] Zhuang D. 2014. The thinking on the design model of the training curriculum of "expert" principals training of primary and secondary schools, take scenario as an example[J]. Journal of Changchun Institute, 30(23): 114-115. (In Chinese)

[351] Zheng Y L. 2009. Research on school improvement based training mode for primary and secondary school principal (Unpublished master's thesis)[D]. East China Normal University, Shanghai, China. (In Chinese)

[352] Zheng J Z, Li C F. 2007. Chinese leadership: Progress, issues and tendency[J]. Journal of China Executive Leadership Academic Pudong, 1(1): 55-62. (In Chinese)

[353] Zheng Y L, Walker A , Chen S Y. 2013. Change and continuity: A critical analysis of principal development policy in Mainland China (1989-2011)[J]. Educational Management Administration and Leadership, 41 (4): 484-503.

ACKNOWLEDGEMENTS

First of all, I praise the Lord Jesus, the almighty, merciful and knowledgeable, for granting me this opportunity and encouragement during the process of the study and to proceed fruitfully, without him I could not go this further. The thesis reaches its designated form due to the assistance and guidance of several people and I would like to thanks them all.

Words are not enough to express my appreciation to my beloved supervisors Dr. Bambang Sumintono (principal supervisor) and Dr. Jaqueline (co-supervisor), who have been guiding and advising me from the beginning till the end of the study, without your kindly guidance and encouragement, I shall never complete my study. I would like to thank Professor Alma Harris and Dr. Michael who gave me the valuable suggestions for my thesis, which was really helpful for my study.

My gratitude also goes to my friends who helped me during the data collection and gave me valuable suggestions; they are Professor Wang Ruiping, Wang Zhengwei, Feng Jiajun, Thomas Mevel, Leong Mengli and Tan Jiaqi. I truly want to thank all the participants during my field work in Henan Province, thank you for your patience and collaboration to provide the information that I needed.

Not forgotten to my lovely family members, my parents, my parents-in-law, my husband Chen Lin and my adorable son Chen Mingbo, thank you for your constantly encouragement and tremendous supports during the long journey of PhD study; you are always the inspiration and motivation in my life.